Healing, Meaning
and Purpose

Healing, Meaning and Purpose

The Magical Power of the Emerging Laws of Life

Richard G. Petty, M.D.

iUniverse, Inc.
New York Lincoln Shanghai

Healing, Meaning and Purpose
The Magical Power of the Emerging Laws of Life

iUniverse books may be ordered through booksellers or by contacting:

iUniverse
2021 Pine Lake Road, Suite 100
Lincoln, NE 68512
www.iuniverse.com
1-800-Authors (1-800-288-4677)

Because of the dynamic nature of the Internet, any Web addresses or links contained in this book may have changed since publication and may no longer be valid.

The information, ideas, and suggestions in this book are not intended as a substitute for professional medical advice. Before following any suggestions contained in this book, you should consult your personal physician. Neither the author nor the publisher shall be liable or responsible for any loss or damage allegedly arising as a consequence of your use or application of any information or suggestions in this book.

ISBN: 978-0-595-45801-1 (pbk)
ISBN: 978-0-595-90101-2 (ebk)

Printed in the United States of America

Contents

Chapter One   Setting the Scene 1

Chapter Two   Straws in the Wind 17

Chapter Three   Our Changing Planet, Our Evolving People 31

Chapter Four   The Evolving Laws of Health and Healing 47

Chapter Five   Beyond the Clockwork Universe 63

Chapter Six   Hidden Harbingers of Health 79

Chapter Seven   Expanding Concepts of Health and Disease 94

Chapter Eight   Recruiting Your Allies 115

Chapter Nine   Creative Self-Integration 130

Chapter Ten   Mind Control 144

Chapter Eleven   Dynamic Relationships:
The Missing Key to Wellness 160

Chapter Twelve   Putting the Pieces Together 177

Acknowledgments 199

Further Reading 201

Chapter One
Setting the Scene

A New Vision of Reality

The scientific world is erupting with profound and unexpected discoveries that are impacting every aspect of our lives. Fueling a flurry of ground-breaking theories, today's findings are reshaping everything that we think about our world and ourselves. Those of us working at science's cutting edge are re-evaluating the very nature of reality itself.

Among the most far-reaching scientific discoveries are those impacting our understanding of the laws of health and healing. In unprecedented numbers, scientists and physicians are attending meetings and conferences to discuss the critical relationship between science, consciousness and spirituality. Such gatherings, accompanied by a growing body of research, carry practical applications for everyone sharing our planet.

> "I ignored an axiom."
> —Albert Einstein (German-born American Physicist and, in 1921, Winner of the Nobel Prize in Physics, 1879–1955): His response when asked to explain, in a few words, how the idea of relativity came to him.

Laws long perceived as unchanging and unchangeable are rapidly adapting and evolving, along with our minds, bodies, relationships, society and our planet. Rather than replacing existing laws, the new laws of healing will both challenge and enhance existing paths to health and wellness. Doesn't it always seem that every time you open a book on health or watch a television program about it, that the advice is always pretty much the same? "Eat right; take some exercise; learn to breathe properly; learn to relax; take time to smell the roses, and avoid smoking and alcohol." All are fine, but, as we shall see, are but partial glimpses of a bigger picture.

Let's take a look at just a few examples of extraordinary findings, which we could call our "Dogma Busters":

1. A central dogma in neurology and psychology has been stood on its head, with recent research suggesting that the brain is far more plastic and dynamic than most people ever realized.

Anybody who has studied psychology or biology has probably been taught that we're born with a certain number of the brain cells known as neurons. Most books will also tell you that throughout adulthood, you lose approximately 100,000 neurons daily, that neurons do not regenerate and that recovery after an injury is impossible. These "facts" have simply been repeated from one textbook to another for more than 50 years and have directed almost everyone's thinking.

We now know neurons regenerate and that we continue creating new neurons into our 70s. Even more extraordinary: We know some specific ways to stimulate new neuron growth. Though the number of new neurons is usually quite small, this constant regeneration occurs in some critical regions of the brain. This new awareness of neuron regeneration is paving a path toward previously unimagined possibilities. We have also discovered that neurons are not the only players in the brain. Small cells called glial cells, which were thought to do no more than to provide support and scaffolding for the neurons, are constantly active and seem to be critical in the development of some types of memory. The brain is far more dynamic and plastic than most people ever realized, and the future for neurology, psychology and psychiatry is extraordinarily bright.

2. Today's genetic revolution has—so far—been oversold, with claims that our genes determine everything about us. While many characteristics are indeed strongly genetically predetermined, like height or eye color,

recent research suggests most genes are switched on in response to environmental changes. Even more startling: When we examine the brain, we find that most genes don't determine precisely how someone will behave, but rather how a person will *respond* to the environment. It therefore appears that both nature and the nurturing we receive contribute to our behavior.

3. We have also discovered that the whole genome is very fluid: Genes shuffle around, sometimes they jump, and they constantly undergo all sorts of other changes. This has been deeply disturbing to those of us raised to believe that genes had to stay rigidly in place or there would be a genetic catastrophe. Yet there is more: A central dogma in molecular biology was that the wondrous molecule called DNA provided the program for RNA, which in turn provided the special codes for proteins to be manufactured within cells. Information would just flow in one direction. But then scientists showed that the process could also run in reverse, with cells modifying and editing DNA. Some viruses can insert themselves into the cell's DNA and hijack some of the cell's machinery. There is increasing evidence that some acquired characteristics can lead to genetic changes, which can then be inherited. Many different kinds of physiological imbalances and ecological stresses can lead to genetic mutations. Now this was regarded as scientific heresy until very recently, and sometimes people who were educated with the "old biology" still find it difficult to accept that our genetic makeup is fluid and ever changing. Biology is not destiny.

4. Physicists and cosmologists have made a stunning discovery: They seem to have "overlooked" more than 90 percent of the universe. This missing piece is being referred to as "dark" matter and "dark" energy. We know very little about it, but it is utterly extraordinary that such long-held views of our universe are so incomplete. Some visionary scientists are already wondering if this dark matter and dark energy may have something to do with the burgeoning evidence for the existence of "subtle" systems associated with the body. These subtle systems appear to be of many types, and in Asia have been given names like qi (chi) and prana, or in the West were called the etheric or the fifth element, after earth, fire, air and

water. We are going to use the term subtle "systems", to be a little more precise than saying "energies", for these subtle systems are composed of the inseparable twins:

1. Subtle energies *and*
2. The subtle fields that carry them.

Without energy, the fields could not actualize, and without the fields, there would be nothing to carry the energy.

5. Some very respectable scientists are taking another look at cold fusion, the idea that we can produce the nuclear furnace powering the sun, right here on earth, at room temperature. Fifteen years ago it was first reported that this might be possible, but then the idea vanished from mainstream science after repeated failed experiments. Cold fusion is now being revisited with new eyes as laboratories around the world once again report something closely resembling cold fusion. If true, and if there is the political will, this could instantly solve the world's energy problems.

6. Consider another new idea called "entanglement." This is an extraordinary quantum physics theory, predicting that particles that seem to be isolated are actually constantly and instantaneously connected through time and space. When initially proposed, this concept appeared so preposterous that many people didn't know whether to take it seriously. Today, growing bodies of scientific data demonstrate that this is a real, robust phenomenon. One possibility presented through this new way of thinking: Scientists are looking at this phenomenon as something that could be harnessed to create new quantum computers, while others are wondering if it provides a theoretical explanation for extrasensory perception and healing at a distance.

7. Our final dogma-busting example involves our interconnectedness—even across continents and between different species. Scientists are unearthing powerful evidence that indicates that human and animal

minds can interact with each other over long distances. Just as the Ancient Wisdom has taught us for thousands of years, we are interconnected.

The Global Consciousness Project based at Princeton has a global network of 65 random event generators around the world. Highly sophisticated analysis has shown that three to four hours before the attacks of September 11, 2001, anomalous readings started being picked up all over the world. Dean Radin, from the Institute of Noetic Sciences, has reported that in the 14 days before the attacks, tests of extrasensory perception began to show a marked decline.

It is pure speculation, but it is possible that this was because people were intuitively damping down their intuition in anticipation of the impending catastrophe. I know from personal experience that most people with any kind of psychic abilities go through a phase of either denying them or damping them. I often hear people say: "How wonderful to be able to pick things up about people." In fact, until you know how to control it, it is not wonderful at all. I have known a lot of people who had genuine psychic abilities, who became overwhelmed by them and got lost in drug abuse or mental illness.

The reason for taking time to discuss these findings is that we have progressively more evidence that there really is a global consciousness that is developing and evolving. The French Jesuit priest Pierre Teilhard de Chardin spoke about his vision of humanity evolving toward the Omega Point, while in India, Sri Aurobindo wrote volumes about the future evolution of not just individuals, but humanity as a whole.

I discern the first signs of global evolution beginning in our own lifetimes. The problems that we see around us are the reactions of a world soon to be replaced by something far more magnificent.

But there is more: Nature can learn. This is a profoundly important concept. If a new chemical is synthesized in one part of the world, it may take time to make it into a crystal, but once that has been accomplished, it becomes easier and easier to make that crystal elsewhere. Once a mouse has learned a maze in one country, another unrelated mouse could learn the same task more quickly in an entirely different part of the world.

> "Discovery consists of seeing what everybody has seen, and thinking what nobody has thought."
> —Albert von Szent-Györgyi (Hungarian-born American Biochemist and, in 1937, Winner of the Nobel Prize in Medicine, 1893–1986)

We could detail scores of other extraordinary "Dogma Busters," but we selected these as the ones that are going to be important to us in this book. Our interest is in health, healing and personal development, rather than an account of a lot of scientific discoveries. Later we are also going to look at some of the extraordinary theoretical work being done throughout the world to realize a vision of an Integral World.

So what does all this mean to you and me? It means we're living in an extraordinarily interesting time, when the veil surrounding our physical world is being torn, allowing us to start seeing ourselves differently.

So how did I come to be working on a new approach to health and wellness? How did I come to realize that some of the laws of healing are changing and evolving as we are evolving? And how did I come to write this book? I am normally extremely reluctant to discuss my own background, but I think that you have a right to know how I came to write this. After all, no idea, no concept, no advance, happens in a vacuum. And if I am to be your guide, you need to be sure that I know where I am going!

The Reluctant Psychic and the Library Angel

From early childhood growing up in England, I've had always had the ability to sense things about people and about coming events. To sense people's "Energies." It was not until I got punished for "telling stories" about what I saw and felt, that I began to understand that not everybody could do this, and I quickly learned to keep it quiet. It was only years later that I discovered that everyone does have the ability, it is just that most people ignore it.

I became extremely eager to find out what this "thing"—this ability—was, and how I could use it to help others. So the decision to go to medical school was an easy one.

Then an odd thing happened. I was due to spend a couple of weeks in Germany during the summer before starting medical school. I went to the local lending library to find something to take with me. As I was walking toward the science section, a book fell from one of the shelves as I was passing. I mean that quite literally. The book fell off the shelf and hit me. The book was Alice Bailey's *Esoteric Healing*. The writer Arthur Koestler once described this kind of happening as the "Library Angel," who helps you find just what you need, when you need it. In Bailey's book I started finding some different kinds of answers, and by the end of the summer, I had read all of her other books that the library had in stock, and with it began to learn that there was something called the "Ageless Wisdom."

So now I entered medical school with my experiences, a newfound source of information and a passion for science. My medical career developed rapidly, but to the chagrin of some of my mentors, I also got trained in acupuncture, homeopathy, Reiki and a few other "unorthodox" fields. I thought it best not to tell them that I was also studying with a number of spiritual teachers, and in the fullness of time, started helping teach T'ai Chi Ch'uan, Qigong and meditation. I became a successful researcher, but I gradually got more and more pleasure from coming up with ideas and funding, rather than doing the work myself. So I became very involved with and eventually became the chair of the Research Council for Complementary Medicine, as well as working closely with the famous Hale Clinic in London and serving the Foundation for Integrated Medicine, which was the brainchild of His Royal Highness, the Prince of Wales.

For many years now, a great many people have been asking me to write about some of the new concepts of health and healing. I was not eager to do it. I already had plenty to do, and I had seen what happened to many friends when they wrote about unorthodox medicine. Eventually I decided to give in for three reasons.

First, despite a lifetime of teaching students, doctors and my patients how to care for themselves, I had a health challenge myself that led me to reconsider whether the methods had gone wrong. The results of that reconsideration were a revelation that I am going to share with you.

Second, it was clear that, despite all the advances of modern medicine, psychology and psychotherapy, there were more unhappy, unhealthy and unfulfilled people than ever, and the only way to help with that was by going beyond teaching a few thousand professionals a year and helping people before they had "fallen off the cliff." That meant showing individuals a whole new way of looking at themselves, and providing the methods for caring for themselves and those around them.

Finally, we all have a need to leave a legacy. For most of us, that means having children and grandchildren. There is also another type of legacy, and one that you can start building at any point in your life. And that is the need to make the world a better place for those who come after us. If I failed to share some of what I have learned and experienced, that would not just be a shame, it would not have been congruent with my own life purpose. So I realized that it was time to sit down at the keyboard and start!

This book will present a program designed to help you open your mind to new possibilities, leading to a healthier, more productive life. "The purpose of life is to live it." A common enough statement. But what does it really mean? Our life's purpose is more than that; it is to reach our fullest potential—which I'd like you to keep in mind as you progress through this program.

Human beings are changing, adapting and evolving in response to our rapidly changing environment. We know that there have been diseases and whole epidemics that have come and gone before. Infectious diseases like the Black Death and rheumatic fever have come and gone for reasons that were never quite clear, and most of us have known people who have suffered the ravages of coronary heart disease, which was virtually unknown in the 19th century, became progressively more common during the first 75 years of the 20th century, but then began to decrease again, even before the improvement in people's lifestyles.

A final example is one of the most terrible illnesses that has ever afflicted humanity: schizophrenia, a severe mental illness during which people lose contact with reality, and lose their drives and mental abilities. This illness probably existed in historical times, but it seems to have increased very rapidly around 1750, at the beginning of the Industrial Revolution. Until now, nobody has known why. But now, the approach that we are going to be using in this book will give us some important clues.

As complementary and alternative approaches to healing gained ground, something strange began to be noticed: Treatments that worked well in the past were often not as effective today. Conversely, treatments that once worked only occasionally started becoming more stable. Among the lengthening list of new forms of successful physical and psychotherapy treatments are Thought Field Therapy, Quantum-Touch, The Reconnection, and Tapas Acupressure Technique.

Many of these techniques have been discoveries, rather than inventions. Physicians and therapists have been pushing and prodding people for millennia. Their powers of observation were often astonishing. So it is unlikely that they would never have noticed some of these therapies, unless the therapies did not work in the past. Although there are some therapies that rely on novel technology, there is now no question we are seeing clear evidence that the laws of healing are changing.

More than any other field, medicine is based on our understanding of human life. If we think we're no more than machines reacting to the environment, then that's how our medicine will be designed. For as we shall see, we are more than just mobile bags of skin and bones forever at the mercy of our biochemical reactions. It bears repeating that biology is not destiny.

You Are a Healer

After more than three decades of working with thousands of medical doctors, alternative and complementary medicine practitioners, healers and people in all walks of life, I have discovered one certain thing: You are a powerful healer. You may not yet know it, you may not yet have found your own gift, but I can assure you that you have it. You and I may not yet have met, though I hope that one day we shall, but nonetheless, I know you to be a healer. Even if you suffer from ill health, you still have this ability. Indeed I have met some skilled healers who have themselves suffered from chronic ill health.

You may have heard the old expression about all healing being self-healing. And it is quite true. In Chapter Two we are going to learn something about this healing force. We shall see that it is not constrained within your body, that it is more than just heat or magnetism, and that it exists everywhere in the Universe. It is more than just the energy fields that flow in your body. It is the Matrix of Active Information, which we call your Inner Light, your Inner Divine Spark. You can tap into this force for yourself, and also for other people. The only thing that distinguishes you from a professional healer is that he or she has usually done a lot of work on himself or herself to become a conduit for this force. The healer may also have worked with someone who has induced the ability in him or her.

There have been reports going back to antiquity that some illnesses could be cured by applying one person's hands to an ailing part of someone else's body: that some people have healing hands. These claims have persisted over thousands of years and in every culture that I have examined.

There is even some scientific research on healing using the laying on of hands. It seems to require intention and a particularly coherent state of consciousness. For many years now, I have, when asked, treated staff members with various forms of "Energetic medicine," primarily using my hands. An extraordinary number of these people have subsequently found they could do exactly the same thing. I have had a number of seriously ill patients whom we have been able to help and who later became effective healers themselves. This has become so well known that we even coined a term for it, "Quantum Induction," to capture the suddenness of the change.

Most mothers know how to soothe and calm their children. That is as it should be. But there is more: I have observed countless mothers stroking key acupuncture points on children's heads, their ears and their backs. Points that are known to soothe and calm. You may have had that experience yourself. I doubt that anyone ever showed you where to touch and what to do; yet you just knew. And what exactly is an acupuncture point? It is an entry point into your subtle systems.

Later on I will be telling you more about what it was that led me to understand some of the changes taking place in the realm of healing and why I chose gradually to move away from treating individuals to helping people care for themselves. For now we know that education is of cardinal importance, though not in terms of communicating facts and figures. Later we shall be meeting one of the kindest people I ever met, the physicist David Bohm, who spoke of "In-forming"—putting information into—the body, the mind, the subtle systems, the relationships and spirituality of us all. The Ageless Wisdom teaches that the education of the next generation should start before conception, continue during pregnancy, and on throughout childhood. Raising children educated like this will revolutionize our world. Not in terms of making them all little Einsteins, but in terms of creating balanced, integrated, harmonized individuals. I firmly believe this sort of education, which forms the core of this book, should continue throughout life.

Does this all sound Utopian? Well, it is supposed to. However, the whole program is a part of an enterprise begun over 30 years ago that has seen people all over the world make extraordinary progress. Many chronically ill people have recovered, while others with every genetic risk for particular illnesses have avoided them. I am robustly realistic, and know only too well the limitations of any system of care. But if you decide to follow through with this program, you really should start seeing rapid improvements in yourself. And then you can start to help those around you as well.

The Five Domains of Life

Beginning with the familiar, we'll look at a model of health based upon five domains. We sometimes use the technical term "Five Interlinked Nested Domains" or "FINDS." What does this mean exactly? It means that in everything that we are going to be working on, we always consider five domains: physical, psychological, social, subtle and spiritual.

An important principle of this interconnected health model is that it's almost always a mistake to look for a single cause for a problem, imbalance or illness. Not only is it usually wrong to think about "one illness, one cause," but it is also usually not enough to use just one therapy or one health maintenance plan: Carefully coordinated combinations are key, for they generate a powerful synergy.

Since the domains are interlinked, physical and psychological health, to say nothing of our social health, and the health of our subtle systems are difficult to maintain without spiritual health. The road to spiritual health begins with understanding and following the natural laws of the Universe, finding your true Purpose and applying both to the service of others. You and I are going to devote some effort into discovering and applying all three in your own life.

We are going to be learning why a popular way of thinking about psychological forces and subtle systems no longer reflects what is going on inside of and around most people.

We will then look at the evidence for saying that humans are adapting and evolving, not just personally, but also in each of the five primary interconnected areas that we refer to as our Five Domains—and how this is closely connected to various stages of healing. We will see how the changing Laws of Healing have necessitated a changing set of principles for maintaining our health and vitality.

Wisdom: the Integration of Understanding

While useful, knowledge and information are no substitute for understanding. Indeed, recent evidence suggests that people who obtain all their medical information from the Internet may actually do worse than those who rely on more traditional forms of information. It is our intention here to provide both information and understanding. When understandings become integrated, we may see the birth of wisdom. When reading, keep in mind there is often more to communication than just the facts. To get the most out of this program, I urge you to let the messages seep into your Being.

There are many fine books, articles and websites about health and healing. However, what I really would like is for you to gain a deeper understanding about these subjects, and that comes not just from reading, but also from gradually allowing the material to expand your cognition and ultimately your consciousness. In the first half of the book, we can, and we shall, do that by presenting new mind-stretching material.

But there is something more. Books have been written and music and poems composed that contain triggers to increase a person's awareness. You have probably noticed how some speakers and teachers seem to be able to communicate a lot more than is contained in the words themselves. It is my sincere hope and expectation that you will find here more than just the words themselves. In the second half of the book I am going to give you the opportunity to become very engaged in applying this deeper understanding as we do a series of exercises and experiments. As we do them, we shall be discovering new perspectives and new insights, and deepening our understanding.

One final point: While I've taught countless people these methods for maintaining wellness, this information may not work for everyone. I have had my failures, and I am suspicious of anyone who tells me that he or she has a 100 percent success rate at anything! As with all forms of treatment and personal management programs, it is these "failures," that continue attracting most of my attention, since they have helped us refine some of these methods. I put "failures" in quotation marks because I am not sure there are ever any failures. Health and illness, success and failure, are all part of the natural cycle of existence, and I hope that I can help you see the play of these cycles in your own life.

Virtually everyone knows the basics of physical self-care, and yet so few people actually follow a set plan to help themselves. Not only do most people never get beyond chapter one of books on health, or cassette one of a tape program, but one of the most commonly owned but least-used item in the American home is a piece of exercise equipment. We have to look at why this is and what we can do to keep you on track.

If you think that I am optimistic about your future, you are quite correct! How can I be so optimistic, with all the constant bad news in the media? Number one is experience, and number two is that the constant depressing news tells me something else. Let's go beyond the simple notion that bad news sells. We are hardwired, genetically programmed, to respond to bad news, because it has survival value. Bad news is designed to have us produce an emotional reaction to prepare us to move. If you have ever seen animals signal warnings of distress to each other, that was the forerunner of negative reporting! It is our intention in this program to show you that your genetic programming is not the only factor driving your life. A key to your life is to transcend the blind dictates of your genes.

Throughout the chapters that follow, and most especially in the second half of the book, I will be suggesting experiments and exercises for you to do. They are designed with one principle in mind: You already have most of the answers. You have access to much of the wisdom that you need, but what you may not yet have is the means to get at it. The exercises have been refined over many years and are all designed to help your Inner Wisdom bubble up and to inform your mind, your subtle systems and your body.

Once you understand the new principles of combining and harmonizing different healing approaches, you will then find the precise steps to help yourself. If I help empower you, your results will be far deeper and more extensive than anything we could achieve by simply offering you instructions or prescriptions.

The reason why I would like to guide you toward some experimentation is this: People normally look at a book or a tape or a CD program for as long as it takes to "get it." To get the gist of what the author is trying to communicate. Then it's on to the next thing. However, I have found from very long experience that there is often a great deal more "meat" to be found later on.

Lecturers are normally supposed to communicate one point during a 30-minute lecture, and two points during a 45-minute lecture. Good, engaging lecturers can often get in an extra point. I am a great believer in the old saying that "If you give a man a fish, you feed him for a day; if you teach him how to fish, he will be fed for the rest of his life." I am going to teach you how to fish. You can do a great deal if I guide you to do a little work on yourself. And then in no time at all, you will discover that you have made a number of great strides toward your ultimate goals of health and wellness for yourself and your family and friends.

We are going to lead into the next chapter with an important quotation from Nobel Laureate Alex Carrel:

> "The future of medicine is subordinate to its concept of the human being ... To date we have studied ourselves only in such a way as to procure fragmentary concepts of what we are. Our analysis began right from the outset by severing the continuity of the human being and his cosmic and social environment. Then it separated the soul from the body. The body was divided into organs, cells and fluids. And in this spirit of dissection, the spirit has vanished."

In this book, we are going to make sure that all these fragments are going to be reintegrated and placed back where they belong.

Chapter Two
Straws in the Wind

The Force

The single greatest Force in the human body is its constant drive to heal itself. Your thoughts and your emotions, your relationships, your environment and your beliefs can affect this Force. Mental, emotional and social experiences and expectations can be transmuted into changes in your physiology.

What Exactly Is This Force?

It is your Inner Light. As we shall see in a moment, it is, technically speaking, the "information" that supports every aspect of your being. From the time you were conceived, you have had an intelligent design plan, which we call an "Informational Matrix." More than just your DNA, it is this matrix, this design plan that maintains the harmonious integrity of your body, your mind, your subtle systems and spirit. When this Informational Matrix becomes corrupted by negative thoughts or emotions, by toxins or other types of outside interference, we can see illness develop. We age primarily because the information systems gradually become corrupted over time.

It is this matrix that underlies the ancient writings about qi (chi) in China and prana in India. Qi is often mistranslated as "Energy," but it really is better thought of as an influence that leads to the production of the energy systems that maintain the body and flow around it and throughout Nature.

Some Words About Qi

I was teaching a class in Integrated Medicine at the University of Pennsylvania, when the unthinkable happened. Usually I am early, but on this particular day I walked in at the precise moment that I was due to start lecturing on Traditional Chinese Medicine. I apologized for being late, and used the reason for being late as an example of our topic. As I explained, I was late because I had been trying to help a very distressed individual with that abnormal and exhausting elevation of mood that we call mania. She was speaking extremely fast and very loudly, and making very little sense. She was restless, moving incessantly and giggling.

"And," I went on, "in the Chinese system, we would describe this as an excess of Yang Qi. Now for those of you attending my psychopharmacology class next week, I shall then be giving you a detailed breakdown of the chemical disturbances in this poor lady's brain that are causing her symptoms. So how can we reconcile these two descriptions of the same person? Well, we would put it this way. The ancient Chinese identified over 20 types of Qi. The first fundamental disturbance is of Active Information. That leads to a disruption of the energy flow in the body, which in turn disturbs fundamental biochemical processes in the brain and throughout the body. Because thoughts and emotions are not generated just in the brain."

These were very smart students, and I got the expected question: "So why is it necessary to bring information and Qi into the equation? Why not just leave it at the level of biochemistry? Surely that explains everything."

I responded like this: "That is indeed the central question. The reason for including these other factors is that they—together with the chemistry—give us a more comprehensive and more comprehensible picture of what is going on here. If we leave out the psychological, the social, the subtle and the spiritual, we are left with an incomplete account of the person, and of the illness. If we leave those factors out of any description of the world, we have to ignore a lot of observations in every realm of science.

This holistic model enables us to generate hypotheses that we can test and treatments that we can try."

Robert's Recovery: Repairing a Ravaged Brain

It was a warm and sunny day in Philadelphia. The stifling heat of summer had given way to one of those bright days that promise a delightful fall season. And then, at 11 o'clock on a Tuesday morning in October, I witnessed a miracle.

It was in the observation room beside the nurses' station on the neuropsychiatric unit of the University of Pennsylvania Medical Center. And with me were many of the staff on the ward and the family of the young man who had been referred to me from central Pennsylvania just two weeks earlier.

The man, whom I shall call Robert, was 34 years old and the CEO of an innovative software company. He was married and the proud father of three young children. Although he had come from a modest background, his intelligence, hard work, perseverance and charisma had enabled him to move from a tiny farmhouse to a nice new home that he had built in central Pennsylvania. It really looked as if he had it made.

And then catastrophe struck. He woke up one morning in September with an unbearably severe headache, followed by strange speech. As the hours went by, he could no longer identify simple things, he was losing the ability to speak at all, and he became more and more disinhibited. The diagnosis at the local hospital was that Robert was suffering from a particularly destructive type of viral infection of the brain.

Though immediately given all the finest treatments available to modern medicine, Robert continued deteriorating. Other consultants came in. He was given medicines to attack the virus, reduce brain swelling and stabilize his behavior. Then a homeopathic physician tried to help. Robert didn't improve.

In desperation, the family asked if there was anyone else to consult. My neurologist friend, who had treated Robert, suggested they have him transferred to my care at the University Medical Center. When he arrived, we rapidly confirmed the diagnosis. From some extraordinarily sophisticated investigations, we found that the virus had already ravaged the brain. Instead of the usual crisp structure and coordinated activity that I normally see in the nervous system, the scans presented a picture of scorched and devastated brain: some areas swollen. Some where brain cells had clearly already died. Random electrical activity. We all felt that, barring a miracle, the outcome was grim and that Robert would likely need lifelong residential care.

The trouble is, I am a little stubborn, so, in addition to his conventional medications, I tried a new method that I had been working on. Based on the idea that it is possible to re-establish the normal "Informational Matrix" of the body, I worked with other hospital staff members, touching acupuncture points, concentrating on correcting the flawed information patterns. One person touched specific points on the feet; the other worked with corresponding points on the head and neck. We did two sessions a day, each lasting about 30 minutes. Within two days, and to everyone's astonishment, he began to recover, and the brain scans improved.

A few weeks later, I ran into one of my friends, a renowned neurologist whom I had asked in to consult on Robert and who had echoed all the gloomy prognostications. He asked me what had happened. I told him it was incredibly gratifying to be able to discharge Robert home last week. "He is almost back to normal, apart from a little difficulty finding some of his words," I said. The neurologist was dumbstruck.

The Wellness Approach

There is nothing new about unexpected or spontaneous healing. In fact, some years ago, one of the pioneers of integrated medicine—Andrew Weil—published a whole book on the subject, with some excellent advice on how to keep healthy and how to induce a healing response. More than 10 years ago, the Institute of Noetic Sciences in California sponsored a comprehensive report on the phenomenon. But this was different: It was planned. Just a day or two later, we had the opportunity to see something similar.

> A 38-year-old man was admitted to my unit after an extremely serious suicide attempt, which occurred during a bout of severe depression. We tried everything I could think of to treat his depression. After several weeks, still nothing. He was mute; he was bed-bound and starving himself. In sheer desperation, we tried the new method that we had been working on. Based on the same idea that it is possible to correct a person's Information System, I worked with one other person and then another, as before, touching acupuncture points on the feet and the head, and simply concentrating on a healthy signal, which would then allow the free flow of energy throughout the system, and that would then correct his biochemistry. Two hours after we had finished, he got out of bed and asked for something to eat. Within another week he was ready for discharge from the hospital.

My first inclination was to publish these cases in the scientific literature, but it was clearly still too early to do so. And we immediately ran into a problem. Most of the newer therapies work differently on different people, which make clinical trials very difficult. If I want to test an antibiotic, it is very easy to design a good study, with endpoints and so on, but far more difficult when we have therapies that work on unseen and controversial domains of a person. Whenever something new like this comes along, particularly something that seems to work where other treatments do not, we have to be extra careful not to give false hope, and no treatment works every time. So the standards of evidence have to be extremely high. It was for this reason that I have gradually moved away from treating people who are ill, to using the same methods for helping people enhance and maintain their wellness so that they can fulfill their potential, rather than waiting until an illness has already struck.

There have been two distinct approaches to health in the Western medical tradition. The first is that the role of a physician is to treat diseases. That is the way that all my colleagues and I were trained. The second approach is to consider that health is the natural order of things. So in the first case we constantly hear the use of military metaphors: People speak of "a war on cancer," "killer cells," "magic bullets," and the need to adopt a "fighting spirit." Sadly this aggressive attitude by the medical profession may be at odds with the wishes and needs of an individual, the family and the other people in a person's life. We have to try to strike a balance between the whole instinct to fight and expressions of healing and acceptance.

In the second case, the philosophy is grounded in the idea that we need to work in harmony with Nature. The maintenance of health and wellbeing comes from re-establishing balance and harmony not just in ourselves but also in our relationships with each other, with society and with the entire environment around us. This is important: The way that we look at illness and ourselves is a direct reflection of our overall worldview. We cannot really try to evolve medicine in any meaningful way unless we have a clear model of what it means to be human.

Redefining Today's Medical Model

The dominant paradigm in medicine is entirely materialist and reductionist. There is no place for purpose or meaning. However, most scientists do not realize that their craft rests on a series of philosophical assumptions that are open to question. And some get really annoyed if they are challenged. Although, interestingly, it is normally not the top-line folks. They have the

> "An open mind is a very bad thing—everything falls out"
> —Lewis Wolpert (South African-born Emeritus Professor of Anatomy and Biology, University College London, and Fellow of the Royal Society, 1932–)

self-confidence to take challenges in their stride, and to see how new ideas and concepts fit together. They also understand that the definition of what is "scientific" in medicine has varied over time. In the early days of the United States, most of the great physicians of the time were convinced that bloodletting and purging were examples of enlightened scientific medicine. But it is now well known that these very practices probably contributed to the death of George Washington.

Happily, there are many people in positions of power and authority who understand that there are problems with the materialist paradigm and are trying to do something about it.

I have had the privilege of having several extraordinary mentors in medicine, others in science and yet others in the Ageless Wisdom. When I was a young doctor, one of my medical mentors was the late Sir John Ellis, one of the best clinicians I have ever known. He was someone who possessed profound clinical wisdom and an approach that at the time was rather unusual. Although an internist, he had been much influenced by a remarkable Hungarian-born English psychologist called Michael Balint, with whom he had worked, and who had first proposed in the 1950s that often the doctor functions as a "drug"—as the actual therapeutic agent—and that the true role of a doctor or a therapist is to help people feel better and lead happier and more satisfying lives.

Sir John used to have a "special clinic," where he would see some extraordinarily tough cases that had been referred by senior physicians from all over southern England. Every few months he would select a young doctor to work with him. Most did not enjoy the work and stayed only a short time, but I loved the challenge and the approach. Although he was very much the conventional dominant patriarchal physician, it was extraordinary to see Sir John in action. He had a remarkable ability to focus on someone very intently, almost as if looking inside them. And then, as if by magic, the person would start getting better. He had induced the healing process.

When I once said to him that he was a good old-fashioned "Healer," he was quiet for a moment. Then a warm, good-natured smile crossed his face. He looked me straight in the eye and said, "Yes. But hardly anyone else has ever noticed. You did, because you are one too. In my 40 years in medicine, over a dozen of them as dean of this medical school, I have only ever found a handful of physicians who had the Gift. But don't you dare quote me until after I have retired!" Even a man as powerful and influential as he, did not want people to think that he was somehow odd or eccentric.

Outdated Research: Digging Deeper

London houses some of the finest libraries in the world, and for five years I spent one or two days each week chasing down the literature about anomalies that did not fit the accepted scientific framework. I still have stacks of reprints from those days. Sometimes I would find information that had been repeated from one textbook to another, or from one popular book to another. Yet when I looked at the original report, it said something completely different or had been mistranslated. Some research keeps getting quoted even after it has been found to be flawed. Sometimes books and papers written in other languages get quoted incorrectly. As a young student I did not know that until I started looking at original papers in French, German and several other languages.

Everything that you and I are going to discuss and discover is based on personal experience and on thousands and thousands of hours of reanalyzing and reinterpreting mountains of information from more than a dozen fields of inquiry. With the passage of time, it has become more and more clear how little we really know about the body, the brain and the mind.

The further I got into these different fields, the more challenging they became. I found that there were hundreds of different forms of therapy and scores of ways of describing people including psychology, sociology, astrology, the Enneagram and the Seven Rays. The list went on and on. So instead of deciding on one system, I decided to start from the other direction. To assume that they all had a piece of the truth, and then to try and find out what it was. There were also a lot of presuppositions that had been passed down for years. I also found an awful lot of theories that made no sense in terms of established psychological principles. Well, sometimes that's a good thing. Many established principles are wrong. But sometimes people had not done their homework.

Let me give three simple examples of concepts that have been taken for granted, but for which there is little good evidence:

1. That there is one cause for an illness. We call this the myth of "unicausality." Apart from trauma, there are extremely few examples of one illness being caused by just one deranged gene or one missing nutrient.

2. That the best way of describing depth psychological phenomena and "Energy" is as a series of flows of water: The "hydraulic metaphor." Metaphors matter. They can define and pattern our thinking and our understanding. At a conference in London in 1988, the writer Katherine Whitehorn used some beautiful language to describe the notion of healing, using a "hydraulic"

metaphor: "The only thing which every form of therapy seems to have in common is a reliance, greater or less, on the springs of healing within the patient; an underground reservoir, if this is not being fanciful, that could be caused to gush forth by a very great variety of drilling equipment." This false metaphor may limit us. As we shall see, if we think of information as primary, and energy flows as secondary, we gain a surprising degree of understanding and balance in our lives.

3.   That it is a good idea to stimulate the immune system. Well, it is a good idea to balance the immune system, but it can get overstimulated, and then autoimmune diseases can follow.

> "We are seeking for the simplest possible scheme of thought that will bind together the observed facts."
> —Albert Einstein (German-born American Physicist and, in 1921, Winner of the Nobel Prize in Physics, 1879–1955)

The Case for Connection

A sad thing that has happened in the last few centuries is a retreat from the understanding that the entire universe is interconnected. How do I know this? First, from personal experience and second because that is precisely what scientific observation has shown us. The deeper that we have looked into nature, and into current explanatory models, the more evidence we have found that there is indeed an entire living network of information that underlies the universe. That feeds, supports, nourishes and loves it. Once we begin to understand that, it quickly becomes clear that there are whole new possibilities for understanding ourselves and for healing our world and ourselves.

Science and the Akashic Field

From the earliest days of this quest, the objective was to try to find some overarching theory to explain how different pieces of information fit together. The Ageless Wisdom speaks of this being the time of the "Avatar of Synthesis," an intense desire to make sense of mountains of data in many different fields. Many others have been working on this too. Over the last 20 years, some of the most astonishingly comprehensive theories have come from Ken Wilber and Ervin Laszlo. We shall be meeting Ken Wilber again a little later, but I would like to say a few words about the work of Ervin Laszlo that directly impacts on the material that we are discussing in this book.

Most of Laszlo's works are quite technical, but just as I was finishing writing my own book in December 2004, he brought out a wonderful volume for a general readership, called *Science and the Akashic Field*.

"Akash" or "Akasha" is a Sanskrit word for the most fundamental of the five elements. So we would have Earth, Fire, Air, Water and Akasha. The "Akashic Record" is supposed to be an enduring memory of everything that has ever happened or *will ever* happen. These terms were widely adopted by spiritualists about 100 years ago, and for that reason, as well as an apparent lack of any kind of scientific proof for a fundamental force, the concept was largely ignored throughout the 20th century. But as Laszlo shows, we were probably wrong to have done so. He picks up on and brilliantly develops a notion that many of us, in particular Deepak Chopra, have been discussing for some time. It was actually the theme of a lecture that I gave at the Society for Psychical Research in London in 1985, but at that time we did not have all the pieces, and the idea remained "on the shelf." Laszlo does a masterful job of pulling in a lot of data that have appeared over the last two decades. And what is this key idea? It is the concept that the primary factor needed to create a Theory of Everything is "information." As we shall see, this is almost certainly correct, and fits in with everything that we are discussing here.

Unseen Data: Energetic Information

When we think about information, we usually think in terms of data, or what somebody knows. But there is more to it. In the late 1940s, a brilliant man called Claude Shannon first talked about information theory, and why information could be a fundamental aspect of nature. We have already seen how the late David Bohm went so far as to call it "in-formation," to illustrate that a message actually "forms" the recipient.

> "God's first language is silence, and all else is a bad translation."
> —Father Thomas Keating (American Cistercian Monk and Priest, 1923–)

When we treat someone with acupuncture or Reiki, it is not so much that we are squirting "Energy" into him or her, but that we are giving that person's whole organism some cleaned-up information that has a positive effect on the person receiving the treatment. The programs that we suggest in this book are designed to induce beneficial changes in the "Informational Matrix" that underlies every part of your being. It has been known for a long time that if people are going to be effective healers, then it is really important for them to have done some work on themselves. Otherwise, they can do more harm than good. We interpret that to mean that if they have not done the necessary preparatory work, then they may be inducing faulty messages. This is very similar to the effects of attending a religious service. People often leave uplifted because they have felt a Divine Presence. Cool, clear, unadulterated Spiritual "Information." The same happens sometimes when they have been in the presence of a spiritual master. There are countless reports of people being transformed simply by being in the presence of some of the great sages like the "Sage of Arunachala," Ramana Maharshi. For 50 years he taught people from all over the world who came to his ashram in southern India. For most of that time he did not speak, insisting that the greatest truths were transmitted in silence. Countless people were transformed by sitting with him. A deep, blissful and joyous feeling that often continued after they left and moved to other parts of the world. I have known many who have maintained these long-term and long-distance connections with teachers like Sai Baba and Nisargadatta Maharaj. Something clearly happens, and it has all the hallmarks of being "nonlocal."

We're All in This Together

This word *nonlocal* has become a bit of a buzzword recently, so let me explain what it means and why it is so very important. It is an idea first proposed by the Irish physicist J.S. Bell in the 1960s. And it is that, at the microscopic quantum level, particles that have been in contact remain permanently connected.

> "There is a continuum which links all living things together so that the smallest cell does not pulsate without its effects being felt in the furthest regions of the universe"
> —Douglas Baker (South African-born British Writer and Spiritual Teacher, 1922–)

Although it has been repeatedly demonstrated in the laboratory, for a long time it seemed no more than a curiosity. The effect was infrequent and unstable and had not been shown to occur except with the super tiny particles. But then data started coming in from surprising sources: The "distant viewing" experiments of Russell Targ and Harold Puthoff in the 1970s; work reported from the Princeton Engineering Anomalies Research (PEAR) Laboratory; some exquisitely clear-cut research by Dean Radin, first while he was at the University of Nevada, and now at the Institute of Noetic Sciences; and finally, the wealth of data on distant healing has really made it seem very clear that these nonlocal effects do indeed occur in the world of large physical objects. Not surprisingly, this research is so important for our understanding of the world, that it has all been viciously attacked. But the fact is that the data keep coming in, and keep resisting the most ferocious attacks.

These concepts are far from being academic. If we can understand one or two fairly simple ideas, it will help us plan our own wellness strategies and guide us in many other aspects of our lives. If we have all been correct all along, and that the missing key has, all along, been "Information," then there are some very important consequences. As Ervin Laszlo says:

> "This concept ... merits being known. First, because the energy-and information-imbued "informed universe" is a meaningful universe, and in our time of accelerating change and mounting disorientation we are much in need of a meaningful view of ourselves and of the world. Second, because understanding the essential contours of the informed universe does not call for having a background in the sciences; they are readily comprehendible by everyone. And last, but not least, because the informed universe is probably the most comprehensive concept of the world ever to come in from science. It is, at last, a truly unified concept of cosmos, life and mind."

A key point for us is this: Despite the *initial* evidence of our senses, and despite three centuries of reductionist science, there is more and more evidence that we live in a wonderfully, magically interconnected universe, in which each and every thing is interconnected with each and every other thing. You may have heard of the "butterfly effect." This was a proposal made some years ago that even very small changes in a system could have massive effects down-stream. So the flapping of a butterfly's wings in Brazil, could, under the right conditions, produce one cascade of effects after another, until we have a tornado in Oklahoma. This notion of interconnectedness takes us even further. If you yell at someone today, then the effects will spread out into the world. If you spend your day in a calm, positive, non-judgmental state, then that will spread out as well. Believe it or not, there is some experimental data to verify that assertion. We are all in this together!

Chapter Three
Our Changing Planet, Our Evolving People

One Hundred Years: The Biggest Shift in History?

In the year 1905:

The average life expectancy in the U.S. was 47.

Only 14 percent of the homes in the U.S. had a bathtub.

There were only 8,000 cars in the U.S. and only 144 miles of paved roads, and the maximum speed limit in most cities was 10 mph.

More than 95 percent of all births in the U.S. took place at home.

Ninety percent of all U.S. physicians had no college education. Instead, they attended medical schools, many of which were condemned in the press and by the government as "substandard."

At a time when the average wage in the U.S. was 22 cents an hour, sugar cost four cents a pound. The average annual intake of refined sugar was 60 pounds per head, up from 7 pounds per head in 1805. (It is estimated to be about 150 pounds per head in 2005. A twenty fold increase in just 200 years.)

The five leading causes of death in the U.S. were:
1. Pneumonia and influenza
2. Tuberculosis
3. Diarrhea
4. Heart disease
5. Stroke

There were only about 230 reported murders in the entire U.S.

Only 8 percent of homes had a telephone, and there were no computers, airplanes or 24-hour lighting.

The human body contained several hundred fewer synthetic chemicals than it does today.

We did not originally evolve to deal with the immense changes that have assailed our planet and us over the last hundred years. If you look back one thousand years, the change is even more stunning. But we did evolve with the ability to adapt to a changing environment. The problem is that sometimes our adaptations occur unevenly, and these underlie many of the strains and illnesses of today.

"Observe constantly that all things take place by change, and accustom thyself to consider that the nature of the Universe loves nothing so much as to change the things which are, and to make new things like them."
—Marcus Aurelius, (Roman Emperor and Philosopher, A.D.121–180)

If we are going to understand ourselves and how to use the evolving laws of health and healing, we need to know a little bit about where we came from.

New Natural Laws

We began the last chapter by remarking that the single greatest force in the human body is its constant drive to heal itself. Now, since we are an integral part of Nature, here is something that should not be a surprise: The single greatest force in Nature is a constant drive to heal itself.

"The major problems in the world are the result of the difference between the way nature works and the way man thinks."
—Gregory Bateson (English-born American Anthropologist and Writer, 1904–1980)

Illness and distress occur when we, our relationships and our organizations and cultures fail to follow the natural laws of self-healing. This is why there has been so much interest in studying the ways in which organisms defend themselves against infections and then applying the same principles to computer security. Or looking at the principles of biological harmony to help us understand how to operate our businesses more efficiently. The point is this: Change and accompanying stress are not random or chaotic, but follow certain rules. Understanding and finding a response to these rules lie at the heart of health and wellness. Because we need to have a clear understanding about health and wellness, we also need clear, self-empowering evidence.

Now here is something very useful: We have a goldmine of evidence that has been largely ignored. To tap this evidence, we need to understand an immensely useful notion. Sometimes Nature does our experiments for us. For example, vascular disease—disruptions of some blood vessels—is much more common in diabetes mellitus. We have a pretty good idea about the chemical and cellular disturbances in diabetes, so we can use diabetes as a model to study vascular disease in general. Examining illness can inform us about how to avoid it, and on the other side of the coin, a study of exceptional human performance can inspire us to understand what is possible for us. Hence all our interest in "spontaneous" healing and in reports of extraordinary abilities to control the mind and the body.

Nature constantly heals itself by maintaining and re-establishing a coherent stream of information. The principle mechanisms by which this stream of information plays out are the three processes of development, evolution and adaptation. We develop throughout our lives, as new informational programs come into play. Humans have the longest period of dependency of any animal species, in part because of the need of the head and the brain to develop after birth, since the mother's pelvis could never allow delivery of a fully developed individual. As children reach adolescence, their behavior may change, from a combination of neurological developments and hormonal changes, which are preparing the developing person to leave the nest. A lot of new data about the development of young people help explain their vulnerability to impulsive and risky behavior. We shall have an even better understanding as we examine the subtle and spiritual aspects of development.

So apart from development, what about adaptation? The way in which Nature adapts can be genetic, biochemical, physiological, behavioral and even cultural. Climate change and diseases have had profound impacts throughout history. The mini Ice Age that affected Europe from 1300 to 1850 was responsible for substantial farming and industrial development. Sadly, Nature sometimes cannot adapt in time, as we can see with the devastating consequences of AIDS in Africa.

There is sometimes a real misunderstanding about what the theory of evolution does and does not say. It is true that some people have used it as a tool to say that there is no need for any form of creation. That everything can be reduced to a few molecules swimming around in a lagoon. Simple molecular models can indeed generate very complex forms and structures. But notice that I have said that they used it as a *tool*. There is nothing whatsoever in the theory, and in all the experiments that have confirmed it, that shut out more subtle and even spiritual forces. All that the theory does is to provide a physical mechanism for how we adapt to the environment.

Looking more deeply at human evolution and adaptation is key to understanding who we are and how we can do better. Evolution means change, but the direction of that change depends on what is useful and adaptive at a particular time and in a particular place. Thick fur is very nice for a polar bear, but would be the kiss of death if he were to live in the Sahara. Evolution is not just constant progress is one direction.

The Case of the Mice and the Marram Grass

Many years ago there was a comment in an article published in the venerable *British Medical Journal.* It described an astonishingly important observation that had been made on the sand dunes of East Anglia in England. Mice who had been poisoned with the anticoagulant warfarin would go out onto the dunes looking for marram grass. They would only stop when they found this particular grass. No trial and error nibbling at any stems of grass that they found. It had to be marram grass. This sturdy grass is loaded with Vitamin K, a natural antidote for warfarin poisoning. This raises very interesting questions. How did the mice know which grass to go for? Clearly they could not have a gene directing them toward finding marram grass, and it's unlikely other mice could have taught them this trick.

There are many examples like this throughout the animal kingdom. From dogs and cats that eat grass when they have eaten something bad, to elephants who eat clay to soothe their stomachs when they have problems with acid. But such explanations fall down when we look at the marram-grass-searching mice. Or other equally intriguing observations: Hedgehogs use a combination of saliva and pungent herbs like tobacco and mint to fend off fungi and pests, while some birds crush ants against their feathers to repel pests. All imply a form of *knowing* what is best.

So why have we lost this ability? Or have we? There is in fact some powerful evidence to suggest that we do have access to a whole seam of knowledge about the world around us. The anthropologist Jeremy Narby studied shamans in the Amazonian rainforest who have found safe and effective herbal treatments among the 80,000 plants available to them. They are usually used in combinations, and to have tested all the plants and all the possible combinations would have taken hundreds of thousands of years. So it cannot have been done by trial and error. I have seen something similar in traditional Chinese herbal medicine, where combinations are invariably used, and once again, if the effective ones had been discovered by trial and error, it would have taken armies of physicians working for countless thousands of years.

But there is more. The annals of scientific research are full of extraordinarily interesting facts. Yet few have tried to take them all and weld them into a coherent picture that will include the subtle and spiritual realms. However, when we do that, we learn some amazing things about ourselves, and the other inhabitants of this body that we call the Earth.

Black Grasshoppers, Pepper Moths and Herring Gulls

In his story *Big Two-Hearted River*, Ernest Hemingway wrote about a character seeing a black grasshopper after a forest fire. And he was quite correct. Faced by a sudden environmental change, a grasshopper can indeed adapt to the color of the environment, changing the pigments in its skin by switching on a specific gene. If he remained bright green in a black environment, it is a safe bet that he would soon feature on someone's lunch menu. This is an example of high-speed adaptation occurring at a deep level of the organism.

The 19th century saw one of the most interesting examples of rapid *micro*evolution. The peppered moth was, until 1845, light-colored. In that year a black peppered moth was caught near Manchester, England. This was a heavily polluted area during the height of the industrial revolution. As pollution increased, more of the black forms were captured. In the most heavily polluted areas, the black form became the dominant variety. There was even a term introduced to describe this phenomenon: "industrial melanism." It was soon discovered that moths that did not darken were more likely to get eaten by birds.

Nearly 200 species of insects changed color as rural pastures gave way to the environmental blight of the Industrial Revolution. Individuals changed color, and so did their descendents. As England gradually cleaned up the mess of industrial pollution, dark moths gradually gave way to light ones again.

Even at the level of the physical body, evolution and adaptation can be extremely rapid. When we look at the evolution of the mind, which will be the topic of the next chapter, we see that change can be even faster and more far-reaching.

In the study of animal behavior, we use the term "releaser," which refers to a stimulus that has evolved to facilitate communication between animals of the same species. The natural world is full of examples of releasers, including brightly colored plumage and behavioral displays of male birds that help them attract mates. A more sophisticated example is the way in which an increase in the amount of light in the springtime causes a cascade of hormones in the body of a songbird, so that he begins to grow the parts of his brain that are responsible for generating his songs. But there is something more. It has been discovered that a wide range of organisms frequently responds more vigorously to releasers that are different from those found in Nature. They are known as "supernormal" releasers.

The European herring gull has a yellow beak, but on one side it has an orange spot. When the gull chick pecks at this spot, the parent regurgitates food for it. But if you paint the orange dot red, the chicks peck far more vigorously. Paint the whole beak red, and the pecking becomes frenzied. This suggests that the naturally occurring stimulus is not the best one for inducing an instinctive response.

You will be able to think of several examples in humans, for instance when cosmetic surgery to "increase this" or "reduce that" is done to induce specific responses in other people. But if a bird has too much plumage or sings too loudly, it might attract predators rather than mates. And some of the consequences of cosmetic surgery might make life difficult if we ever had to revert to the sort of environment in which we evolved.

"What we see depends mainly on what we look for."
—John Lubbock (English Statesman, 1834–1913)

Why is this important for us? Because it suggests that there is a powerful *potential* evolutionary force. We have always thought of evolution as an organism's blind response to something in the environment. But what if the response comes first? A bird develops the possibility of having an orange beak, and then Nature "looks around" for a way to use it: to find a stimulus to release it. If that is indeed true, it suggests a far more sophisticated and far more wonderful basis for behavior. That, far from being a simple set of responses to things going on in the environment, an organism develops and stores capacities and potential responses so that it can be ready to deal with environmental change. All of which suggest Purpose.

As I am writing this, we have all been horrified by the devastation that the tsunami visited on the lands of the Indian Ocean. You may have seen reports in the media that, although there has been an appalling human toll, animals appear to have escaped. After closely reviewing reports from the regions about the impact on animals, I've found that the animals that survived ran away before the disaster struck. In the literature there are countless reports of animals who seem to sense when a disaster or catastrophe is about to occur. The most striking examples concern earthquakes, when animals have been reported to go into hiding up to 12 hours before the earthquakes strike. In Southern China, animals have actually been used as an "early warning system" for earthquakes. There have been attempts to explain this behavior by theorizing that the animals sense changes in ionization of the air, or the releases of gases from the Earth's crust. Neither seems likely here, and I attribute the animals' survival to a kind of "sixth sense," implying that some animals have access to modes of knowing that most humans do not. But we are going to show you that you can, with a little training, access this rich seam of information.

The Dancing Genes

You will remember that we mentioned in Chapter One that we now think of genes as being far from the fixed structures depicted in high school textbooks. It is more accurate to think of the dancing genes, in constant motion in response to the environment and our mental states. Your appearance and the way you metabolize and behave are the product of your genes, your environment and your experiences. Let us begin to look at this a little further.

A person's fat distribution is largely genetically controlled. It has now also been shown that the composition of the diet can help determine where fat is laid down. Katherine Tucker and her colleagues at the Friedman School of Nutrition Science and Policy in Boston have spent years looking at the physical consequences of different diets. She has found that people who consumed a lot of refined carbohydrates tended to store more fat in the abdomen, even without a large change in weight. And it is this fat inside the abdomen that is linked with many illnesses. Interestingly, people who ate more whole grains, beans, fruits and vegetables were less likely to have a change in waist circumference.

> "In all affairs it is a healthy thing now and then to hang a question mark on the things you have long taken for granted."
> —Bertrand Russell (Welsh Mathematician, Philosopher, Pacifist and, in 1950, Winner of the Nobel Prize in Literature, 1872–1970)

The most mobile genes are those involved in controlling the immune system. There has been a strange and paradoxical observation that the best way to prevent allergies in children is to expose them to the allergy-causing agents ("allergens"). For instance, the more pets a child has, the less likely he or she is to develop allergies later in life.

Genes are important, but with the exception of some inborn metabolic problems, they rarely spell inevitability. Although genes play an important role in determining who develops breast cancer, so can diet. Eating a high-carbohydrate diet seems to increase the risk of developing the illness, probably by raising the levels of insulin in the body, which can cause cells to grow abnormally.

One of the most exciting examples of the environment modulating gene expression has come from some amazing experiments on one of the genes responsible for controlling the brain chemical acetylcholine, involved in everything from memory and attention to sweating. Nicotine works on acetylcholine receptors, which is why smokers sometimes claim they can concentrate better after smoking a cigarette. The new discovery is this: Stress—both physical and emotional—can change the way in which one of the acetylcholine genes manufactures its proteins. This is the most recent example of the mechanism by which the mind can affect genes. And it may provide the link between stress and Alzheimer's disease.

In conventional medicine, it is often useful to define and classify illnesses. So we will try to determine whether or not someone has streptococcal (strep) throat or a viral infection. The former can be serious and warrants antibiotics, while the latter will likely improve without antibiotics. When we classify an illness, we can either think of it as a "category," like strep throat or a heart attack, or we can think about it as a "dimension." So instead of seeing illness as a separate entity, we think of health and illnesses as lying on a spectrum, running all the way from being healthy and well, through mild degrees of just not feeling "right," to being severely ill.

This second way of thinking is particularly useful when we are thinking about psychological problems. The world is full of people who are a little bit obsessive, or who get bad mood swings, but they are not bad enough to be called an "illness." In fact, having some of these traits can be enormously beneficial, and they have continued in the population because they have a survival advantage. If I need to have surgery, I sincerely hope that my surgeon will be mildly obsessive, rather than discovering a few weeks later that he had forgotten to do something he should have!

In January of 2005, some of my colleagues in Edinburgh, Scotland, published an important paper, after studying people at high risk of developing schizophrenia. Many of the people who were at high risk of developing the illness did not, although some had transient and partial symptoms. We also know that some family members—the carriers of the genes—may also suffer from some specific symptoms. This shows us again how the genes do not control everything: Many people suffer from mild cases because their environment or personality helped protect them from developing a full-blown case. These findings also give us important clues as to how we may be able to reduce the risk of an illness expressing itself. This demonstrates that diagnoses are not always cut and dried. Medical professionals are sometimes unable to reach a definitive diagnosis, needing to wait and see how things develop. With a few notable exceptions, whatever your genetic risk of an illness, it is not inevitable that you will suffer from it, however strong your "genetic loading." Later we will be looking at specific techniques for helping you avoid some of these difficulties or for preventing and even reversing them if you are already in trouble.

Evolution in Human Health and Disease

A popular and valuable approach to understanding illness has been to apply evolutionary principles, known as Darwinian medicine. We soon discover that many illnesses are a result of adaptation that occurred during evolution but which cause problems in the modern world. Scientific medicine has accumulated a lot of information about diseases and health problems, but it is usually content with explanations about how we become sick or what causes a disease. Until recently, we rarely asked the "why" questions:

Why do we feel pain? Or get allergies? Why have some inherited diseases remained in the population? Why are depression and anxiety such extraordinarily common issues? Why can treating symptoms neutralize our adaptive defenses, like coughing, sneezing, pain, fever and vomiting?

> "The ultimate and highest purpose of science is to understand ourselves and our place in the universe."
> —Sir George Porter (English Chemist and Former President of the Royal Society, 1920–2002)

Darwinian medicine tries to deal with these questions and many more, helping us understand the basis for some illnesses, and how we may prevent them. While we want to go beyond fixing just the body, it is a good idea to see how far we can push our understanding of the physical. Many golden nuggets of information will provide a background to the wellness programs that form the core of the final part of this book.

Symptoms are physiological responses. We can go further and say that they are a response to a "perturbation" in the matrix of information that holds us together: the "Informational Matrix." Symptoms represent the defenses of the body. We could think of examples like pain, fever, coughing, nausea, vomiting, diarrhea, sneezing and inflammation that evolved either as defenses against injury or to protect against infectious diseases. Many of these symptoms can be uncomfortable. But evolutionary responses and adaptations care about *survival,* not about comfort. If we over-treat these defenses, then we may end up suppressing the body's defense systems.

Some influential voices in homeopathic medicine have taken the position that most diseases result from the medical profession's suppressing illnesses. There is some truth in that, though I would certainly not go so far. Scientific medicine has helped with many diseases. On the other hand, we are all familiar with the over-prescribing of antibiotics, resulting in resistant bacteria. So taking an antibiotic for every sore throat is not a good idea. It sometimes looks as if pain thresholds and pain tolerance have gone down dramatically in recent years, simply because even young children are used to getting analgesics for even the most trivial problems.

Nobody knows whether pain thresholds really have changed, and nobody would want to go back to the days of needless suffering, but could the reliance on "better living through chemistry" be detrimental to our personal health and the health of the nation? Or lead people to the notion that a tablet contains the solution for all our ills? So if we feel unhappy, we turn to a stimulant drug? This is important for us all to think about.

Let us look at three examples.

1   Fever is an adaptive response to infection. Raising the body's temperature will help to destroy pathogens. Treating a fever may make us feel better, but it also undoes eons of evolution.

2   Morning sickness and food aversions are common in pregnancy. It is now widely believed that these are defensive reactions designed to protect the fetus against toxins in the first trimester of pregnancy.

3   Many chronic illnesses are associated with anemia. It is now thought that this also is a defensive reaction. Not to chronic illness, but to the problem that was far more common during evolution, and that was infection. The liver pulls iron out of the circulation so that bacteria cannot use it for their own growth.

During evolution, our bodies adapted to gaining weight as quickly as possible so that we would have fat stores ready for times of starvation. Sugar, fat and salt were rare, and when encountered, our ancestors would eat all that they could. So today, we may still have that legacy of finding sugar, fat and salt tasty and appealing. Moving slowly and avoiding unnecessary exercise is a good idea if you are trying to conserve energy. Not if you are able to eat to excess at the same time.

Some disease-causing genes have been maintained in the population because they have survival value. The best-known example is the sickle cell gene. If someone has two copies of the gene, it can lead to a horrible illness, but carrying just one copy of the gene confers protection against malaria. Carrying one copy of the cystic fibrosis gene is thought to confer protection against typhoid and cholera. Two copies and we can see the development of an often-devastating illness. The list goes on and on.

A brief discussion about the evolutionary origins of psychological problems will set the scene for our later work together. Some types of depression have been strongly associated with a hibernation response, in that people's metabolism changes, they sleep excessively, and they develop carbohydrate cravings and weight gain. Anxiety also clearly carries evolutionary roots. The question is always why a normal adaptive response becomes an overreaction and leads to illness.

While I don't conduct animal experiments and rarely even discuss them, one study is important to us. Some years ago an experiment was done with small guppies, dumped into a tank with a ferocious predator: small-mouthed bass. During the 60hour experiment, the guppies were separated into three groups:

1   Bold—They showed little or no fear and made no attempt to hide. None of them survived.

2   Ordinary—They swam away from the predator, and 15 percent survived.

3   Timid—They actively hid from the bass and 40 percent survived.

Clearly being overly brave does not confer a survival advantage. It is important to remember that the next time somebody exhorts you to conquer your fear. Conquering some of it is good. Trying to eradicate all of it is not. Later on we shall be talking about a very helpful tool called Thought Field Therapy (TFT). When I first saw TFT being done, it seemed so illogical that I went to California to try to debunk it. But instead I became a firm advocate after it cured me of a fear of heights. The only problem was that after my treatment, I ran to the top of the hotel where we were meeting and leaned over the railing, proclaiming: "This is wonderful. I could never have done this before!" Friends called me in, saying: "That's quite enough now. There is a reason for a little bit of anxiety, you know." And they were, of course, absolutely correct.

Panic disorder and even paranoia can be seen as a form of false-alarm mechanism. It would be easy to continue making the point that an evolutionary perspective helps us understand a great deal about health and about illness, but we have seen the most important issue. Illness can be only half understood if we ignore our evolutionary origins. And if illness is only half understood, then it is difficult to know how to avoid it. Let us now turn to the last of the great groups of problems that we need to understand so that we can see how to help ourselves.

This is the only chapter that, I believe, needs a quick review in place of the experiments and exercises that will follow most of the other chapters.

In these last few pages, we have encountered several concepts that may have been new to you, and so we are going to cover some of them again before we finish.

We learned about the extraordinary rate of change in every area of our lives.

We learned about some of the new factors impacting our bodies and our minds, and how the ways in which they interact with us obey rules.

We discovered that there are three key processes of change: development, evolution and adaptation.

We then went on to find out about some extraordinary animal behaviors that cannot be explained by our current biological model and that may offer evidence of extrasensory abilities.

We went on to look at the "dancing genes," learning that genes, although important, are not the fixed and unyielding structures of the schoolbooks and that they are engaged in a constant interplay with the environment. There are very real possibilities that we can modify the expression of our genes in many, many situations.

We also made mention of the "dimensional" way of looking at illness: that health and illness lie on a spectrum and that many people have partial or transient types of illness, that may prove amenable to all sorts of different interventions.

Chapter Four
The Evolving Laws of Health and Healing

Our health and our wellness are the result of an interplay of neurobiology, of culture and of choice, of subtle systems and of spirit. We now need to look at some of the reasons how we discovered that our world and some of its laws are changing. If all I do is state it as a fact, then you could, and should, ask me how I know! As I am going to show you, understanding is always much better than trying to follow someone else's prescription.

Redefining Toxins

Though we have all heard about "toxins," I would like to extend the concept in this way: Instead of just thinking of them as poisonous substances, we need to see them as rogue information systems that supply us with incorrect or aberrant signals. Whether we are thinking about cancer-causing chemicals in the environment or whether we are thinking about light or noise pollution, each of them provides a potentially damaging signal. Each of us has a different informational structure, so how we deal with toxins will vary. And one of the major determinants of our own informational structure is our psychological state and our level of consciousness.

Dealing with toxins is an essential part of maintaining our wellness and will become an indispensable part of the combination programs that we will be constructing in the second part of this book.

Let me give you an example: Environmental factors are now generally believed to contribute to many tumors. In a recent report, the World Health Organization estimated that environmental factors are responsible for between one-quarter and one-third of the global burden of disease. Since the creation of inorganic and organic chemicals in the late 19th century, the global community has faced an enormous rise in the production and subsequent exposure to environmental chemicals, many of which are potentially toxic. The concentrations of many of these chemicals remain quite low. Now, remember how in the introduction we mentioned the positive power of treatment combinations. The other side of the coin is the negative power of toxins: Combinations of chemicals may produce significant health hazards not generally seen with small concentrations of individual chemicals.

Every day we are being exposed to many synthetic chemicals that can produce unfavorable health effects. But more than that, since the invention of gas lights, and even more so, of electric lights, overexposure to light has begun to appear as a problem. Our bodies run on a system of interconnected biological cycles and rhythms. Most are dictated by exposure to sunlight and to moonlight. *Constant* exposure to light, particularly artificial light, can produce aberrant signals that disturb our natural rhythms. There is good evidence that loss of our normal rhythms is associated with some mood disorders, as well as with resistance to the actions of the hormone insulin. We now know there is a close link between obesity and the number of hours that a person sleeps each night. If artificial light reduces the number of hours that a person sleeps, they become more insulin resistant and lay down more fat stores, even if there is little change in the number of calories consumed.

But before we leave the subject of toxins, we must be very clear that although they can simply be chemical toxins, they may also have more subtle aspects, or be entirely subtle or energetic. Let me give you an example: Several years ago, I had been working on my computer for many hours. It was in the days of the old computers with those enormous monitors. A friend who was a homeopath called, and I said that the work had exhausted me. "Tell me more," she said. I gave her a list of odd symptoms that I attributed to sitting hunched up all day. "No," she said, "Those are classic "phosphorus" symptoms. You should take some." So based on the homeopathic idea of "like curing like," I took some homeopathic phosphorus, and the symptoms vanished in a matter of minutes. Well, one case proves nothing. But this was interesting. The homeopath knew absolutely nothing about computers, and certainly not that the *inside* of the screen would have been covered in phosphorus-containing chemicals. There was no possibility of the chemicals escaping and causing me a problem. That means that it must have been some emission associated from the phosphorus that was disrupting part of my own informational matrix. It was that disruption that was corrected by the homeopathic remedy. In case you are wondering, we did go ahead and do a double blind study with me as the single subject. And the phosphorus worked every time.

The list of "toxins" is almost endless and may push the limits of a strict definition of "toxin," but not when we think of them as disturbed, or rogue, sources of information. We could easily add loud, discordant music; tactile stimulation by strangers in crowded places, and, of course, the constant sexual stimulation that assails everyone, whether he or she wants it or not.

Mankind's Metamorphosis

Why should we be constantly assailed by these environmental stresses? This is, of course, the million dollar question. If, as many would have us believe, we live in a meaningless mechanical Universe, then it is "Just One of Those Things." But I do not think so. And as we continue, we are going to look at more and more evidence to suggest that our Universe is a far more vital place, and that there is a profound Purpose underlying the lives of each one of us.

In engineering, there is an expression of "testing to destruction," of seeing how far we can push something until it breaks. Well, I do not think that we are being tested to the point of breaking, but instead, that the insights of Darwinian medicine, of the New Genetics, of toxins and of the remarkable ability of animals and ourselves to adapt, to find what we need to survive and to escape catastrophe, all point us towards something else.

These stressors are an invitation to develop and to adapt in a positive direction: We are all part of a metamorphosis.

Let me give you an example of how this works. Several years ago, I was teaching an introductory course on neurology to a group of phenomenally intelligent medical students who had just arrived from the Universities of Oxford and Cambridge to complete their clinical training. Now, neurology is often regarded as one of the most taxing and difficult things to learn in medicine, but with a few simple principles, it can become quite easy. The problem we had was this: The students had become accustomed to learning their material by rote memorization. Most were very good at it. The trouble is that that form of learning really is not best in medicine, since it can easily lead to inflexibility, particularly at a time when medical knowledge is expanding so rapidly. What we need is to provide people with "pegs" on which to hang their knowledge. We need to supply them with concepts and principles that they can apply whenever new facts come their way. We resolved this by using a technique that we call "overwhelm learning." By inundating the students with more details than they could ever hope to remember, while *also* giving them the principles, the problem was solved. They learned the principles because they had to, and all aced the tests at the end of the course.

The accelerating rate of change is a form of "overwhelm." Humans are naturally equipped with a number of coping systems. Most are hard-wired into the body and into the brain, but some of them do not get used as often as they should. As a species, we are highly flexible and highly adaptable, and these characteristics are among the most important attributes that lead us to our current position of dominance. Change is natural. Change is to be welcomed. Change leads us to grow. Even so, it is no surprise that some people find change frightening and react by becoming rigid and defensive. Our task is to remain flexible in the face of change. How do we do that? By understanding what is going on and by having a series of coping strategies based on the laws of health and healing that we are discovering here.

Are We Really Changing?

The conventional wisdom has been that human consciousness has been evolving rapidly over the last 50,000-100,000 years but that the human body has changed little. That might have been true if there were no connection between our minds and our bodies, and if the massive environmental changes of the last few hundred years had had no impact on us. But, of course, neither of those things is true. As our minds, our relationships and our cultures have changed, so have multiple aspects of our organisms:

- As we have seen, each of us is now the receptacle for literally hundreds of synthetic chemicals to which our ancestors were never exposed.

- We evolved to utilize specific foods for our nourishment, with others that could be taken and utilized if the primary foodstuffs were unavailable. But how many of us are eating the foods to which we adapted over millennia?

- We did not evolve to deal with poor-quality air and water.

- We are bombarded by stimuli and by demands that were completely unknown in history.

Our physical bodies and our minds have indeed changed beyond all recognition over the ages. So it is no surprise that the physical and psychological illnesses have changed and that we need new methods to maintain our health and wellbeing. And since the Universe is alive and intelligent, it is also no surprise that the laws of health and healing are changing. Therefore, we need to think differently about how to maintain our wellness. We are going to look at one particular model of development, which will help us get oriented.

Spiral Dynamics

The problems of the modern world appear to be so overwhelming, the pace of change so frenetic, that most people struggle to understand what is going on around them or seek the certainty of faith. This is important for us as we establish the new laws for health, healing and wellness, since we are obviously all a part of this world and the world reflects our psyches in more ways than one.

It would clearly be incredibly valuable if there were a comprehensive integrated approach that could help us to understand how everything is connected to everything else, and which could then allow us to align and channel energy into appropriate solutions that would work not just for individuals, but also for organizations, for businesses and for humanity as a whole. That such a theory might exist sounds hopelessly Utopian. But in fact there is an intriguing and quite revolutionary model that not only appears to be able to tie together many apparently irreconcilable differences but that also has extraordinary correlations with other systems that have been developed over the last few thousand years.

The model is called "Spiral Dynamics," and it represents a revolutionary approach to the development of consciousness and human value systems. Since our bodies and our minds are so closely interlinked, the model can also help us understand change and development throughout all of our systems.

Memes

The word *meme* was first introduced by the Oxford University biologist Richard Dawkins, who used it to mean things that are transmitted or broadcast through culture. Good examples would be songs, ideas or fashions in clothes, which are quickly disseminated through a culture, rather like a virus spreads around a population. These are now called "little memes." Spiral Dynamics takes a broader view. Each level of development is represented on a spiral and is called a "ValueMeme" (vMeme), which expresses itself through the "little memes." You will normally see "vMeme" abbreviated to "Meme," with a capital "M" to distinguish it from the "little memes." Each Meme is a code, or a system of information. This code can be biological, psychological, social or spiritual and is the glue that underlies and holds together every aspect of our lifestyle and culture. Every form of cultural expression is a manifestation of it—our forms of government, architecture, creative arts, sports, our scientific models and our sense of identity. As a matter of convenience and convention, each vMeme has been labeled with an arbitrary color, as we will see in just a moment.

The reason for briefly looking at this model is that the human body, mind, social situation, subtle systems and spiritual nature are not static. Neither are they finite. They change as the conditions of existence change. Apparently new systems are forged in response to these changes in our world. I say "apparently new systems," because they are already there within us in embryo. As we saw with the astonishing ability of animals to switch on genes that are there in the organism, waiting for their chance to come do their work, these systems exist as a series of "potentialities," waiting to hatch when they are needed. Even as new systems begin to manifest, the older systems stay with us. Changing times produce changing minds. Changing minds produce changing bodies. Changing minds and changing bodies have changing needs for maintaining health and wellness. But always within are the remnants of the old. So we need to have a bigger, broader and smarter way of dealing with the changing laws of health and healing.

When a new system or level is activated, the change in all the Five Domains has a profound impact on the world around us. All of our relationships, and indeed society as a whole, are the fruits of our psychology, our beliefs and our own energy matrix.

Through the ages we have been told of the profound importance of the Mystic Spiral as a template of the Universe. So it is something of a shock to discover that a spiral vortex best depicts the emergence of human systems as they evolve through levels of increasing complexity.

The germ of the idea began over 50 years ago when Dr. Clare Graves, a professor of psychology, became frustrated by all the conflicting theories being offered. He resolved to get to the root of what differentiates people, why they see the world so differently, why some change and others do not. And why they react in varying ways to physical, emotional and social challenges. This frustration led to decades of research first by him, and then others, most prominently Dr. Don Beck. Gradually, other research from neurology and the social sciences was included.

According to Spiral Dynamics, human nature is not fixed. It changes as the conditions of existence change. And since our minds and our bodies are so intimately interrelated, it follows that this evolutionary change will have consequences for every part of us: Physical, psychological, social, subtle and spiritual.

When our life circumstances change, we have the built-in capacity to adapt and to develop more complex cognitive and emotional responses to handle new problems. An exceedingly useful concept is the "complexity quotient" (CQ), which measures our ability to adapt to changing complexity. It is another way of thinking about a person's "capacity." Successful leaders, winning athletes and healthy individuals are extremely flexible and have a high CQ. They can raise their game and adapt quickly. On the other hand, they also have the ability to let go when the pressure is off. After recovering from a mental breakdown, the psychologist Carl Jung was known not only for his remarkable scholarship, but also for his extraordinary ability to relax and to become childlike and to think up all sorts of games for his children. These are signs of a well-rounded, balanced and integrated personality. Sometimes we see people in whom this ability goes haywire, and they overcompensate with drugs, alcohol or risky sexual behavior.

The old ways of thinking and behaving never disappear. We carry them within us and call on them when necessary. For every one of us, the key is to discover the axis around which we circle: our center of gravity. This is the level at which we operate most of the time and which is activated in times of stress. It is easy to behave in an educated and enlightened way when we are in a calm, stress-free environment, but it is how we react under stress that not only is crucially important, but also helps define us as individuals.

Each Meme is not simply a level, but appears as a wave of development, building on the one below and becoming progressively more expansive and complex. It is essential for us to realize that we are not saying that one level is superior to another. Each is adapted to its environment. I remember hearing Warren Buffett say how perfectly he was adapted to corporate America yet how poorly he would do in most other settings!

The Memes: The Eight-Stage Spiral of Development

The first six levels are "subsistence levels," marked by what we call "first-tier thinking." Then there occurs a revolutionary shift in consciousness: the emergence of "being levels" and "second-tier thinking," of which two major levels have so far appeared. Here is a brief description of all eight levels.

First Tier: The Six "Subsistence" vMemes
1. Beige Meme:

This is the instinctive, survivalist Meme that appeared about 100,000 years ago. It is the unemotional basic survival level of an intelligent animal we call "primitive man," complete with finely developed instincts that have partially atrophied in us today. At this level of development people used their instincts and habits just to live day to day. Food, water, warmth, sex and safety had priority. They formed into bands to protect and perpetuate life, they lived off the land, and there was no distinct concept of self. Their existence was largely automatic. We have all been through this phase of development. It is always present inside us and can come out in people struggling with chronic and persistent mental illness, or severe Alzheimer's disease. Anyone can regress to this level when faced with catastrophe or illness. It can also be the level at which people function when they have become chronically bored, and have lost all zest for life, and all sense of purpose and meaning.

2. Purple Meme:

As survival needs are met, new connections form in the brain. Whole new systems begin to "come online," not only in the brain, but also in the psyche and in the subtle systems. This is the magical-animistic phase, which started to be seen around 50,000 years ago. People began to recognize and plan for dangers, so they began to band together for safety and to share food and responsibilities. This is the basis for kinship. For people at this level, the world was a magical place alive with spirit beings and mystical signs, over which they had no control. Individuals began to become aware of a distinct self, but it was subsumed in the group. This is the time when storytellers kept the inherited wisdom alive. This is sometimes described as a wonderfully holistic time, but really it is not. People have magical names for every part of the landscape but no name for the land itself.

We have all passed through this phase in childhood, and some people still function in this Meme. We might think of street gangs or athletic teams as good examples.

3. Red Meme:

When safety has been assured, people begin to question their leaders and reach for personal autonomy. This is the impulsive and egocentric Meme, which first started manifesting about 10,000 years ago. If we look back in history, here we see the stories of powerful archetypal gods and goddesses. Until now, the sense of self was weak, but now it emerged with a vengeance as something distinct from the tribe. Feudal lords had slaves and protected the weak in exchange for obedience and labor. It is the Meme of instant gratification. People would do or grab whatever made them feel good without regard for others. There was no sense of guilt, no remorse, and no concerns about consequences. If something went wrong it was somebody else's fault. If thwarted, people would become angry and violent. The biggest fear was of losing face.

The majority of the world's population lives at this level—not because they choose to do so but because that is what their life conditions demand. All the Memes have their positive and negative aspects. For example, Red is not all bad: It is also extremely creative and it gives people the strength to fight to defend themselves. It gets things done, inspires heroic acts, breaks with limiting tradition and opens up new pathways.

You will recognize people who, even as adults, are primarily at this phase of development. During personal development, it occurs during the "terrible twos," and again in the rebellious years of adolescence. And of course there are rock stars who have become professional exponents of the Red Meme!

4. Blue Meme:

This is the Meme that we associate with an ordered existence under the control of "ultimate truth." There is only one right way to think and the virtuous are rewarded. It is typically described as the purposeful, authoritarian and absolutist Meme, and it is often also called the Meme of mythic order.

The move to Blue occurs when people become desperate for two things: for order to replace anarchy and for reason to explain their suffering. So now life has meaning, direction and purpose. There is a code of conduct based on absolute and unvarying principles of "right" and "wrong" and of good and evil. Violating the rules has severe, perhaps everlasting, repercussions. This meme first started to appear in large numbers of people around 5,000 years ago. This Meme is seen in Puritan societies, in the England of Charles Dickens and in the English "public schools." It can underlie both charitable good deeds and religious fundamentalism. The expression of the Blue Meme is one of the potent causes for some of the Ego-fears that we shall be exploring in Chapter Ten.

5. Orange Meme:

This is the Meme of the achiever and the strategist, which first showed itself in large numbers just about 300 years ago. At this level, the self begins to escape from the "herd mentality" of Blue, and seeks truth and meaning in individualistic terms. People at this level begin to question things that were previously unquestionable, to seek new and better ways of doing things and to rebel against constraints. People become objective, mechanistic and scientific in the classical sense of the word. The world is seen as a rational machine with natural laws that can be learned, mastered and manipulated for one's own purposes. The Meme is highly achievement oriented, especially toward materialistic gains. Success is highly rewarded. People have developed the ability to keep track of multiple interests and shift attention between them, and are mobile, pragmatic, independent and in control our lives. People feel that they stand or fall by their own efforts and talents.

This was the Meme of the Enlightenment that shaped the world of today. It is an astonishing fact, with enormous relevance to all of us that the greatest advances and breakthroughs of the Enlightenment were made by no more than one thousand people.

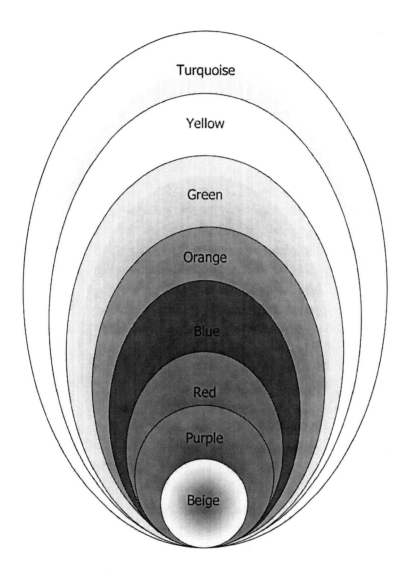

*Figure 1. A diagrammatic representation of the Memes,
indicating their increasing development*

6. Green Meme:

This wave is the egalitarian Meme, or the Meme of community, and of the sensitive self. It started to appear some 150 years ago. People whose center of gravity is in the Green Meme feel that the human spirit must be freed from dogma, greed and divisiveness. Relationships, bonding, dialogue and networking are central to them. Feelings and caring supersede cold rationality. They are likely to be sensitive to ecology, and to value the sanctity of Life and of the Earth.

At this level, people begin to understand the downside of Orange. There is more to life than material success and possessions: they do not on their own bring happiness. At this stage people need and seek a purpose, and they try to make peace with themselves and to bring peace to society by resolving inequalities. This is the Meme of ecology, humanistic psychology, cooperative inquiry, human and animal rights, and diversity movements. Experts estimate that 10 percent of the world's population is at this stage, although the figure may be twice as high in Western Europe and parts of the United States.

We are all mixtures of different Memes. But if our center of gravity is primarily in one of these first-tier memes, it can be quite difficult to understand the thinking of any of the others. If there are people in your life with whom you can never agree, they are probably centered in a different Meme. Let me give you some examples that might strike a chord in your own family or friends. Red might think that Blue is repressive, while Blue thinks that Orange is pushy, and Orange thinks Green is idealistic and unrealistic. Green sometimes thinks it has all the answers and criticizes Orange, failing to recognize that it was Orange that produced the wealth that Green wants to share with everyone. Green cannot see that the drive and expertise of Orange can be harnessed to resolve the problems that Green has identified. It will only take a moment to see that kind of tension at work all the time in contemporary politics.

With the completion of the Green Meme, human consciousness is poised for a quantum jump into "second-tier thinking." Clare Graves referred to this as a "momentous leap," where "a chasm of unbelievable depth of meaning is crossed."

Second Tier: The "Being" vMemes
7. Yellow Meme:

This is the wave of integration. It first started manifesting 50 years ago, although interestingly it was predicted much earlier in the Ancient Wisdom. In this wave, people understand that chaos and change are natural and inevitable. Therefore flexibility, spontaneity and functionality have the highest priority. Life is seen as a pattern of natural hierarchies, systems, forms and values. And armed with that knowledge, our ability to cope with complexity becomes greater than the sum of all the earlier six stages put together. The world is no longer perceived only from the human scale. Instead it is seen from a total or universal perspective. As people reach this level, they live fully, treasuring the magnificence of life above material possessions, and they rate knowledge and competence above power and status. And because we understand the fundamental patterns of life, and how to think and direct them, we can do more in less time and with less expenditure of energy.

We can see the whole picture, how each Meme builds on the preceding one and how everything fits together in one enormous never-ending spiral of life. We can see what each individual, or organization or country needs to help it evolve to the next level. As an example, the power, the force and the energy of Red needs to be channeled, not repressed. We want to foster the evolution of all Life.

8. Turquoise Meme:

This is the holistic Meme, which began to appear in the 1970s. It is the Meme of global synthesis and renewal. There is a perception that the

Universe is a single dynamic organism composed of an elegantly balanced system of interlocking forces, and that the Self is both a distinct entity and also part of a larger whole. If somebody asks if people at this level are superstitious, they might respond: "No, but I do know that there are complex interactive forces, which are usually invisible but which have a powerful effect on our lives."

Each one of us is a composite of these different Memes. Each Meme is associated with its own strengths and weaknesses, its own powers and pathologies.

As an experiment, I would like you to start working out where you would place yourself in this scheme, and also where you place other significant people in your life. Do this not just in terms of psychology, but also from the point of view of:
Body
Social relationships
Subtle systems
Spiritual orientation

Later on, we are going to develop the idea of relationships far beyond our normal models, and this will be a good first exercise.

Let's finish this section with a quotation from the person who started this whole revolution in thinking, Dr. Clare Graves:

> "What I am proposing is that the psychology of the mature human being is an unfolding, emergent, oscillating, spiraling process, marked by progressive subordination of older, lower-order behavior systems to newer, higher-order systems as man's existential problems change."

Chapter Five
Beyond the Clockwork Universe

The Limitations of Mechanical Models of the Body

It is now calculated that the sum total of all medical knowledge is doubling every three and a half years. We began our discussion with a few "Dogma Busters." We're now finding that our concepts of how biological systems work are undergoing profound change. The physical body needs to be honored, respected and even revered. But simple mechanistic accounts of a human being are simply insufficient. At the most basic cellular level, organisms have the ability to organize themselves. Not surprisingly, this is called "self-organization," a dynamic principle that underlies the emergence of biological forms. Another astonishing characteristic of living systems is their ability continuously to renew themselves and to regulate this process so that the integrity of the structure is maintained. The technical term for this is "autopoiesis." Illness can occur when these natural processes break down.

Self-organization and self-renewal are fundamental to the maintenance of both the structure and the function of the body. For example, if you break your leg, the tissues grow back in more or less the correct place, although you may have a scar to show for it. Taking this for granted, we often forget how miraculous this is, leading to an obvious question: Why doesn't this process occur with all diseases? Or could it? The answer is that when it comes to healing, it is unwise to speculate about limitations. Any experienced clinician has seen wonders aplenty. When we change our focus toward maintaining wellness, the sky is the limit. It is quite well-known that the body's molecules are recycled every four or five years. So the molecules constituting your body today are entirely different from those that you had five years ago. With the exception of most of the brain's neurons, most cells also undergo a constant turnover, so there have to be precise systems for ensuring that the molecules and cells end up in the correct places.

Practically all organic processes are organized in cycles. We are rich with biological rhythms ranging from periods of split seconds for electrical activities of neurons, to seconds for the heartbeat and respiration, to minutes for the ultra-short ("ultradian") rhythms, to hours for circadian rhythms and then days and weeks and even years for the periodic cycles. Our cells, bodies, emotions, cognitions and subtle systems all dance to their own rhythms. This has been talked about in Chinese and Ayurvedic medicine for centuries, but it is only in recent years that Western medicine has begun to realize the importance of these cycles. While we can explain some of the cycles in biochemical terms, coming up with plausible explanations for others entails a re-envisioning of biology. Subtle and spiritual energies are nested within these systems.

Star Wars and T'ai Chi Ch'uan

George Lucas knew what he was talking about when he introduced the idea of "The Force" into the Star Wars movies. Legend has it that he got, or refined, some of the ideas from mythology master Joseph Campbell. Despite being able to sense and feel some sort of energy in myself and in other people and animals since early childhood, I remained highly skeptical that there was some unknown force at work. Perhaps it was all just body heat or electricity. Finally, after being thrown by my T'ai Chi Master from 15 feet away, I could deny it no longer, and I can now teach most people to sense their own and other people's energy fields quite easily.

The Critics' Catechism

"Everything was fine until this point in the book, and then you spoiled it by getting into all that woolly stuff about subtle systems and spirituality… There's no need to even consider them. The laws of physics can explain everything in the Universe. And we already know what they are. Behavior is no different: Just a series of genetic programs and reflexes. So why are you wasting your time on all this?"

> "To avoid criticism, do nothing, say nothing, be nothing."
> —Elbert Hubbard (American Writer and Philosopher, 1856–1915)

Many of my colleagues in academia have been making similar comments to me for more than 30 years. At one time I argued or showed them research to buttress my position, but after a while, trying to persuade everyone seemed a bit of a waste of time, and I carried on with my work without bothering to discuss the matter. While resistance lingers in some quarters, top medical, scientific and engineering experts I've known, along with complementary and alternative medicine specialists, are usually very receptive to new ideas along these lines. By contrast, I once knew a professor who made the extraordinary statement that something without an immediate scientific explanation could not exist! I may not understand precisely how my computer works, but I can observe that it does, and there are many people who know much more than me about the workings of the machine.

> "The unexpected and the incredible belong in this world. Only then is life whole"
> —Carl Jung (Swiss Psychiatrist, 1875–1961)

A Visit to Vulcan

I think a short story from the history of science is useful here. The positions of some of the outer planets in our own solar system and those circling other nearby stars have been deduced from perturbations—small wobbles—in the orbits of other planets, or of the stars themselves. These are caused by the gravitational fields of these "hidden" planets. During the

19th century, astronomers noticed some apparent wobbles in Mercury's orbit, prompting construction of clever models to account for the phenomenon. One theory involved a small planet inside Mercury's orbit, named Vulcan. The idea was that this small planet was whizzing around the Sun, and every time it passed Mercury, Vulcan's gravity would pull the planet slightly out of its orbit.

It was not until the beginning of the 20th century that Albert Einstein proposed a totally new way of looking at the Universe, which finally explained the astronomers' observations. There was no need to invent the planet Vulcan. The apparent disturbances in the orbit of Mercury were just that: apparent. They weren't real but were instead the result of light being bent by the gravitational field of the Sun. Correct observations, wrong explanations.

So it is today within medicine. Observations about what we call the "Extended Mind": extrasensory diagnosis, nonlocal effects, and the efficacy of some forms of unorthodox medicine are being made every day, and it is wrong to reject them just because we cannot explain them using current scientific models. People who instantly dismiss subtle systems, or the importance of spirituality have usually not done their homework: the evidence for all of them is becoming utterly overwhelming. At the back of this book, you will find references to hundreds of books, and many websites that I have carefully sifted and checked. They provide powerful evidence to support everything that I am saying. I have not included many hundreds of scientific papers that also support these concepts. If you would like them, just let me know!

Both biology and psychology have suffered from a bad case of "physics envy" for many years. Because physics has been supremely successful, many scientists have tried to apply physics models to everything. Sadly, this has in general not worked very well. The physics that govern purely physical phenomena are fundamentally different from those that govern organic life, and the principles of organic life are quite different from those governing psychology. Yet other principles come into play when we work with the subtle systems and spiritual energies. If I remove my shoes and socks, and walk around barefoot for a few weeks, my feet will develop protective calluses. This is a simple adaptive mechanism that comes into play in response to a change in the environment of my feet. If instead I drive around in my car for the same few weeks, sad to say, my tires would not grow thicker! While my feet and my tires are both subject to the same laws of physics, the reactions of my feet are also shaped by natural adaptive responses.

"Neither the testimony of all the Fellows of the Royal Society nor the evidence of my own senses would lead me to believe in thought-transference, as it is impossible."
Hermann von Helmholtz, (German Physicist and Physiologist, 1821–1894)

Nature, Health, Business and Society

While these four may seem like strange bedfellows, all are governed by some of the same laws and principles. Understand one, and in most cases that understanding can be translated into the others.

Information is a form of energy, and energy cannot exist in a vacuum, so in order to express itself, it needs to flow and combine with other information. When information combines, it can generate new levels of meaning and order. Consciousness underlies this information, which helps explain why, when we're talking about health and wellness, we usually talk about them being partly a reflection of our state of conscious awareness. This was why we just spent some time looking at one aspect of the development of consciousness, because people functioning at the level of the Beige Meme need a different form of input from people expressing the Turquoise Meme. Last night I dealt with a horse that had bad colic, a serious problem in horses. He needed straightforward physical treatments, together with some simple work on his subtle systems. We did not need to get too involved with some of the issues about meaning and spirituality, which would form an essential part of helping the Turquoise individual.

> "Creativity, as has been said, consists largely of rearranging what we know in order to find out what we do not know ... Hence, to think creatively, we must be able to look afresh at what we normally take for granted."
> —George Kneller (American Psychologist, 1910–1999)

A healthy functioning system is described as being "open," which means it constantly exchanges energy and information with its surroundings, and this is the foundation of creativity. Whether we are dealing with a biological system, the Silk Road to China or a modern entrepreneurial business, the principle is the same. The biggest changes and the most profound and creative insights always arrive when there is cross-pollination between previously separated realms of information, knowledge or expertise. Whether dealing with cells, organizations or cultures, creativity and innovation tend to stagnate when information is locked into separate silos. What is more, critical events always happen at the edge, the boundary, the membrane of a system. Whether we are looking at a cell or a society, that is where most of the action takes place. Would you want to watch a movie or a play where nothing happened, and where there was no prospect of change? I doubt it, because that would be so grossly abnormal!

Let's look at an example. A hugely important illness is type 2, or maturity onset diabetes mellitus. The fundamental problem is that cells in the liver, and then in fat and muscle, become resistant to the actions of the hormone insulin, which normally facilitates glucose flowing into many of the body's cells. One way of thinking about the fundamental problem is that the free flow of the information delivered by the insulin is unable to mix with and inform the cell. Similarly, a key difficulty in some forms of depression is that some cells in the brain's serotonin systems don't exchange information, in the form of the chemical serotonin, with the next system of cells in line.

We have commented on the similarity of the principles underlying healthy bodies, healthy minds, healthy businesses and healthy societies. Experts on computer safety are examining the ways in which animals and plants protect themselves against predators and parasites to find new insights into how to protect computers against viruses and hackers. The blossoming field of Integral Studies is successfully applying principles derived from a deep study of psychology, human potential and development, to inform such disparate fields as business and medicine. If we really understand the principles in one realm, we can begin to apply them in many others, the trick being to understand what *additional* laws are at play in each realm.

Before we move on from this concept of information being energy, I would like to suggest something to you. This might initially sound fanciful, but another manifestation of information and energy is money. Critics often say that it is incongruous for people on the spiritual path to possess financial concerns. However, all the principles of material abundance can be reframed as allowing an open flow of information and energy. Hence the rationale for charitable giving and tithing.

The Biofield

Biofield is a word about which you are going to hear a great deal in the years to come. It is the term that we use for the organizing Informational Matrix, which is the underlying field of life itself. It is your Inner Light. If you are not functioning at your best, or if you're ill, this means your Inner Light is being hidden and not expressing itself.

We have just seen that information is a form of energy. Although we use the term "energy," I must issue a word of caution. The term itself is fuzzy, conveying multiple meanings, with many people discussing "energies" and "vibrations" with little clarity. There is a potent reason that this matters:

When healers only visualize energy flowing from them into a receiver, like water flowing from a pipe, they are limiting what they can do to help. When we use self-healing, it is essential to use the bigger idea of the Informational Matrix, to help us focus our mind and our attention.

For centuries, most of the traditional forms of healing have relied upon the notion that there is a "vital energy," an "essence," a "life force," forming the basis for a person's health and healing. There can be no doubt that many healers do generate some force, and many of us can help people experience some flows of this force with just a little practice. We now come to the reason why, a moment ago, I highlighted the problem of physics envy. We saw that different laws come into play when we are dealing with my tires or my feet, and I could show you that yet another set of laws is operating when we look at psychological processes.

When we are looking at healing energies, we find that there are several types. Some are explicable in terms of recent novel discoveries about the structure of the human body, but others cannot be explained so simply. The subtle systems of your body and the forces that we recruit in distant healing are something else again. Distant healing and extrasensory perception, to which it seems to be linked, obey a new set of laws. Even events far apart in space can occur simultaneously, and the healing effects or the communications do not diminish over distance. Every *known* form of energy obeys the "inverse square laws." The further apart a transmitter and a receiver are, the weaker the signal. This does not apply with distant healing, or, for that matter, with extrasensory perception.

In the late 19th century, the scientific world felt that there was no need for anything like a life force, and that all would be explained by physics and chemistry, as it was then understood. So all mention of a life force was simply removed from the scientific view of the world. To even mention it was to invite ridicule, and for a century most people in the scientific community regarded the idea of a life force as archaic and quaint, on a par with ideas about the earth being flat, or the existence of an ether that transmitted light.

The discovery of the structure of DNA was thought by many to signal the end of the discussion. But it turns out that DNA is not the whole story either. We have seen already that genes are not static structures and that even our emotional states can influence the expression of specific genes.

Morphic Fields and Morphic Resonance: A New Science of Life

The English scientist Rupert Sheldrake has sparked more than his fair share of controversy with a revolutionary theory about the organization of Nature. When his first book was published in 1981, it was famously described in the journal *Nature*, as a "best candidate for burning." Rupert's ideas sprang from his own highly conventional work on plants. Dissatisfied with the conventional account that biological forms develop from a genetic code, he proposed that the development of embryos—for example the growth of a baby or the growth of a tree from a seed—depend not just on the information inside them, such as genetic code, but also on organizing fields of information from outside, which he called "morphic fields." The word *morphic* comes from the Greek word *morphe*, which means, "form." They contain the information to dictate form, pattern, order or structure. Rupert has likened DNA to the building materials for a house. They will stay in neat piles unless an architect has designed a plan and formulated a course of action and there are workmen to follow the assembly instructions.

Every molecule, each type of crystal, and every organism has its own morphic field. The organization of behavior, like the instincts of a dog, depends on similar organizing morphic fields. These fields carry the memory of an organism.

Not just the memory of what it has done, but the cumulative memory of its species, which determines its form. This cumulative memory depends on a process called morphic resonance. This resonance allows the field to learn. The field grows with experience. The more often a pattern is repeated, the more likely it is that it will become stable. Every time an object comes into existence, it adds its own information to the overall morphic field. So in effect, Nature is habit forming. Like the philosopher Alfred North Whitehead, Sheldrake has said—and I totally agree with him—that the *laws* of Nature are more like *habits* of Nature.

Secondarily, these fields are creative, for otherwise nothing would ever change. Which is why, as we learned in Chapter One, once a crystal has been prepared in one place, it is much easier to repeat the trick elsewhere. Or once a rat has learned to run a new maze, rats elsewhere can learn to do it much faster. This idea is very like Jung's idea of a collective unconscious, except that it is not confined to humans. It is found throughout Nature, even in rocks and plants.

In recent years, Rupert Sheldrake has been recruiting armies of volunteers to test his ideas of what he now calls the "extended mind." He has done experiments on animals who seem to know when their owners are coming home unexpectedly and to test whether people can tell when they are being stared at. In each case the experiments have been overwhelmingly positive.

If Nature can learn, then it can learn from the things that we think and do. It helps us explain why the laws of healing can and have changed, because, as we have seen, almost everything else is changing. Nature is learning to respond to novel forms of treatment that use information and the subtle systems of the body. It gives us part of the mechanism by which the laws of healing are changing. It is because Nature is learning new tricks.

Messages in Water

The information matrix of water molecules can hold a memory. The last decade has seen a series of remarkable reports from scientists in Japan, headed by Dr. Masaru Emoto, who have been taking photographs and making videos of the formation of ice crystals in pure, natural water. Our bodies are more than 70 percent water, and so anything that impacts the water in our bodies could have a major effect on our health and well-being. There should be nothing unusual about experiments involving ice crystals, except that the team began to discover that replicable patterns developed when music was being played. Well, that also was not too much of a surprise: We have all experienced the vibration of music, and it could easily alter the freezing of water.

But more was to come. Beautiful and inspirational classical music produced beautiful, delicate and elegant crystals, while water exposed to violent heavy-metal music resulted in ugly fragmented crystals, if they formed at all. The scientists then began to catalog the effects of writing different words and exposing the water to them. Finally they have described the ability of water to absorb, hold and even retransmit human feelings and emotions. Water from clear springs and water exposed to loving words show brilliant, complex and colorful snowflake patterns, while polluted water and water exposed to negative thoughts produced incomplete, asymmetrical patterns with dull colors. At first this all seems like a really bizarre idea. But, once again, the key point here is that the results were replicable.

Why do we become so concerned about replication? Some years ago I was at a lecture in London where someone was showing some Kirlian photographs that were supposed to show the aura around the body. Some of the pictures were striking, but my old friend, the late Professor Arthur Ellison, asked the question in many people's minds: "Why did you select these pictures?" "Because they show the best effects," we were told. "And how often do you get such nice effects?" "Oh, about once every couple of weeks."

When we hear of someone picking just one picture out of many, or of an effect that only occurs when one particular individual was present in the laboratory, we always have to ask whether or not we are looking at a real phenomenon. The problem with understanding the extended mind and how to use subtle information systems and subtle forces has been this. In the past, so many reports and observations have occurred only sporadically. It is only in the last thirty years that many of these phenomena have become more stable and reproducible.

The experiments with water are tremendously important and need urgently to be repeated by other scientists. But just think: If they are correct, and expressing love and good will can change the structure of the most important substance on the planet, the implications are awesome. I think it highly likely that the observations are correct, for this reason: The techniques that you are going to be learning do undoubtedly work, and this is the best theory yet as to why.

We need now to look at the notion that the heart is more than a pump. There have been a number of highly controversial reports of people who have received heart transplants also receiving memories from the donor. Some of these reports certainly seem to ring true, but this issue needs further study. But this brings us to an important concept that we are going to be able to use.

More than just a pump, the heart is a physical location of an aspect of our emotional functioning. In Chinese medicine, the heart is known as the repository of *Shen*, or Spirit. It is also an important endocrine gland, with evidence that it is also a sensory organ with a sophisticated system for receiving and processing information. The neural network within the heart enables it to learn and remember. The heart constantly communicates with the brain, influencing key areas involved in perception, cognition and emotional processing. You or someone you know may have had a baby, in which case you or she will have had intrauterine cardiac monitoring. Normally the baby's heart rate varies from minute to minute. Some 40 years ago it was discovered that if that variation stopped, it could be a harbinger of doom. Obstetricians knew this, but the rest of medicine forgot about the observation until 1991. Since then, there has been enormous interest in the phenomenon of heart rate variability (HRV) in the general population, because if it is lost, it can be a potent predictor of health problems. HRV reflects the tone in the autonomic nervous system. If this system becomes unbalanced, it can have effects on most of the major organs.

Now we see another link between modern science and the Ageless Wisdom. The most important contribution to the parasympathetic nervous system comes from one of the largest nerves in the body, called the vagus, or wandering nerve. In the old teachings, this is called our psychic antenna. We all have one, but not all of have relearned how to use it. Many psychic stressors can produce physical effects via the vagus nerve. It is interesting that when doing acupuncture or energy healing with people, it is very common for them to get a slowing of their heart rate and to have abdominal rumblings, which are sure signs of vagal activity. Psychics often get problems with their intestines while working with people, not from upset, but because they are exercising their skills. The heart also communicates information to the brain, and indeed throughout the body, through its powerful electromagnetic field. The magnetic component of the heart is around 5,000 times stronger than the magnetic field of the brain and can be detected at a range of several feet. For some years now, we have been seeing a stream of fascinating research emerging from the Institute of HeartMath in California. Brain rhythms synchronize to the rhythmic activity of the heart, and when people are feeling love or appreciation, their blood pressure and respiratory rhythms become entrained with that of the heart. Sustained positive emotions produce a state of coherence throughout the body. But this is where it becomes even more interesting. The electromagnetic field of the heart can transmit information between people, up to a range of about five feet, and one person's brain waves can synchronize to the heart of another.

Recently, an English engineer named Jon Whale has measured and described what he calls the "Assemblage Point," the major entry point of energy into the human body, which is found at the center of the back and the front of the chest. He has even compiled some evidence to suggest that physical and psychological illnesses can follow if it is out of position or not flowing properly and that it may be possible to correct disturbances in this Assemblage Point. This provides more evidence for the existence of important forces beyond the physical body.

The Physics of the Biofield

When looking at the laws of physical phenomena, there are four known forces: gravitational, the weak force, electromagnetic and the strong force. If morphic resonance, extrasensory perception and messages in water exist, then we need to be looking for another force. The eminent engineer William Tiller, from Stanford University, has proposed the existence of a new fifth force to explain certain features of life. Perhaps this is the "dark matter" we met in Chapter One. There are a number of other investigators who have suggested other candidates. For the last two decades the brilliant biophysicist Fritz-Albert Popp has been working on a remarkable phenomenon. Cells and whole bodies emit coherent light, which he calls "biophotons." It has been suggested that this light, which has been recorded coming from the hands of some healers, may be the organizing principle in cells. Others have suggested that the biofield is simply electromagnetic or perhaps something produced by previously unknown systems in the body. The answer is most likely a combination. Figure 2 below, represents a good way of synthesizing all the different approaches to the biofield.

Informational Matrix

The Thought Field

The Main Centers, and the Chakras

The Flow of Energy in the Channels and Meridians

The Electromagnetic Field

The Liquid Crystalline Matrix of the Body

Biochemical Reactions

Figure 2: A simplified linear model of the interrelationships
of some of the key components of the esoteric anatomy of the body

We can think of the biofield as a holistic or global organizing field of life. A holographic plate, like the one you might see on your credit card, distributes information throughout a hologram, the biofield communicates information throughout-the organism and is central to its integration. It is the ultimate regulator of the body's biochemistry and physiology. I did not choose the holographic comparison by chance. There is very solid research that suggests that we may at our central core all have a holographic structure. Knowledge about the biofield and its relationship to emotional, physical, mental and spiritual wellness is only just beginning.

We have bodies beyond the physical, which involve realms of mind, soul and spirit. They really are bodies, with their own ensemble of organs, though most of us have never learned how to use them. As an example, in the Wisdom teachings, we speak of the Golden Eyes of Spirit to denote one of these sets of higher faculties. Some of the people who have worked with the methods in this book have discovered them for themselves.

Chapter Six
Hidden Harbingers of Health

Our Subtle Form

Most of my early teachers were Jesuits and Anglican priests, and then I had the privilege of learning from theosophists, folk from the Indian traditions and one Sufi Master. So I was steeped in the idea that there are seven great planes of being: Physical, Astral, Mental, Buddhic, Atmic, Monadic and Logoic, and that more or less fit in with my personal observations. The whole system becomes very complex, with each of the seven planes being broken down further, into solid, liquid, gas, and various types of etheric. As time went by, I wanted to avoid some of those emotionally charged terms like "astral" and "etheric" and instead went along with a simpler model of gross, subtle and causal as the three great states of being. This is the terminology most widely used these days, and will, for now, give us enough of what we need in order to understand more about the changing nature of the laws of healing.

Many people these days have heard about the "chakras" of Indian mysticism. If you go into any large bookstore, you will probably find a few books talking about them. Having studied several hundred of these books in a number of different languages, I have found that there are striking variations in the descriptions of the chakras. The numbers vary from four to seven to hundreds. They are usually described as colored wheels of energy located in the body and having something to do with various nerves or endocrine glands. But then we start running into trouble. The descriptions of the numbers of chakras, their position, colors and functions show extraordinary differences. I have known many people who have told me that they can see them, and I have no reason to doubt them, although that does not prove that they exist. After all, I have seen many people who have drunk excessive amounts of alcohol tell me about seeing bugs or pink elephants (yes, such people really do exist); and of course a lot of people have seen all sorts of things under the influence of psychedelic drugs.

As I mentioned in the introduction, I have also been able to sense energy fields and chakras since early childhood. Back then, I never thought of it as a gift, but more as a burden. I have now learned that this is not uncommon in children, though most lose the ability, or at least stop talking about it, around the age of seven. I have no idea why I continued being able to do it, many years before I knew what "it" was. However, when I did discover how unusual the ability was, I began to read voraciously on the subject, and it was one of the things that motivated me to go to medical school.

Many of the descriptions of the rotation of the chakras appeared to be the wrong way around: They seemed to spinning in the opposite direction from what I had seen. Could this perhaps have been because reports were from looking at others rather than sensing them in themselves? Next there seemed to be an association between the way that someone had been trained and what he or she saw, and also a relationship between a person's cognitive style and what he or she saw. Chakras are certainly not "in" the body, but associated with it. It has always felt to me that they are composed of all the Seven Planes that the Ancients told us about. When I examine them, each chakra seems to have a gross physical aspect, then a subtle, and then I can often feel the more rarified aspects, which seem to stretch out to infinity, and which I think of as the causal realm. So I tend to feel them as a complex series of forces, not just simple pinpoints in space. I have looked at thousands of people over the last three decades and have become quite good at telling where people's major areas of development are, and the results have sometimes been very helpful in diagnosis.

The Strange Case of the Missing Chakras

But apart from all the variations, which I think that we can resolve to everyone's satisfaction, there is another even more important issue. I have made a deep study of Chinese esoteric anatomy, and looked in detail at accounts of the anatomical, medical and philosophical systems of many of the North and South American Natives, and of the Aborigines of Australia and Polynesia. And in none of them is there any mention of anything that looks like the chakras. There are some things that look vaguely similar, but nothing the same. Many contemporary scholars have tried to point out ways in which, say, the Chinese and Indian systems can be made to fit together, or the Chinese and the Mayan, and they have had some success. But of course it is now 2,000 years later, and we are left with an enormous question. Why the differences? There are several possible reasons:

1   Perhaps the chakras don't exist at all, are just part of Indian mythology and were never meant to be anything other than metaphor. Possible, but unlikely.

2   Maybe they are no more than shared delusions. Again, possible, but highly unlikely. We could all be deluded, but after sorting out the inconsistencies, we still seem to be talking about the same things. I can train someone in the basics of feeling chakras in just a few hours.

3   Perhaps some cultures simply didn't notice them or were not interested in them. That really seems very unlikely. I have too much respect for my ancient colleagues to believe that they could have missed something if it was there.

4   So that leaves another possibility: that the chakras had simply not developed sufficiently in some of those cultures to be accessible to the seers and physicians of the day. That seems to me much the most likely. I spend a lot of time around animals, and they usually express just two or three chakras, although when they spend a lot of time with humans, they often become clearer. The Ancient Wisdom teaches that one of our tasks is to help the evolution of the other kingdoms of nature. Some of my own teachers had cats and dogs that had achieved extraordinary degrees of development.

Clearly there are plenty of people who can perceive chakras, but, as with any kind of perception, what you see and feel is colored by your knowledge, background and perceptual style: some people are visual and others more tactile. I have known people talk about using chakras for healing, and as soon as they are asked about which system they favor, they got a bit flustered, often confessing that they did not know that there were different chakra systems.

If you are planning to work with a therapist who does energetic work, it is a good idea to ask the person which system he or she uses, why he or she favors that particular one, and what evidence he or she has to support their approach. The answers will help you decide if this is the therapist for you.

Spiritual Teachings and Spiritual Practice

We live in a spiritual universe. The very word *spiritual* can be used in many different ways. There are two main schools of spiritual practice. Either it serves as a source of comfort, or it is seen as something transformative, something that is not comforting at all but which seeks to remake the world.

Many people whom I have known have spent a great deal of time on the minutiae of the finer points of spiritual philosophy. There is nothing wrong with that, so long as it does not stop you from doing something constructive, not just for yourself, but for others too. For many of us who have spent a great deal of time with spiritual seekers, there has been a nagging concern. Over the last four decades since Eastern spiritual practices started becoming widely adopted in the West, we have noticed that so many spiritual seekers are profoundly self-centered, seeking personal enlightenment rather than being concerned for the good of all.

I have been extremely interested in the way in which currents of thought develop (those "little memes" again) and how people become receivers of these mass effects. There have been multiple examples of simultaneous discoveries in different parts of the world, and less obvious ones, like all the "split brain" work of the 1960s, coinciding with the cross-pollination of Eastern and Western cultures. So it can be helpful to see if people are responding to some sort of emotional or intellectual current. In this case, I see a real, deep-seated current of spiritual yearning, which some people pick up on more than others.

After studying the Ageless Wisdom and countless philosophical and spiritual traditions, it soon became clear that the teachings often took some translating. Not just because some were in other languages, but also because so many of them were culture bound. What do I mean by this?

It has been striking how often the time and place of the teachings has led to things being included that tell us more about the time and the culture than about the underlying truths. For example, the theories based on hydraulic metaphors came from a time when water was the main commodity, and teachings about spiritual radiations coincided with the discovery of radioactivity. Sometimes cultural biases can be a problem.

One teacher whose work I like very much came from a time and from a part of the world where there was little gender equality. In the midst of some sublime teachings, he expressed firm views about what was and what was not allowed in sexual relationships. Many teachers who have realized some extraordinary spiritual truths continue to harbor some firm ideas about the world. I have known some who espoused extraordinary political philosophies, and others who were misogynist or homophobic. Many others have suffered from severe physical problems. The explanation for these disconnects is to be found in the understanding that we are all developing or moving along a series of developmental lines, and some are more developed than others. It is my intention to help restore your health, wellness and vitality so that you can then make your own decisions about whether or not you would like to follow such a radical path.

An important question is: "What is health?" In answer, we have within medicine three classes of definition:

1   The medical, which is more or less an absence of illness;

2   The social, by which we think of health as a result of appropriate social adaptation and harmony; and, finally, what we might call

3   The Utopian, which considers health as "complete physical, mental and social well-being, and not merely the absence of disease or infirmity," to use the words of the World Health Organization.

But there are other ways of thinking about health. In more traditional cultures, health is often defined as peaceful, undisturbed existence, while we in the West tend to think of health more in terms of feeling good, being fit and performing well.

Traditional, alternative and complementary approaches to health have taken a rather broader view, seeing health as a more vital and overarching state of being that involves finding your place in the Universe, living in conformity with universal laws and principles, and being fully integrated.

We are going to consider health as an expansion and deepening of consciousness, of being in control of one's energy and time, of finding a greater and richer meaning to life and of reaching new levels of connectedness with others and with the Universe. But we are also going to see that it is an aspect of a duality.

Dualities

Most of us live move and have our being in an ocean of false dichotomies:

Black	White
Good	Bad
Male	Female
Yin	Yang
Right	Left
Fun	Fulfillment
Health	Disease

False dichotomies can cause turmoil, and turmoil can lead to a degradation of the coherence that is the deepest path toward freedom and health. Our first task is to move beyond the concept of dichotomies or opposites, toward the idea of dualities. Dualities each contain aspects of its twin, and to a greater or lesser degree each constantly transforms into the other.

The concept of either/or is peculiarly Western, and goes back to the Greek philosopher Aristotle, who was also the originator of the false idea that we have only five senses. In the East, there is far greater tolerance of the idea that two states can exist simultaneously. With it, is a far greater acceptance of uncertainty. In most people who have grown up in the West, uncertainty is a potent cause of anxiety. This is so important that we will later be looking at some techniques for flourishing in the face of uncertainty, and we will show you how your Inner Light is most likely to become manifest in your life during times of uncertainty and transition. Uncertainty and transition are to be welcomed, for if you live constantly within your comfort zone, it is unlikely that you are fulfilling your full potential.

In a dichotomy we are automatically drawn towards judging one part of the dichotomy as inferior. This tends to happen because of our social and tribal evolution, when it was important to understand the pecking order. So we have a tendency to label things unnecessarily.

A critical aspect of our own development is to recognize false dichotomies, to understand them as dualities that we need to integrate within ourselves, and ultimately to transcend them. Transcending duality can be extremely powerful. Consider for a moment a classic example of transcending normal yes/no thinking. You have likely been taught some of the techniques of lateral thinking, and they all revolve around the idea that it is possible to learn to think outside the box. Lateral thinking is not only a very useful practical tool, but there is evidence that it may stimulate the brain to grow.

Dividing people on the basis of gender is a classic false dichotomy. For in truth we all contain male and female elements: male and female dualities. The healthy individual integrates and thus transcends them.

Some false dichotomies have arrested the development of otherwise useful systems of knowledge. Let me take an example of pleasure/pain. This has been the basis for many psychological systems for at least a century. Yet even Sigmund Freud himself wrote that there is more to human motivation than this. Considering pleasure and pain as dualities that transform into each other in a constant dance helps us understand why neither can exist without the other.

Another example is fight/flight. Most people have heard about these two reactions to threat, without perhaps realizing that we have known for many years that there is a third option, which is *freeze*. Or you may have heard about the sympathetic/parasympathetic dichotomy. Long thought of as two parts of the autonomic nervous system that maintain a dynamic balance in the body, it is now thought that there is a third part of the autonomic nervous system, which is involved in social adaptations. Healthy functioning needs all three to be integrated into one harmonious whole.

Let me give you another example of a false dichotomy. I still sometimes hear people talking about individuals who are "left brained" or "right brained." This is fine as a metaphor but not as a fact. It is true that language is more highly represented in the left hemisphere of the brain in right-handed *men*. But language is bilaterally represented in women. The truth is that we cannot neatly divide up the functions of our brains, and we need both sides of our brains if we are to function at our best.

When duality loses its dynamism, we face rigidity, imbalance and an inhibition of the natural healing mechanisms of the body and the mind.

Once we have accepted and integrated our dualities, we can then use them. We may ultimately begin to experience that there never was any duality. Those who have had the revelation of non-duality, find that their minds are liberated from time, and many of the deep fears that hold others back begin to evaporate. It is difficult to be fearful if you realize that you are one with the Universe. After that, you begin to develop a deeper perspective about life, and it can then really begin to express itself in you. You begin to see that astonishing creative potential that runs through our lives but that most people normally do not even notice.

Storytelling and Meaning

Human beings are the consummate meaning generators in the Universe.

One of the most remarkable things about people suffering from severe mental illness is that while the rest of their lives may be falling apart, they are busily trying to understand what is happening to them. They will often produce extraordinarily creative explanations for their problems, even while many of their other cognitive abilities are collapsing. Our brains and our minds are wonderfully adapted to making meaningful patterns. From the simplest attempts to make sense of pictures made up of a few dots, to attempts to produce coherent accounts of our worlds. Sometimes these meaningful patterns become deranged, and then we are set up for chaos in the Five Domains.

> "He who has a 'Why' to live for, can bear almost any how."
> —Friedrich Nietzsche (German Philosopher, 1844–1900)

Since the time of William James, the issues of will, purpose and meaning have attracted little interest within mainstream psychology. Although they sometimes reappear in another guise when we talk about drives and volition, I have many colleagues who feel that these are issues that lie outside the remit of science. I firmly believe that this is incorrect. If you are reading this, it is highly likely that you feel that you have a will, and you may have found or be looking for more purpose and meaning. You simply know intuitively that these things exist. Meaning provides context, and from context flows the real richness of life. Meaning fuels the alchemy that can transform an event into an experience. It is remarkable that in psychology there is either little interest in meanings, or else people go to extremes to try to find esoteric models of meaning. Parables and myths make deep meanings accessible.

The real meaning of freedom is the ability to choose how you will react in response to any situation. You choose the way to think about a problem; you establish your point of view and your way of behaving. It saddens me that so many people whom I see function "on automatic:" they live in a world of habitual responses. As long as you are concerned about what others think and say, you are responding and will never be free. And I promise that you can be different. You can choose how to run your physiology, how to inform your body about your needs and wants. That last one takes a bit of practice, but, within certain limits, it can be done. The ultimate goal of any form of personal development, of psychotherapy and indeed of medicine, should be to remove restrictions from people. Freedom unlocks human potential.

The work of the Austrian psychiatrist and Holocaust survivor Viktor Frankl has quite rightly become popular in recent years. Perhaps more than anyone else, he was convinced of the importance of meaning as a motivating factor. He felt that it was important for people to commit to meaningful goals and values, and to be constantly aware of the meaning in all things. However, he was also eager to point out the futility of becoming so entranced by a particular outcome that we lose all perspective and can trip ourselves up. He also emphasized the importance of extending ourselves, to becoming more than we are now. This is one definition of the transpersonal or spiritual domain. Frankl saw mental health as deriving from ultimate meaning, or spiritual values.

Storytelling is one of the most fundamental and enduring needs of human beings. It is an art that defines us, and provides a narration of our worldview.

We all constantly tell stories about ourselves and our relationships, and these help define who we are. Our stories shape virtually every human endeavor: in medicine, in law and in business. Stories are the vehicles of meaning.

Why do we tell stories? Why the constant need, and what does it mean when the whole process breaks down? It has clear evolutionary advantages to be able to tell good stories, not only for social cohesion, but also as a device to pass on wisdom. We all have a need to leave a legacy. This is a fundamental biological drive, and the neurological machinery of that drive has been hijacked by the mind, so it is also a fundamental psychological drive. The stories that we tell are a device to help us make sense of the world about us. To provide us with meaning. To tell or write a story is to express our individuality and to make connections with others. When our stories become inconsistent with our memories and our beliefs, trouble is usually looming. Many of us have been very concerned about the constant pressure on people to "be real" or to "be genuine." If this involves undermining a person's story without providing a coherent and meaningful new one, it can be a recipe for disaster.

Most people have constructed a personal story that may not entirely tally with objective reality, not that they are lying or faking, but because memory is highly synthetic. The idea that memory works like kind of continuous video recording of events has been shown to be quite incorrect. We constantly synthesize and interpret our lives and try to inject meaning into them. It is when these stories become inconsistent, or we believe in a story about ourselves that does not fit that we can run into trouble. Part of the task of maturation is to separate our fantasy stories from the reality of our lives. This has to be done carefully. Simply exploding a personal story without due preparation can be very destructive. Driving a Bulldozer through a lifetime of experience and coping strategies can be risky for the person with the history, as well as the driver.

Our minds and our brains break down when we no longer manage to make sense of the world around us. It is essential for us to have a coherent story. But there is more to this. A story is a communication with ourselves and with others. It is one of the many streams of information that define us. One of the key things about our stories is that they reflect not just our memories and our experiences, but also the power of our questions.

"The biggest disease today is not leprosy or tuberculosis, but rather the feeling of being unwanted, uncared for and deserted by everybody."
—Mother Teresa of Calcutta (Albanian-born Indian Nun, Humanitarian and, in 1979, Winner of the Nobel Peace Prize, 1910–1997)

I want you to become somebody who narrates the world differently. I want you to start recalibrating and transforming your world by your questions and by the meanings that you attach to them. Because that is the key to what the healthy do. We now need to move to our next topic: the pathology of meaning.

Diseases of Meaning

We have to deal with a huge problem in our perception about health, wellness and disease. Most of us think of health and disease as a dichotomy, as two sharply different states. But in reality, health and disease are part of a duality of healthy functioning. As with the other dualities that we have looked at, each contains the other, each is necessary for the other, and each gives rise to the other. Disease is a healthy response of an organism striving to maintain its equilibrium in the face of disruptive forces, like negative thoughts, unbalanced relationships, environmental toxins, poor nutrition and so on. Disease can initiate a process of transformation; it has meaning. And instead of being brought low by a feeling of powerlessness, this realization can help people become stronger, to live more fully and with more understanding. This way of looking at disease can be applied to any of the chronic illnesses, and even to environmental problems like community violence. Understanding a disease for what it is can be empowering, and even transformative.

"That which doesn't kill us makes us stronger."
—Friedrich Nietzsche (German Philosopher, 1844–1900)

Despite living in one of the most affluent, educated and liberal eras in history, paradoxically we are seeing ever more people with chronic and largely incurable diseases. This is in part because of aging and increased longevity, and the transformation of once often-fatal diseases like diabetes into chronic lifelong problems. But there is also something else. Viktor Frankl concluded that in concentration camps, it was having a sense of meaning that determined survival. We are going to be applying that insight. It is inevitable that we are all going to get some sort of illness at some time. After all, nobody ever actually dies of old age. But maintaining a sense of meaning, and a purpose, can be critical to maintaining health, and dealing with disease if it does arise.

A lack of meaning in life is associated with psychopathology, while positive life meaning tends to insulate us against some of the problems that are part of life. It is likely that sources of personal meaning like strong religious beliefs, membership in groups, dedication to causes, having life values and possessing clear goals influence the processes of stress and coping.

"To be a person is to have a story to tell."
—Karen Blixen, a.k.a. Isak Dinesen (Danish Writer, 1885-1962)

Writing and Rewriting Your Own Story

Empirical research has shown that writing about painful experiences can enhance immune responses and promote physical, psychological and social well-being. It is extremely likely that it can also help buttress your subtle and spiritual bodies. Therefore, we are going to take the first steps toward writing our own life story. And now I have to let you in on a secret. Your memory is not just a video of your life events; it is dynamic and malleable and is constantly being edited. So we can change our stories, and with that, remove some of the restrictions that they have imposed upon us. This is not an invitation to enter into a fantasy world or to start lying to yourself or to other people, but is instead an incredibly valuable tool to help us release the Inner Light.

It is a good practice to think through your stories every day. If you care to write about them, that is even better. We need to answer the question: "What are the stories that have defined who you are and how you act?"

When we think about our relationships, isn't it true that the ones that matter the most and have the most emotional charge attached to them are those in which our stories are intertwined? How often have you met an old friend, after a gap of many years, and found that you no longer have much to talk about, because your stories have diverged so far? How many people maintain family relationships even when their respective stories have nothing in common? Maintaining a relationship out of duty is unfair and disingenuous. Either the stories need to be repaired, or the relationship is doomed.

As an exercise, I would like you to examine some of the dominant stories that have determined some of your personality and your character. And I would then like you to write a brief story about how you would like your life to be.

To help you get started, let me make some suggestions:

- What is your favorite type of story?
- What is the first story about your family that you remember hearing?
- What are your favorite stories about yourself as a child?
- What are your favorite stories about yourself as an adult?
- Who are the key characters in your life story?
- How many of the key characters know each other?
- Does your life story have a plot line?
- Could you create a better one?
- What stories would you like others to tell about you?
- How would you like your story to end?

Chapter Seven
Expanding Concepts of Health and Disease

Meaning and Purpose

The overemphasis on scientific analysis and reasoning at the expense of wisdom and intuition has driven our culture to an alarming state of imbalance. The duality of being and doing has become profoundly unbalanced. Can the whole of psychology be explained by learning and reflexes, or do our deepest experiences point us toward a conscious experience that transcends space and time? The answer is undoubtedly the latter.

We are next going to look at purpose: your master motivator. But first it is important to say a word about purpose in the Universe at large.

Purpose is found throughout Nature. DNA manifests its purpose when it provides the information to initiate protein synthesis that might ultimately lead to life's becoming organized and perpetuating itself. We manifest purposes when we eat, have children, create art or establish societies. But the key point is this: Until we understand that purpose-driven Universal laws are emerging, and until we consciously align with them, our sense of purpose remains personal and we are unlikely to have found our Higher Purpose, or our Destiny. When we align with these Purpose-driven Universal laws, life flows, and we can really talk about being in the "Cosmic Groove."

"Life isn't about finding yourself. Life is about creating yourself."
—George Bernard Shaw (Irish Playwright, 1856–1950)

Something that can be forgotten in the debates about meaning, purpose and creation is that one of the characteristics of Nature is a continuous movement toward the evolution of increasingly complex structures and functions. So we should expect that our own lives, relationships, cultures and institutions should do the same. And it is purpose that guides and directs this movement.

One of the most important tasks is to find your own purpose. Because I can assure you that you have one.

Purpose gives us direction, clarity and power. We have already said that real power healing happens when we are coherent and organized. Purpose is just such an organizing force. Purpose is not just something static; it is a dynamic process that re-emerges every few years as we grow and develop, and again during major life transitions.

That is when we ask the Big Questions:
Who am I?
What's the meaning of life?
What should I be doing with my life/career/relationships?

Questions of purpose often have a catalyst, and in a moment I'll give you a remarkable example of a catalyst.

There is evidence that a sense of purpose is hardwired in the brain. A complete absence of purpose is a powerful cause of depression. One of the best explanations for the number of people who develop serious illnesses or die shortly after retiring from work is that they have lost their sense of purpose. Some of us have a strong innate sense of purpose. For others it comes as a result of a life event. Once we have found our purpose we must take action on it. A sure sign of having found your purpose is that taking that action is constantly enjoyable and fulfilling.

Your Integration Journal

Memories of resolving to keep a diary on New Years' Day and losing interest around January 5th had given me a rather jaundiced view of keeping a journal. But some years ago I rediscovered the value, not of slavishly writing out everything I could think of, but of using it as a tool. I am going to be making some suggestions for exercises and experiments for you to try out. I have designed them to be used more than once so that you can keep track of your progress. Your Integration Journal is the perfect place to keep a record as you advance. Nothing breeds success like more success, and you will be inspired if you see measurable changes in your attitudes, psychological well-being, and physical and spiritual health.

> "The unexamined life is not worth living."
> Socrates (Athenian Philosopher, 469–399 B.C.E.)

It's a good idea to find a journal with a cover that you like, and paper that is pleasing to you so that using your journal will be a constant source of pleasure: an adult reward. You may even want to have two journals, one for your private use and another for sharing insights with others.

When you have done the experiments, played each of the games, or answered the questions I give you, more questions will inevitably occur to you, and the journal can become the repository for all your insights. I will also let you in on a secret: Most of the major advances in physics have come not from logical progression, but from mystical revelation: Albert Einstein and the theory of relativity, Max Planck and quantum theory, Erwin Schrödinger and wave mechanics; the list is a long one. Bertrand Russell once said of Einstein, that the problem in understanding him was not a difficulty with his logic, but with the freedom of his imagination.

> "There is no such thing as a logical method of having new ideas ... Every great discovery contains an irrational element of creative intuition"
> —Sir Karl Popper (Austro-British Philosopher, 1902–1994)

If you give the experiments and exercises a little bit of time and take care to record your results, you should quickly find an improvement in your intuition and insight, and who knows what new ideas and concepts may come to you.

I am always pragmatic about trying any new method. If after two weeks you have failed to find any benefit, then feel free to discard it.

An Evaluation Experiment

It is very helpful for you to have an idea of your own sense of meaning and purpose. I am going to ask you to rate yourself using this small questionnaire. I have spent many years designing and working with rating scales, and they can be valuable, *but only insofar as they can go.* Few of them are used in diagnosis, and our intention here is for you to use this scale to point out areas that may need work. I am also extremely aware that these scales are not for people suffering from some illnesses, like mania or depression.

It is essential that you do not just do this evaluation on your own. It will also be extremely useful if you can ask loved ones, friends and co-workers to do this as well. You can use it to keep track of your own progress by repeating the rating after you have finished this book and you have been following some of the recommendations for a few days.

If your score is:
Over 50: You already possess a high degree of meaning and purpose in life, so some parts of the program will be easy for you.

30–50: We can easily help you construct a more fulfilling life.

Less than 30: We shall need to do quite a lot of work together, but you and those around you will be impressed by the positive changes

1. I am enthusiastic about life.

Always 5 4 3 2 1 Never

2. Life feels constantly exciting.

Always 5 4 3 2 1 Never

3. I have very clear goals and aims.

Always 5 4 3 2 1 Never

4. Making plans for the future is fun and pleasurable.

Always 5 4 3 2 1 Never

5. I always know what to do when I have a problem

Always 5 4 3 2 1 Never

6. I feel that I have a lot more things to do in life.

Always 5 4 3 2 1 Never

7. I feel that my life is full of purpose and meaning.

Always 5 4 3 2 1 Never

8. My life is full of constant unpredictable changes.

Always 5 4 3 2 1 Never

9. My personal existence feels meaningful and full of purpose.

Always 5 4 3 2 1 Never

10. Each day is constantly new.

Always 5 4 3 2 1 Never

11. I have discovered clear-cut goals and a satisfying life purpose.

Always 5 4 3 2 1 Never

12. I have a clear mission in life.

Always 5 4 3 2 1 Never

13. I can see a clear reason for my being here.

Always 5 4 3 2 1 Never

14. If I should die today, I would feel that my life has been very worthwhile.

Always 5 4 3 2 1 Never

A Horse Called Aidan

Everything in the Universe has a purpose, and it is clear that one of our goals—indeed, *our* purpose—is to find our personal purpose, as well as the purpose of those around us. At the end of the book, we shall be talking about the importance of relating to animals. One of the reasons for suggesting working with them is this: If they have come into our lives, then that is for a reason too, and we need to find it.

Let me give you an example. We have a young Irish horse called Aidan. He is a wonderful fellow: innocent, ever curious and ever loving. If we could spread those qualities around the world, we would see the end of the world's problems in days. In the horse world, the best horses are bred for one particular discipline, to have one skill set. Aidan was bred to be a hunter. He has feet the size of dinner plates and has never taken a lame step in his life. But then something unexpected happened. He is a product of 300 years of breeding, but now we see a wild card. It turns out that he also has all the classic features of an "eventing" horse. So much so, that some are already predicting that he might eventually go to the Olympic games. Anybody who has ever done any gardening or who knows the most basic genetics will tell you that sometimes "wild types" turn up.

So what happened here that is different? He was bred as a hunter, and by some of the best breeders in the world. He was trained as a hunter. He was brought to the United States as a hunter. But then what? Somebody else came on the scene, named Kim Littrell, who realized that he could be something else. Within the last week, the man who found and sold Aidan traveled to the United States from Ireland, and admitted his perplexity. This man is one of the finest trainers in the world and has an uncanny way with horses. And he is convinced that this "hunter" is now, all of a sudden, an "eventer."

So what happened? Remember what we said about the dancing genes? Despite all the breeding, Aidan is now something else. Is he just a "wild type"? Some sort of genetic aberration? No. He still has all the physical attributes of the hunter. So this is not just a matter of genes.

What happened here is that somebody found his True Nature, his Purpose. What the Ancients used to call a Being's "Name." Like all creatures, Aidan was created for a purpose. He was created to be an outstanding eventing horse. The fact that he was bred to have the DNA of a hunter is a mere bagatelle. He had the potential to transcend his DNA and to rise to be something else. His True Nature has been discovered. As a horse, he has his own Journey, his own Path. As humans, it is our responsibility to ensure that he can walk that Path.

Could this tale all be some sort of anthropomorphic fantasy? That we see Aidan as human, and that this is all magical thinking?

Not at all: This story is not a metaphor. It is something that is happening here in our home today. I am not projecting onto the horse or trying to make this event something that it is not. I am just presenting a set of facts.

It would be easy to say that all of this is a coincidence, but I do not much believe in coincidence. "Coincidence" is a lazy response to Life's mysteries.

What was needed to find Aidan's nature? Was it that by chance he found himself surrounded by people who were sensitive to his Purpose? Did he surround himself with people who were sensitive to his purpose? The answer to these questions is yes: Both are correct.

I would like you to ponder on this. You might even want to put the book down for a little while to intuit and think your way through this story, and to ask when a situation like this might have happened in your life. It could be very important for you. And we shall then begin to help you find your purpose.

Clarity and Purity of Purpose

"Those who follow that part of themselves which is great are great men; those who follow that part which is little are little men."
—Mencius (Chinese Philosopher, c.370–c.284 B.C.E.)

We have spent time looking at the mighty trio: Purpose, Meaning and Will. We are now going to start using them. But the way in which we use them is different from most recommendations. Purpose is crucially important, and so are the steps involved in manifesting it. You have a personal purpose and also a transpersonal or, if you prefer, a Divine purpose. I say that based on experience, study and interacting with tens of thousands of people. It is the higher purpose that, once you have found it, will support and sustain you for your whole life.

I have been very struck by the number of books and seminars that have all promoted a single idea, or at most two or three concepts. Learn this, or master that, and you will be successful beyond your wildest dreams. I am sure that you have seen the same thing: Live more passionately; generate a burning desire for something; have an unshakable belief that you will be successful; set clear goals; create a plan of action; persist; affirm; visualize; give yourself permission to succeed; have a positive mental attitude. The list goes on and on. I am quite certain that each of them is correct and that each has helped a great many people, but in our changing world, mastering any one of these will not be as effective as using all of them together. The way of the Integrated Individual is to have all these aspects working in coherent harmony, with all parts of you, even the negative, unified and working together. What these various aspects need is a glue to organize them.

That glue is Clarity and Purity of Purpose, which activates your Will, and gently requests the Universe to help you. It may sound rather old-fashioned and idealistic to talk about Purity of Purpose, but the fact remains that actions must always be carried out from the purest of motives. Whatever their philosophical, religious or moral orientation, few people would really disagree about that. If you are really, truly, honestly doing something from your highest ideal, it is far more likely to succeed than if you simply have a clear goal that you want to get rich or famous. Today we are going to start working on finding that ideal.

The first of my schoolboy friends to become really well known was Douglas Adams, who wrote that wonderfully amusing satire *The Hitchhiker's Guide to the Galaxy*. When the computer, Deep Thought, is asked for the answer to "The Great Question of Life, the Universe and Everything," it computes away for seven and half million years before coming up with the answer "Forty-two." The problem, the computer points out, is that nobody ever actually knew the proper question. The Universe will not be able to help you unless you are very clear about what it is that you need, and about what you will be able to contribute with what it gives you.

I am sure that as a child you played the three wishes game: that you could have three wishes bestowed upon you by a passing leprechaun or genie. Well, I would like you to do this as an exercise. You are allowed three wishes, and, no, one of the wishes cannot be for another three wishes. But I want the wishes to be transpersonal, not for you personally, but for other people whom you know, or for your society or the world as a whole. I would like you to rank your three wishes in order of priority. Forget for a moment that this is a child's game. I have specifically chosen it because it is so well-known and it has a morphic field attached to it. Record these wishes, and you have taken another important step toward finding your purpose.

The next way of prioritizing your goals is to play another game: I would like you to list the 10 books, the 10 pieces of music and the 10 people that you would like to take with you to a desert island. You can also use these lists to help you locate the preponderant Memes at work in your psyche.

"Someone who is truly directed by a high ideal is never discouraged. The mere presence within him of this high ideal that feeds and guides him makes him happy. He knows, he feels that he is walking on the right path, that nothing will ever hinder his progress, and this is enough for him—even if he takes some wrong steps on this path …"
—Omraam Mikhaël Aïvanhov (Bulgarian Spiritual Master, 1900–1986)

I have one final exercise: If you had the chance, and if there would be no possible consequences, is there anyone or anything in the world with which you would like to "get even?" This may sound like a very odd question, but it is important. I have seen countless people destroyed by the corrosive effects of deep festering resentments over some perceived slight or injustice. When we get to the next chapter, I am going to want you to keep this list in the forefront of your mind, as something to be disposed of.

Questions, Questions

Inasmuch as humans are the consummate meaning generators, we are also the consummate questioners. The quality of your questions determines the quality of your life. Whether you are learning algebra, working with someone in a business, trying to work out why a relationship is not going the way that you had hoped for or working on a new theory of the Universe, the key is to ask the right questions. I was once coaching somebody who was having a lot of trouble with passing a particular examination.

"How do you actually do your studying?" I said.
"Oh, I just sit down with the book and try to remember everything I read," was the reply.

"The only stupid question is one not asked."
—Unknown Author

I was astonished. Here I had a highly intelligent person who had already obtained a medical degree, and he had never been taught a fundamental skill. I made a simple suggestion. Since the best types of learning are based on understanding principles and making associations, I recommended that every time he read something, he should ask: "How does this fit in with everything else that I know?" And if it did not, then to question what it was about his models that could not accommodate the new facts. So his models needed to change and to expand, and then the facts began to be linked and associated. By building some coherent stories, he went on to conquer the problem in just a few weeks.

If you are meeting somebody, whether for the first or the hundredth time, whether in a business or any other kind of setting, the quality and structure of your questions will provide the context and the meaning for the relationship that develops. Most people have heard that it is good to be interested rather than interesting. That is absolutely correct. Why is that? Because good questions help another person to tell his or her own story. That is important to everyone, and with your help, they may even find new nooks and crannies that will help both of you.

> "It is not the strongest of the species that survive, nor the most intelligent, but the ones most responsive to change."
> —Charles Darwin (English Naturalist, 1809–1882)

I am ambitious for you. I want you to inject more meaning into your life, and I want you to transform your life. I have had the incredible privilege of knowing many extraordinary people. I have learned from all of them that it is their stories and their questions that are key. Each has constructed an empowering narrative of his or her life, and each could take a problem in virtually any field and find a new way of looking at it. The art of good questioning starts with a real interest in the answer, together with flexibility and an absolute absence of any prejudice or any preformed ideas.

Asking a question to get an answer that you want is unwise. It is best to get the other person to find the answer within him or herself. I am now going to ask you to engage in an activity that has helped innumerable students to get better at this.

To start on the road toward finding and refining your own purpose, I offer some questions that I would like you to work on regularly. It is essential that you do not do this alone, but that you do this exercise with any people with whom you are close. Ultimately it will help you define your personal, familial and group purpose, and from this you will create your mission statement.

I have dealt with a great many couples, families and groups, who, within their unit, all had different plans and aspirations, and they created chaos until all the cards were on the table.

These are 23 questions that I suggest you work on regularly, even if just for a few minutes each day.

1   Who am I?

2   Why am I here?

3   What do I want?

4   If I had a part in choosing, then why did I choose to be here in this time and place?

5   Where do I belong?

6   What are my Core Needs?

7   What are my Core Wants?

8   What are my Core Beliefs?

9   Am I being true to my Core Beliefs?

10 What would I do if I had no obligations and I had an endless supply of energy, time and money?

11 What makes me happy?

12 What are my main gifts and strengths?

13 Am I using my gifts and strengths to the fullest? If not, why not?

14 What are my challenges?

15 What is it about me that I would most like to improve?

16 Am I exceeding my own expectations? If not, why not?

17 What do I have to give others?

18 Am I giving it? If not, why not?

19 Whom do I love and who loves me?

20 For what do I want to be remembered?

21 Have I had a positive impact in the world? If not, why not?

22 What is my legacy?

23 What would I do right now if I had a Magic Wand? Would I do it?

These are 23 questions to ask when faced with a challenge.

1 What predisposed me to develop this problem today and not yesterday or tomorrow?

2 What precipitated the problem?

3 What is supporting or perpetuating the problem?

4 How much of the problem is my fault?

5 Is this problem part of a pattern?

6 Is it really a problem, and why do I need to solve it?

7 Can I reframe the problem?

8 What resources do I have at my disposal?

9 What resources or information do I need to obtain?

10 Am I asking the correct questions?

11 What am I assuming about this situation?

12 What would happen if I challenged those assumptions?

13 Do I know all the laws and rules governing the problem and its potential solutions?

14 How can I look at the problem from another perspective?

15 How would a wise being from another planet solve this problem?

16 How will I see this problem one year from now?

17 How will I see this problem 10 years from now?

18 What are my choices?

19 What am I missing or avoiding?

20 What action steps make the most sense?

21 What is possible?

22 What can I learn from this situation?

23 What would I do if I had a Magic Wand?

Medicine: Alternative, Complementary, Integrated and Integral

At last count there were over 500 types of "alternative" or "unorthodox" medicines. Many techniques and methods appear to be mutually exclusive: How could the same back pain be caused by a disk problem, a muscle problem, a psychological problem, an "energetic" problem or some karmic issue? So some years ago, I decided to look at the whole issue of differences from the perspective that they are all right and that each has a part of the puzzle. I helped initiate some of the first multidisciplinary meetings at which conventionally trained physicians discussed patients with homeopaths, acupuncturists, psychotherapists and so on. It was helpful but seemed to get us no closer to a dream of a comprehensive new model of health care.

Some people have said that there is no need to develop any new models of medicine or new techniques. After all, we already have a large enough toolbox. But that cannot be quite right. After all, the world is still full of people with physical, psychological, social, financial and spiritual problems. One of the great difficulties of many of the more unorthodox therapies is that they take a lot of time. Many of my friends who are alternative practitioners like spending hours with each patient, and obviously the patients like it too. The trouble is that it is scarcely feasible to spend many hours with every sick person in the world.

So we decided to look at the common denominators that could form the basis for a comprehensive program of self-care.

First, it became clear that a key component of any good therapeutic interaction was the relationship between the therapist and the patient. We also know that social factors play a central role in an enormous number of diseases.

Second was the ability of the therapist to instill meaning and to teach some problem-solving abilities to the individual. So it was important to think in terms of helping people establish their purpose in life.

Third, it soon became clear that different therapies are quite specific to where people are developmentally. What do I mean by that? We all go through a series of developmental stages in life. Since the mind has such a powerful influence on the body, the state of mind and the state of consciousness will have a major impact on the expression of illness and the maintenance of health. At the extreme end, we learn in the Ageless Wisdom that there are a number of predictable illnesses that can befall people who are engaged in intense spiritual practice.

> A 31-year-old woman was referred to my clinic in London from a small town 300 miles away in Cornwall. She had first presented to her family physician almost a year before, with symptoms of palpitations, sweating, weight loss, anxiety and insomnia. Diagnosed with an overactive thyroid gland, she was referred to an endocrinologist in a nearby hospital after exhausting the possibilities of natural medicine. The endocrinologist was a good physician whom I had helped train. Unable to find an obvious explanation for the overactive thyroid, he started a standard conventional treatment plan. But absolutely nothing worked. He wanted to give her treatment with radioactive iodine, but she declined and asked if she could see someone else. My name came up, and she made the journey to London.
>
> It turned out that she was a yoga and meditation teacher, and had been working very hard on activating her chakras, using a combination of yoga postures, breathing, meditation and visualization. She had done quite a good job, except for her throat chakra, which was wildly out of control. I suggested that her spiritual practice might actually

be the cause of her troubles. She was initially aghast, asking how that could be, since she was using an ancient and natural process. What we decided to do was to temper her practice with some specific exercises to rebalance her subtle systems. The results were remarkable. Within three months, she was able to discontinue her thyroid medicines. She did not want to make the long journey back to London for follow-up with me, but as luck would have it, I was in Cornwall at a meeting on holistic health about a year later, and she was also present. She told me that she was doing extremely well, and I saw she had no obvious signs of an overactive thyroid. We are well aware that some illnesses come and go, and naturally, her overactive thyroid could come back. But I doubt that it will. This was what used to be known as a "disease of discipleship."

The "Energies" of Healing

We owe an enormous debt of gratitude to the psychiatrist Daniel Benor. Like most people trained in Western medicine, he was very skeptical about spiritual healing until he saw a tough case that failed to respond to conventional medicine but was cured by a spiritual healer. He then started to study spiritual healing and has written the standard textbook on the subject, which runs to FOUR volumes. He once told me that the evidence for spiritual healing is stronger than the evidence for almost any other field of unorthodox medicine and stronger than the evidence for quite a number of practices in orthodox medicine!

I can attest to that. I review articles that have been submitted for publication to quite a number of major medical journals. I am known as something of a "hawk." If there's a mistake, I am usually good at finding it. Several years ago I was sent a now-famous study of the influence of distant prayer on the recovery of patients in a coronary care unit. I was certain that I would find a flaw in it, but after three days of intense work, I had to conclude that the study was sound. And it is now one of many. Prayer works, whether or not the recipient even knows that he or she is being prayed for.

The physician and writer Larry Dossey has been an important voice in medicine for over two decades. He has identified three eras of medicine. Beginning in the middle of the 19th century, Western medicine began to adopt an approach based on concepts drawn from the classical, mechanical, Newtonian concept of the Universe. As a result, medicine developed a mechanical view that is still the predominant model today. Dossey calls this Era I, or mechanical or physical medicine. In the middle of the 20th century, it began to be realized that thoughts, emotions, attitudes and beliefs can impact the body, which led to a radically new perspective: what we now refer to as mind-body medicine. Dossey calls this Era II. We are now living in an extraordinarily interesting and exciting time, when empirical evidence, like the research on distant healing that we just mentioned, is forcing us to recognize the emergence of Era III, or *nonlocal* medicine. Unlike the first two Eras, the nonlocal perspective acknowledges that your thoughts and intentions may affect the functioning of other individuals, at any distance, and with or without the awareness of the recipient.

Building upon the concepts that we have been developing here, the key to successful treatment is to use a judicious combination of the best of each of the three Eras.

Several years ago, driven primarily by frustration with the squabbling between different schools of conventional and unorthodox medicine, and our failures to help so many people, we began to develop an expanded model of medicine. In Europe my colleagues and I called this "Integrated Medicine." "Integrative" was the term more commonly favored in the United States, and it was a similar concept. What we were aiming for with the European model of Integrated Medicine was something even more comprehensive than the system being developed in the United States, and more akin to what is now being called "Integral Medicine."

It is my intention to guide you toward better care for yourself and your family, so I think it will be helpful if I show you how this works. We can then show you how to use the system in your own life.

Integrated Medicine is designed to expand the model and the method of conventional medicine, and restores patients to the central position in an ongoing dynamic healing process. It revolves around the notion that human beings are, as we have seen, a composite of interlinked physical, psychological, social, subtle and spiritual natures, and that each of these needs to be understood.

Homeostasis, the ability to maintain a constant internal environment, is a key component of each level of your body, from the biochemical processes within cells to your subtle and spiritual bodies. These innate mechanisms can be recruited even at late stages of an illness. There are differences between treatment and healing, and successful healing requires the participation of the individual to mobilize the innate healing energies of the body.

From the earliest days of the development of this model, we conceptualized healing, and the maintenance of wellness as a process of "education," to empower the individual, first to re-establish health, and then to maintain it. I put the word *education* in quotes, because we conceive of it in a much broader framework than we normally use: not just communicating facts, but rather transmitting information to help rebuild the Informational Matrix and to allow your Inner Light to shine through.

We also emphasized that practitioners would benefit and be more effective if they were themselves healthy in mind, body and spirit, actively engaged in working on themselves, had been trained to acknowledge and use intuition, and could comprehend metaphor and analogy. The key to all this was to be able to give the person being treated, clear, unambiguous healing signals. We also discovered that one healer can often induce another to become a healer. On one of my units, we discovered that many members of the staff became able to treat others, and even some of the people who had come for treatment began to be able to treat others. We coined the term "quantum induction" for this process, in recognition of its similarity to a process sometimes observed in quantum mechanics.

Combining Treatments and the Pyramid

The use of combinations is absolutely central to working successfully with the new laws of healing. These are not random combinations, but are carefully tailored according to the specific needs of the individual. The combinations work in synergy to address every aspect of an individual's being and their precise developmental level.

The first point is that the approach needs precision. Let me give you an example from the field of nutrition. Some years ago, I was making a series of short films for television. One was about the use of vitamin supplements by older citizens. The producer felt that it would be a good idea to recommend that low-income elders should be advised to take any supplements that they could get. I pointed out during the rehearsal that it was sometimes better to take nothing than to take small amounts of one vitamin, for that can lead to an imbalance.

The precise amounts of a supplement are important, as is the combination. I want to give you an example of this. I have recently seen supplements being sold that claim to improve sexual performance. Some contain the amino acid L-arginine. That's fine; L-arginine is a precursor for the vasodilator nitric oxide, which is involved in the mechanics of sexual arousal. There is just one problem. For L-arginine to work, you need to take about 9,000 milligrams. Most of the supplements give you only 200 to 500 milligrams. I have also seen supplements that contain mutually antagonistic vitamins, and others that are missing key components, for instance calcium supplements that do not contain magnesium. I shall have more to say about this important issue in the future.

The second, and crucial point is this: Different forms of therapy work at different levels of our being. Returning to our basic concept that treatment needs to be directed toward gross, subtle and causal realms, I have represented a few of the treatments that operate at the different levels. Each therapy corresponds to one of the planes of being from the gross to the subtle to the causal. The information carried by each therapy resonates with the corresponding plane. The list is far from exhaustive but starts to give you a flavor of the way in which we conceptualize treatment, and how it is very different from the systems typically used in the past. We will spend the rest of our time together examining how exactly to put this information to use.

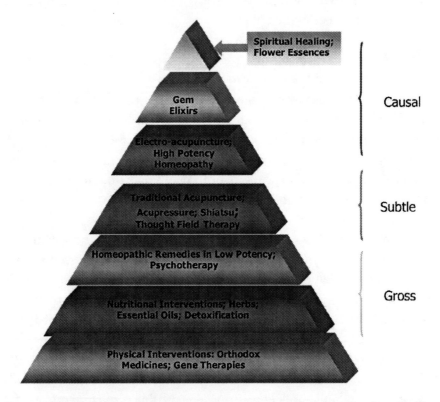

Figure 3: The Healing Pyramid, indicating how some treatments can be aimed specifically at certain domains of the individual

Chapter Eight
Recruiting Your Allies

The Power of the Will

> "Perhaps the only limits to the human mind are those we believe in."
> —Willis Harman (Former President of the Institute of Noetic Sciences, 1920–1997)

We have just seen how meaning and purpose have been largely neglected by academic psychology in recent decades. The third of the neglected trio is the Will, surfacing in psychology books under the guise of "volition." Intuitively we all know this is important, and it will help us on our journey to maintaining health.

When we put energy into something, it implies a level of personal involvement and effort. Ernest Holmes, the originator of Science of Mind, said: "Where the mind goes, energy flows." This is precisely the same statement found in traditional Chinese medicine, that mind acting with intention directs the qi. With our model, you will see that intentional mind directs the information field, which causes the qi to flow. Meaning stimulates the will; boredom cripples it. The will needs a purpose. Why do we feel so happy and cheerful when we are planning a vacation? Because we have a purpose that involves a vision of the future, and purpose is very much involved with a future perspective. Peak experiences, those sudden feelings of intense happiness and well-being, generate surges of meaning, which can propel your will to great heights.

The key to success in any endeavor is purposeful action—not being busy, but working with purpose, clarity and focus. Willpower is the force behind energy and focus. Knowing how to use your will is the key to preventing your past from becoming your future.

The Italian psychiatrist, Roberto Assagioli, who created a field of therapy known as Psychosynthesis, wrote a classic book on the will. He identified the importance of the will in many key areas of our lives, teaching us that besides a strong will, skillful, good, and personal wills are also important. Assagioli is thought to have been one of the grandparents of the burgeoning field known as neurolinguistic programming (NLP). He was also a personal student of the theosophist Alice Bailey, whom we encountered in the introduction to this book. Many believe that NLP was a gift from the people behind theosophy who try to help and educate humanity.

Can we learn to strengthen our Will? The answer to this is absolutely! For the will is strengthened by use. Whenever you create a challenge for yourself and you overcome it, your willpower is strengthened. This is why so many successful people rapidly excel in more than one field. It is crucial to have a firm purpose for yourself and a clear focus while aligning your thoughts and emotions. Next, practice integrity with yourself. And it *is* a matter of practice. Ensure that when you say that you will do something, you do it, or keep quiet and don't promise. Keeping your word is not just a matter of integrity and will, but it will also help you cure yourself of making promises you cannot keep and that most corrosive of illnesses: the disease to please. Saying something to please another at your own expense is often a result of one of the Ego-fears that we are going to be examining in Chapter Ten.

We are also going to be looking at how to deal with some of the factors that can undermine your energy and your Will.

Energy Management Is the Key to Healthy Living

The idea of linear time flowing like a river from the past into the future is a decidedly Western culture-bound idea. It is also very clear that there are many different types of time, ranging from physicists' and astronomers' concepts of time, to subjective time familiar to all of us. There never seems to be enough time for anything. We multitask, trying to pack more into each day. Time is always limited. If you live your life under the rule of the clock, you will live your life constricted and constrained. The emphasis on time as the determinant of our activity is very recent and can be traced back to the Industrial Revolution. Before that, people tended to follow the natural rhythms of nature. We absolutely need to be aware and to honor time. If I ignore or do not respect time, I am not going to be able to catch my plane or take a meeting. But here is the secret: Time is limited, while energy is not. The key to success lies not so much in time management but in energy management.

Linear clock time is very much the realm of your physical existence, with far less impact in the other dimensions of your existence.

Every one of our bodies, each domain of life, has an attached energy that we need to preserve, amplify and channel. We each have a source of endless energy and power as long as we do not needlessly dissipate it. The key to healthy functioning is harmonious, coherent integration of all aspects of our lives, which allows the information to express itself and the energy to flow.

As we develop and mature, we learn the importance of not succumbing to instant gratification. Equally important is to never become a *victim* of the sensations of the moment. The really successful do not complain or explain. Whatever is going on around them, they never flinch. Complaining reinforces the belief that you are a victim, disempowering and distracting your energy.

Focus on possible solutions, rather than on the problem. If somebody keeps repeating how much a thing hurts, or how they worry about the upcoming examination, or how they worry about money, those are all negative cognitions that will lead to negative outcomes. Do not look for a way out of a situation but for a way through it. It is exceedingly important not to focus on things that are beyond your control. Work on the things that you can control, and use techniques appropriate to the task at hand.

Just recently, I was two weeks into a three-week lecture tour of Asia. Someone said to me that I must have a tough constitution to be able to deal with the constant changes of time zones, the constant changes in temperature and diet. But actually the real answer is that I simply continue, whatever the level of adversity. Some of the most powerful people in history simply did not acknowledge—or even notice—hardship.

Will you need food and rest? Will you need the nourishment of other people? Yes, of course, but in their time. The real trick is learning to listen to your body, to know your mind, and to trust your spirit. And gradually you will also be able to listen to the gentle voice of your other bodies. They contain all that you will ever need: the Matrix, and ultimately your true strength.

I was once traveling from the Taj Mahal in Agra to New Delhi. It was incredibly hot, and, as usual in those days, the air conditioning on the bus was not working. I was with a group of young travelers from Europe and the United States, who began complaining about the heat as soon as they got on the bus. Four hours and 146 miles later, several of them had heat stroke. Those of us who just carried on with life, drinking water, getting some salt, and carrying on with our project, were just fine. The complainers were scattering the very energies that would have kept them healthy. Believing that you are doomed can sabotage everything that the Universe would like to do to help you. I say, "Would like to do," advisedly. If we remember everything that we have said so far, we have seen that we are, of course, part of the Universe and that the most powerful single force in our body is a constant urge to heal itself. And the Universe is not chaotic, but self-correcting, meaningful and purposeful. So it follows that the Universe ultimately wants to see you living as you should, without the limitations of age and illness.

There is a well-known story of a poor homeless man who found his way into a refrigerator car on a railway train. He got trapped inside and died of hypothermia—even though the refrigerator unit was switched off. He literally died because he thought that he was going to die of the cold, and his body had all the classic signs of death by hypothermia. As I started exploring the scientific literature, I found many examples of similar observations. It took a lot of sifting to find credible or repeated reports, but they were there. There were an astonishing number of reports of people who showed dramatic physical responses in response to hypnotic suggestions. For example, people persuaded that they had been burned showed all the signs of a physical burn. Some of the most extraordinary reports demonstrated that it was even possible to suppress an immune response in the skin.

> Many years ago I had as a patient, a young man in his mid-forties. Intelligent, fit and healthy, this police inspector experienced odd symptoms that never quite added up. It was obvious that something was wrong, but despite a massive number of investigations, we could not pinpoint it. He helped on the investigation unit, serving meals and helping elderly and handicapped patients. We discharged him with no clear diagnosis, concerned that we would be seeing him again. Less than two months later he was back, with an ominous yellowing of his skin and eyes, called jaundice, which has been known for thousands of years as a sign of a diseased liver. This time it was easy to find that he had a liver full of cancer. On hearing the news, he paused for a moment and then asked if he could have a private room and if he could see his wife and lawyer. He made peace with his wife and family, put his affairs in order, and

took to his bed. He was dead in less than a day. Yes, he had cancer. But I have seen thousands of patients who were in much worse shape and who lived for decades. Apart from the jaundice and the tumors in his liver, there was no obvious physical reason why he died. Except that he had decided that it was time to go.

In the East, there is a venerable tradition of advanced and enlightened people entering "Maha Samahdi." Literally deciding when it is time to go on to the next world. One of my early influences was a famous theosophical writer in England. In 1970, he did exactly this. He announced when he was going to pass on, and he did. Surrounded by his loved ones, they meditated together, during which he quietly left this world. He was of advanced years, but there was absolutely no physical reason for him to die then and there. Except that he willed it. After a lifetime in medicine, I have seen countless people who decided that it was not yet time to go. Many did not get "cured" of their illness. Instead they learned to coexist with it. Now it gets interesting: In virtually every case, the common factor was that they still had something to do, not usually for themselves, but tasks or responsibilities for other people.

To what extent are we really able to control our bodies and our minds? Some writers would have us believe that we can control absolutely anything and that we can each create the Universe around us. I have seen some extraordinary consequences of changing a belief system and have access to an extremely powerful system for manifesting change, but there are problems with that extreme view. If I want my team to win and you want your team to win, doesn't that create a sort of metaphysical logjam? Whose view prevails? I am in no doubt that millions of people locked into concentration camps wanted out with all of their might. Some of the most intelligent, educated, creative and, above all, motivated people were unable to vaporize the gates and fences. Yes, liberation eventually came, and I know of endless metaphysical or karmic explanations for what happened, but on the day-to-day physical plane, people suffered terribly. We have been told that if you want money enough, then you can manifest it. Well, indeed you can, though it rarely turns up in any way that you might expect. I have never yet met anyone who manifested a pile of $100 bills on the night-stand! We have to be realistic about what can and what cannot be done, and not try to tell the Universe how to produce a result.

There is another difficulty with the extreme view of what we can create with our minds. I have seen countless people mired in guilt because they had been told that they had created their own illness, and that the only reason that they were not better was a lack of faith or commitment in their ability to cure their problems. While it is always good to try to understand why an illness has occurred, to see what meaning it has for us, what it may teach us, it is rarely helpful to pile guilt onto people suffering from illness. It can also lead people to avoid the very treatments that may help them.

The key to understanding this important issue is that the Universe does not so much give you what you want, as that the Universe gives you what you *deserve*. Rather than telling the Universe what you want, listen and ask the Universe what *It* wants. The best way of ensuring a positive outcome is through a constant alignment of your will with the clarity and purity of your Higher Purpose. We are going to be going through some very specific steps for doing that, but first I would like to say something about a word that has, for a long time, had unnecessarily bad press. The word is *stress*.

The Positive Power of Stress

There is an old observation in psychology that relates several types of performance to the level of arousal. Arousal is a major aspect of many theories of learning and is closely related to other concepts such as anxiety, attention, agitation, stress and motivation. The essential idea is that if you want to do something well, a little stress is very helpful, but too much leads your performance to collapse. The original findings have been much debated since they were first described in 1908 in relation to habit formation, and the basic concept is important for us. Stress is often demonized as an enemy, when it is nothing of the sort. It is our *reaction* to stress that is important and that involves all the five domains.

A degree of stress provides the motor for achievement. It can provide us with energy, but what we must not do is then needlessly dissipate it. Your energy is a resource to be stored, protected and used in a planned and coordinated way. Some fine meditation teachers provide stress management training. But I have known people who have rushed from work, eating en route, to catch the class at 6:30 in the evening. After an hour of bliss, they then go rushing off home. This is not a recipe for success. The key to managing stress is to provide and structure a whole-person response to it. Doing a weekly meditation class and trying to catch a few minutes during the week can sometimes be frustrating.

There is a remarkable tendency for some illnesses to develop not at the peak of stress, but during the "let-down" period of relaxation. I first learned about this phenomenon during a year spent working in a migraine clinic in London. The clinic had a lot of traffic on Monday mornings from people whose weekends had been ruined by headaches, and we were very busy with schoolteachers at the beginning of the summer break. There is quite good evidence that many different types of illness, particularly those that can be stress related, some painful conditions and some autoimmune diseases, can flare up during a period of relaxation. It is probably related to levels of arousal, and it is important to know if you are one of the people who react this way, because if you are, then routine stress management may backfire on you. If you are one of these people, it is a good idea to change your arousal levels slowly and not to allow them to rise too high in the first place. Using techniques like the 60-Second Peace Technique, which we shall shortly be showing you, can keep your arousal level down and prevent the calamitous roller coaster of high stress/let-down collapse.

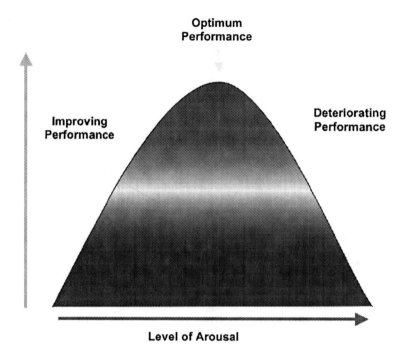

Figure 4. The Yerkes-Dodson Graph, showing how, while some arousal enhances performance, too much can cause performance to deteriorate

An Important Exercise

I would like you to consider everything that is draining your energy, in each of the five domains, and I would like you to record these items. We shall be returning to this list a little later.

How Many Senses Do You Have?

The Greek philosopher Aristotle declared that there were only five senses, when in reality, there are more than 30 additional sense qualities associated with touch, and countless others associated with taste and smell. One reason smell is often so evocative is because it is the only sense not filtered in the region of the brain called the thalamus. Instead, smell is processed directly in an area of the brain that is intimately involved with memory. There are other senses too, including balance. Some people can also feel electrical fields. Many, if not most, people can be taught to dowse for water and sometimes for other objects too. Part of the reason that some are biased against arts like dowsing is purely because of the old prejudice that we have five senses. From what we have seen already in the case of the mice and the marram grass, and the animals escaping the tsunami, other species, and probably many hunter-gatherer people, do possess sensing abilities that would be foreign to most of us. Difficult to test in a laboratory, but there are countless reports of less technologically developed people being able to sense things like water and game, sometimes over considerable distances.

We can train most people to sense their own body subtle energy systems. It usually takes somewhere between five minutes and an hour, and in general, women and children usually learn to do it more rapidly. Some people can also sense the flows of energy in others, though this skill usually takes longer to develop, although if you train with a Master, his or her ability will often rub off, and you will be able to do the sensing very rapidly. It is a little like listening to an orchestra. If you are with a musician, he or she will be able to point out a particular instrument to you, and then it is easy to pick it out in the midst of a cascade of music.

The Mind: Subconscious, Unconscious and Overself

Writers sometimes mix up subconscious and unconscious processes, so I thought that we should sort out the differences. The subconscious refers to mental activity and impulses that occur below the threshold of active awareness. The subconscious mind is also called the "pre-conscious" mind and it includes all the regulatory biological processes. Unless something goes wrong, you are not normally aware of the activity of your heart; it is controlled by the subconscious.

It is now widely thought that there is constant feedback between the body, particularly the nervous, muscular and endocrine systems, and the brain. Even those small clot controllers—the platelets—play a part in this internal symphony: Their membranes and their biochemical processes are so similar to those of neurons that for years they have been used in experimental work as neuron look-alikes. As with all the other processes that we have been looking at, there is not a one-way street from the brain to the body. The body constantly informs the brain. The level of voluntary control that some people have shown over the body is staggering. In the early 1970s, Swami Rama demonstrated that he could stop his heart for about 20 seconds while remaining conscious, and I have seen examples of people who can briefly stop most of their neural activity while remaining fully aware.

The unconscious aspect of mind and personality holds thoughts, desires, images and urges of which the individual is not aware. Carl Jung broke this down into a personal unconscious, which contains unconscious mental contents unique to the individual, and a collective unconscious, which contains ancestral memories and images from humanity's history. The collective unconscious has many similarities to Rupert Sheldrake's ideas of morphic resonance. The idea also has echoes of the Ageless Wisdom. Jung, like Assagioli, was a student of these teachings. It is widely believed that many bad habit patterns originate in the unconscious mind and are maintained within the subconscious. The subconscious is extremely powerful, and learning to work with it is an important part of our work here.

The Overself has been given many names: Higher Self, Soul, Inner Genius, and Daemon. It is that part of you that connects directly to, and is part of, the spiritual realms. It is eternal, immortal, universal and infinite. Attaining knowledge of the Overself, and thereby accessing your Inner Wisdom, should be an important life goal, since it contains the wellspring of knowledge, which you can use all the days of your life. The Higher Mind expresses a Higher Will, and we reach our finest expression, when we find and work with that Higher Will. We will begin to discover how to do that by seeing the world more clearly.

An essential long-term goal is to accept the Universe as it is, for it is many of our false perceptions that create havoc in our lives. As you come to accept the Universe as it is, you leave less of a footprint in the world because you recognize that you are part of a beautiful dynamic, flowing world, rich with meaning and purpose. I was in the lobby of a large hotel in Portland, when I spotted the Dalai Lama, dressed in his customary clothing, in earnest conversation with some aides. The place was crowded, loud and bustling, and nobody even noticed him. That was a beautiful example of somebody whose lifetime of practices and experiences has led him to perceive the world as it is.

Judgment is hard-wired into our social brain, yet it is something that we have to transcend. Making judgments about events and people can be a source of much suffering. You will now see why we began with a discussion of the plasticity of the brain. If the brain were not so plastic, if our genes were not so ready to respond to changes in our environment or in our thoughts, we would be doomed to spend our lives at the whim of millions of years of evolution. But as it is, we can do something about it. As a human being you have an almost unique ability to make conscious choices about your life. Not judging is a good one to add to the list.

Multiple Intelligences

In 1976, I had the privilege of spending the summer studying the brain and behavior in Boston. One of the staff members was an extremely bright young psychologist who was talking about some quite revolutionary ideas. His name was Howard Gardner, and several years later these ideas became known around the globe as the theory of *multiple intelligences*.

For many decades, intelligence was associated with logic and with verbal and mathematical abilities, despite the fact that intelligence is really the ability to respond to novel situations and to learn from experiences. Conventional tests of intelligence (IQ tests) predict success in school and to some degree in higher education but fail miserably to predict how people will get on in the real world. Gardner's view was that our culture has focused too much attention on verbal skills and on logical thinking, while neglecting other ways of knowing, learning and behaving. When he first proposed the idea that there were other intelligences, he counted seven types. The number has now grown to nine, and there has been much speculation that there may be a number of other intelligences waiting to be discovered. We have even reached the stage of being able to suggest neurological correlates for each type. Even before Gardner came up with these ideas, some unconventional schools, for instance the Rudolf Steiner and Montessori schools, have been trying to foster learning and creativity by catering to an individual child's different learning styles and different rates of development.

This whole notion is extremely helpful to us for two reasons: First, it helps us understand how we learn and behave, and second, we can use it to discover the balance of our strengths and weaknesses in different domains. If someone is being educated only to use logic, when that person is naturally more adept at learning through doing things physically, he or she is unlikely to flourish. We all have all the intelligences, and we can strengthen intelligences that are less developed. The advantage of doing so is to help us balance our lives.

These are the major types of intelligences and the styles and strengths of people with each type:

1   Verbal and Linguistic—These people demonstrate strength in the arts of language: speaking, writing, reading and listening. They're often successful in traditional learning environments, with lectures and didactic courses, because their intelligence lends itself to traditional teaching and to books written using concise but evocative language.

2   Logical-Mathematical—These people display an aptitude for numbers, reasoning and problem solving. They will likely also do well in traditional education, where teaching is logically sequenced, and they will be

looking for books and notes that follow a logical linear sequence. They often have difficulty with metaphors and abstract ideas.

3 Visual and spatial—These people learn best when things are visual and organized spatially, relating to eye-catching charts, graphs, maps, tables, illustrations and art.

4 Bodily-Kinesthetic—They tend to experience learning best through activity, such as games, movement, hands-on tasks and building things. It is often difficult for them to sit still, so as children, they may have been labeled as being fidgety or overly active, or even as having attentional problems.

5 Musical and rhythmic—The best way for them to learn is through songs, patterns, rhythms and musical expression. There are countless examples of extraordinarily successful musicians who dropped out of school and were labeled as failures, simply because their gifts were not recognized.

6 Interpersonal—These folk are people oriented and outgoing, and do their learning cooperatively in groups or with a partner. As children, they may have been described as overly talkative or social because their style did not fit the traditional mold.

7 Intrapersonal—These people tend to be particularly in touch with their own feelings, values and ideas. Often reserved, they often learn things and relate to the world with rapid intuitive insights.

8 Naturalist—These people tend to love the outdoors and animals. They also like to pick up on subtle differences in meanings. People in whom this type of learning predominates have often not done well in traditional education, with its emphasis on verbal and logical learning strategies.

9 Existential—These people tend to want to place any new learning into a broader context, asking, since childhood, "Why are we here?" and "What is the meaning of life?" questions.

So there we have the nine types. There have been recent attempts to explore the possibilities of there being others, particularly spiritual and sexual intelligences, and there may well be. But for now, I would like you to use this scheme to find out what *mixture* best describes you. We have not found many people whose center of gravity is purely in one type of intelligence. I would then like you to ask this question: "How would my life have been different, if my parents and teachers had known about this when I was growing up?"

And then, "How can I use this information in the future not just for me, but for all the other people that I know?"

Chapter Nine
Creative Self-Integration

A Tool and a Journey

People are often surprised when they discover they're ill or unable to perform at their peak. But it shouldn't surprise us at all. Much of the time our minds and our bodies each march to their own tune, disorganized, out of kilter, and at the whim of a barrage of corrupted energy and information.

Happily, the organism possesses its own profound wisdom, waiting for the order to coordinate and move forward as an integrated whole. The whole always becomes greater than the sum of the parts. We can achieve things previously perceived as impossible, exceeding our own limitations and expectations. Once we achieve this state of coordination, we are then able to do something remarkable. Instead of just slowly crawling forward, we are able to start what we call phase shifting, to achieve extremely rapid transformation.

A football team would not succeed without coordination. Players constantly practice, not just to hone their personal skills, but also to improve the ways in which they play together. I have met thousands of kind souls who have found life unbearably difficult because they have never mobilized all their resources. They have preferred to remain "free spirits," and then they have become disappointed when things do not work out for them.

How do we emerge from the fog of the disorganized mind and body into the clear brilliance of the moment?

Meditation can help integrate your mind and your spirituality, and usually will help integrate your subtle systems or subtle bodies, as they are sometimes known. But we know that many spiritual masters had terrible health problems, and we have all met fine meditators whose personalities were not that well developed. Many of us around the world have been trying to address these paradoxes for many years now. In the field of human development, perhaps the most interesting is called Integral Transformative Practice, and I have details in the bibliography at the back of this book. Since the mid 1980s, in the arena of health, we have been working with something we call creative self-integration.

> "No human yet exists who can use all the potential of his brain. This is why we don't accept any pessimistic estimates of the limits of the human brain. It is unlimited."
> —Petr Anokhin (Russian Neuropsychologist, 1898–1974)

Creative self-integration is both a tool and a journey toward a greater sense of personal well-being and self-discovery. Each of us has potential access to infinite inner wisdom and limitless capacity to develop and to grow so that we may be better able to serve others. The power of a single person who accesses his or her full inner potential is stunning. When it happens to groups of people, the results can be beyond imagination. Remember how we commented that the Enlightenment was the product of the collective work of no more than one thousand people? Remember also that Rupert Sheldrake's theoretical and research work has shown that Nature can learn. In 1976, researchers associated with the Maharishi Mahesh Yogi first described that in communities where there were large numbers of serious meditators, crime rates went down as the number of meditators went up. This has become known as the "Maharishi effect," and some of this research has been published in highly reputable journals. As you can imagine, it is controversial and has stirred up some heated arguments. But mounting research is pointing to evidence of a global consciousness that is developing and evolving.

Beyond a Cookbook to a Philosophy of Life

When I was first being persuaded to write this book, I asked many people what they would like to see in it. A common theme was that they wanted to be told precisely what to do to regain and maintain their health and wellness.

But there is a problem with just giving out a set of prescriptions. Because they provide no flexibility, they do not give you the chance to use your own resources, and they disempower you. One of the fruits of the Chinese Cultural Revolution was the creation of the "barefoot doctors"—peasants who provided basic medical care throughout much of rural China. They had little training but had a set of manuals that told them exactly what to do with most common ailments. And when they came up against something that was in the book, they were fine. But because the practitioners had not been trained on the basic principles of anatomy, physiology or subtle systems, the system had no flexibility. If somebody had a chest infection, with the same signs and symptoms that appeared in the book, then everything was fine. But if a person had symptoms or an illness not in the book, he or she was out of luck. Within the medical field, there has been a lot of discussion about the value of trying to use treatment algorithms. Insurance companies love them, but many doctors do not, simply because they can fail to take sufficient account of human complexity.

Therefore, we have been laying out the principles for you, so that you can make your own decisions. You will also be in a better position to respond as new information comes forth and as the laws of healing continue to evolve and change.

The IPCRESS System

The IPCRESS System is something that I developed over 15 years ago to organize many types of activities in the field of health and wellness. It has even been used to restructure part of a healthcare system in the United Kingdom.

The mnemonic stands for:
Information
Planning
Coordination
Relevance
Effectiveness
Setting End Points
Strategy

So let me show you exactly how to use this ongoing organic process.

Information: Your Resources

You are going to be using your Integration Journal for this whole process. I want you to describe very precisely why you want to maintain your physical, psychological, social, subtle and spiritual health. It sounds so obvious that of course we all want health, but I would like you to be very specific in what it means to you personally. I do not want you to use any of the language of lack. What do I mean by that? A very good way of sabotaging your efforts is to use statements like "lose weight," or "give up smoking." Your brain automatically responds to those negative terms by blocking them. Why is that? Because we have, over millions of years, evolved and adapted to socialize so that we can acquire the things that we need for survival. Any statements of lack immediately run counter to our programming. Although it is our goal to transcend our survival genes, it is unwise to start anything with a fight.

This is also a good place to raise an important issue: pleasure. Pleasure is good for you. Finding purpose and meaning, experiencing pleasure and laughter, and exercising your autonomy and free will are some of the building blocks of a healthy, well-lived life.

One of the more distressing aspects of advice about health is that most of it has become a great long list of "thou shalt nots." We are constantly exhorted to be abstemious. Yet that advice has created enormous problems. Not only does the brain react negatively to any form of restriction, but also if we consider for a moment, there is a reason why many pleasurable things are exactly that, pleasurable. Trying to eradicate all of life's pleasures is not only counterproductive, but it may actually damage our well-being. Quite obviously, nobody would suggest that smoking cigarettes is a good idea, or that drinking to excess is good for your health, but many of the "forbidden" pleasures are fine in moderation. After many years of running obesity and diabetes clinics, I have consistently found that people can achieve much better results by going for balance, harmony and moderation, rather than trying to encourage people to think that they have to live in constant deprivation. Having seen patients in many different countries, I always find it interesting to see how cultural norms impact the advice that professionals give to patients. As an example, most of the European physicians that I know see nothing wrong in recommending that people can enjoy an occasional glass of wine.

Now let us move on with our inventory. What resources do you have already? We need to do a detailed inventory of your strengths and weaknesses. However, I need to make an important point. I have been disturbed about the way in which so much advice has, in recent years, been couched not just in the language of lack, but also in the language of weakness. "You need to find and root out all your weaknesses", is something that I hear constantly. Yet this is like getting up in the morning and saying: "Today's going to be a lousy day." You know then what sort of a day you will have. Focusing on problems usually exacerbates them. Always think in terms of solutions. When I am working with an individual or a group or a team, my focus is not on the problems, but on the strengths of each individual, and then the strengths of the group. This is most certainly not because I wear rose-colored glasses. I am extremely realistic, and I know that the best way forward is to deal with challenges by integrating them from a position of clarity, positivity and strength. What do you know already about how your body operates? Who can help and support you in your journey? What usually stops you from doing a diet or exercise program, or getting a regular physical, dental work or spinal adjustment? Answer these questions as precisely as you can.

Planning

What single step can you take every day to find out more about your resources, and how can you increase them? We are going to use the information and the exercises in the next three chapters to help us continuously improve our abilities in this area.

We can now begin to reap the harvest of the work that we did in Chapter Seven, when we began to find the Purpose of our life. We need to ask these questions:

Why exactly do you want to move towards health and wellness? What exactly is your motivation?

Keep working at this until you have this absolutely clearly focused in your mind.

Coordination of All Your Resources

We need to see precisely how to work on each aspect of our life in order to leverage all our health assets. Otherwise we simply have a random assortment of health tips. This will become easier as the last three chapters unfold.

Relevance to Your Outcome

For every action that we are going to take, I want you to make a note of whether or not it is going to help you achieve your aims physically, psychologically, socially, subtly and spiritually. Anything that fails to move you positively toward your goals is draining energy from them. If you do not feel that the spiritual or subtle domains are pertinent to you, then, for the time being, they are not relevant for you. I mentioned treating a horse with colic: He needed physical and subtle treatments and a lot of kindness. He was not suffering from a crisis of meaning.

Effectiveness

Are the techniques that I am going to use effective? If I am going to take a medicine or an herb, or if I am going to have acupuncture, have the techniques been used for treating my condition or for preventing me from getting sick? What's the quality of the data?

Setting End Points

Though we might prefer to think about the value of focusing on the journey itself, in reality, most of us find it much easier if we have some clear, quantifiable end-points. Describe yourself one year from now. Ask yourself, how can I tell that I am moving toward my goal? Here is where your Integration Journal will really help, because you are going to have an ongoing record of change for the better. It is essential to record a realistic objective and how you are progressing toward it. We will spend a little time on this in the last chapter.

Strategy

Here we are going to record the precise plan of action: exactly how we are going to move forward over one day, one week, one month and one year.

Developing Your Intuition

One of the most valuable things that you can do for yourself is to learn to develop your intuition, for then you access your Overself and its infinite repository of information. It is the Overself that is indivisible and shared with every other sentient being. Following the plans in this book, leavened by your own intuition, will enable you to make rapid progress.

There is more than one type of intuition. At one level, intuition is simply a way of associating different sensory inputs that are usually below the threshold of awareness. It is a process that occurs very rapidly in regions of both the right and left sides of the brain that deal with associations between different senses and integrate them with our social skills. Women tend to have rather better peripheral vision than men and they routinely activate more of the association areas of the brain connected with vision. Since vision is our predominant sense, it is likely one of several reasons that women *in general* have been shown to perform better on tasks that underlie intuition. As with all gender differences in the brain, any variations show up only when we look at the statistics of groups of people. Biology is not destiny. There are plenty of men with excellent peripheral vision and intuition, and women who have not developed those skills. We call this first level of physical intuition, the intuition of the ego ("lower") mind. When people talk about having a "gut instinct," they are talking not about an instinct, but about a physical intuition. It is an important cognitive ability that we all have to some degree.

The second type of intuition is of a different order, and it is what we saw activated in the great physicists who were picking up transpersonal insights about the Universe. These intuitions come from the same realm where Mozart said he heard the music that he took down almost as dictation, and the same realm where the great philosopher and scientist Emanuel Swedenborg had his conversations with angels. These are the insights of the Overself, or the Higher Mind.

Learning to develop either type of intuition will help develop the other: cross-training at its best. And your intuition will help guide you to make the best choices for maintaining your health and wellness. Intuition is a skill that can be developed. It will improve automatically if you trust it, if you manage to spend a little time in silence and solitude, and if you practice any form of "witness consciousness." This is another one of those techniques that came out of the Indian traditions in which I was raised. The idea is that by watching yourself, or anything that you are doing, you can gradually slip away from the constant control of the ego mind, or lower mind. It is why watching your breath or watching your thoughts can help you develop your intuition. Recording your intuitions in your Integration Journal will help you enormously to keep track.

The key to intuition is to be open to the possibility that it exists and that it *can* help you. Constant cynicism and constant overstimulation of our senses oftentimes leaves us deaf, dumb and blind to the signs of Universal purpose that surround us. You need to open your body, your senses and your mind to receive. What do I mean by opening your body? You must always scan your body for tightness, or for constrictions, before you do anything. The upright military posture or a hunched over posture is guaranteed to prevent the circulation of energy into your head. When you perform these games, make sure that you are neither hungry nor full. It is best to do them about two hours after a meal. Do not use caffeine, alcohol or nicotine before doing them. It is also best not to have drunk any soda for the two hours before doing them. It is hard to hear the sounds of your Overself if your brain is addled by stimulants or artificial sweeteners.

1   The first thing about intuition is to notice it in your life. List five lucky hunches that have turned out to be correct over the last year.

2   Now start with simple "guesses." I want your initial experiments to be easy, and, when you get positive results, I do not want you to become discombobulated. You may remember when Luke Skywalker said to Yoda "I don't believe it," Yoda responded: "That, is why you fail." I have seen countless people give up because they couldn't explain their new insights within their current belief system. So it is best if we start with some experiments that, if we get them right, *could* have a perfectly straightforward explanation.

Which elevator is going to arrive first?
When I get to the mailbox, is it going to be empty or full?
Who is calling on the telephone?

What is in this letter or package?

Will the Dow Jones Industrials go up or down today?

Once you have had some practice, we'll then go to next level:

When, exactly will the next elevator arrive?

How many letters are there in the mailbox?

Who will the next telephone call be from?

How many points will the Dow Jones Industrials go up or down today?

"Coincidences are God's way of remaining anonymous."
—Unknown Author

---

3. As a daily practice, start looking for meaningful coincidences in your life, and then record them in your Integration Journal. As you start, you may not find many, but you will find more and more as you practice. Deepak Chopra has developed an outstandingly useful system around becoming aware of the coincidences in one's life, which he calls "Synchrodestiny." One of the things about developing your intuition so that you can make more informed choices about your life is that it rarely says something only once. The marvelous thing about intuition is that it keeps sending you messages until you "get it." The form of an intuitive insight is a function of your own style of communication and will often correspond to which of your multiple intelligences is most developed. Occasionally the more verbal people will hear their intuitions in terms of their internal conversation, while the logical types will detect some shift in perception. People who are more visual will more likely obtain their intuitions from images, while those whose center of gravity is more with emotional, may just get strong gut feelings, and the body-kinesthetic types more often feel intuitions in their bodies.

A 43-year-old man was seriously overworking. He was a highly successful and very logical businessman, who enjoyed physical activity. First of all, co-workers told him to slow down. He ignored them. Then he started getting insomnia and warning nightmares. Still, he carried on. Finally, as he was rushing, he slipped and fell, injuring his back. He was unable to work for over a month. Then he "got it"; if he had been listening to his intuition, he could probably have avoided that injury.

How do you know when to trust your intuitions? How do you know when coincidences are meaningful? The key word there is *trust*. It is very important that you learn to trust yourself. And that comes as you try these practices and as you receive external, objective validation of your experiences. When you start getting more correct answers, the whole process feeds itself, and you will soon find that you simply "know" when you have had a genuine intuition, supplied courtesy of your Overself.

The most difficult thing, always, is knowing whether an insight or an intuition has come from your Overself or whether it's just wishful thinking, or your imagination playing tricks on you. I have found four strategies to be very useful:

1. Always be certain that you are prepared to hear whatever answers you receive. When we discussed the art of questioning, we talked about the importance of not dictating answers by using loaded questions. Exactly the same applies here: You must be prepared to surrender your decisions to your Overself.

2 Use your intuition to evaluate your insights. Do the insights feel "right" to you? If you feel a tension associated with an intuition or an insight that is often a good sign that it is not correct. Are you getting any external feedback about your intuitions? How are people around you reacting to you and what you are doing?

3   Allow your intuitions to come in their own time. Your Overself does not work on the same time scale that you do: It exists in what Eckhart Tolle calls the "Now," the timeless realm. It is a really good idea to detach from the outcome of your questions. Go out for a walk, let your mind relax, do something completely different. And in the same way that your memory sometimes supplies you with a piece of forgotten information hours later, so it is with your Overself.

4   Never leave any of these experiments and exercises without also writing down an action that you are going to take as a result of an intuition. This is exceedingly important. If you ignore the promptings of your intuition, it is deeply disrespectful to your Overself. Using your Integration Journal will help you check and recheck whether your intuitions were borne out, and you will rapidly begin to trust yourself more. One final word here: Do not fall into the trap of waiting to be told what to do. I have known students of many systems who have become totally passive, believing that they should not do anything at all until they get a clear message from their Overself. The most extraordinary case that I have come across is of a man who graduated from medical school in 1978 and has never worked because he is still waiting for that personal message from his Overself.

The Sixty Second Peace Technique

I constantly meet people who tell me that they have no time to pray or meditate. So this is a simple one-minute technique that most people find very helpful, and before long, they usually find that they want to do it for more than a minute and that they do begin to find the time for meditation and prayer.

Sit down in a comfortable position. For this technique, it is best to have your feet flat on the floor and your spine straight. Put your right hand between the thumb and forefinger of your left hand, and then gently place your right thumb in the middle of your left palm, and your middle finger on the outside of the left hand. Place the tip of your tongue on the roof of your mouth.

- Close your eyes, take a deep breath into your abdomen, and say the word *Peace* as you slowly let your breath out. You can either say it aloud or in your mind. Do this several times, until you begin to feel calm and centered.

- Now call on your Overself to make itself known to you. Call it by any name that feels right to you. Gently quiet your thoughts, and as you breathe in, draw in stillness, and as you exhale, let go of any negative thoughts or feelings.

- As you do this, feel yourself being enfolded by the strength of your Overself. Many people like to feel themselves being gently held by wings or arms. The point is to do what feels right to you.

- The whole cycle should only be for 60 seconds, though I guarantee that as you start doing it once or twice a day, you will soon want to extend the time. It gives a tremendous boost to your energy and creativity, and by doing it for such a short time, you will be able to pour all your efforts into it.

Rooting Out Resistance to Change

We have all had the experience of wanting to change something about ourselves or about our lives, and then doing very little about it. I am not thinking about people who procrastinate, but the way in which many people like to stay where they are, unwilling to take a step outside their comfort zone.

It is never easy to change our mind about anything, as long as we remain *attached* to a particular belief, outcome or line of reasoning that can cause us to be inflexible and intolerant of new ideas. There are several barriers to emotional, personal and spiritual freedom, and attachment is one of the most potent.

There are 12 major reasons why people do not change, however much they need to do so:

1 Being unaware that change is possible

2 Having entrenched belief systems

3 Having an emotional or habitual attachment to particular ways of doing things

4 Feeling comfortable about where they are

5 Fearing change or the consequences of change, like losing face or risking ridicule

6 Having intellectual reasons for maintaining the status quo

7 Being unaware of information to support the need for change

8 Being unconvinced by the necessity for change

9 Having blockages or perturbations in their energy fields

10 Having a life story that does not leave room for change or for evolution

11 Being unaware of the rewards that can flow from changing

12 Not knowing how to harness resources to accomplish change

Please take out your Integration Journal, and spend a few minutes examining which of these 12 factors may be at work in your life, and then record the results.

In the next chapter, we are going to start looking at ways to overcome some of the major barriers to getting integrated and getting and staying well.

Chapter Ten
Mind Control

The Evolutionary Basis of Behavior

We are the fruits of an evolutionary process that has allowed us to become the most adaptable species on our planet. If only we all allowed that incredible attribute to manifest in our lives. Because of our amazing ability to learn, anything that increases our understanding, whether we obtain it from intellect or intuition, leads to our being stretched. Anything new leads to growth within the brain, and if the new is something positive, it can help expand both our cognition and our consciousness. We house multiple interlinked systems dedicated to functioning as social animals. During our early evolution, a big problem for humans was competition with each other. Therefore, much of recent brain evolution has been a response to social living. Social intelligence—the ability to interpret social situations—is crucially important, with some even suggesting that language and ego mind originally developed to aid social tasks.

After social intelligence, a second major contributor to our social functioning is the "somatic marker mechanism" (SMM). Over the last decade, Antonio Damasio, from the University of Iowa, has been developing an extraordinary concept. He has been looking at the way in which bodily changes are represented in the brain in the form of what he calls "somatic markers." According to this view, the way the body responds to a situation lets the brain know how the individual feels about an experience. That marker can then be used in future emotional assessments. This could be the basis of gut reactions. This mechanism supports social intelligence, integrating somatic or body states corresponding to emotional responses with the social situations that triggered those emotional responses in the first place. Emotions are then seen as body states represented in the brain.

Humans and perhaps some apes are aware of these emotions, and when we are aware of our emotions, we call them feelings.

"Who reigns within himself, and rules passions, desires, and fears, is more a king."
—Thomas Middleton (English Playwright, 1580–1627)

Let's look at an example: fear. Everyone talks about fear, and everywhere you see books and magazines espousing the virtues of facing or conquering your fears. All good advice, but let's stop for a moment. What exactly is fear? If you are confronted by a threat to your survival, your body activates physical arousal to prepare it for action. You know the sensations: Your heart races, your hands and feet go cold as your blood is diverted toward your muscles. The brain continuously monitors the body, receiving feedback about what is going on. Fear is the emotional state that occurs when the brain recognizes the physical state of arousal, and then generates the appropriate behavioral adaptation: fight, flight or freeze. If a saber-toothed tiger is chasing us, fear is a reasonable response. It is not reasonable when we get all the signs of arousal but there is no tiger.

When we have a meaningful interaction with someone, it causes us to have an emotional reaction in the body, which is fed back to the brain and stored together with the way the person acted. This is intriguing, because it gives us a way of understanding how we use our emotions to tell us about someone else's mental state, and how we might guess how that person will behave.

One of the most frightening things that can happen to a person is if he or she is threatened and cannot move: The SMM is being short-circuited. Carefully controlled stilling of the body with Yoga or T'ai Chi feeds back to the brain to calm it, and the body-based therapies, like Feldenkrais or Rolfing can help rewire the somatic marker mechanism.

Ego-Fears

Pain and fear are powerful instinctual defenses designed to protect us. People who lack them are seriously handicapped. In my work I have seen countless people with nerve damage lose the ability to feel pain, and have unknowingly cut or burned themselves. Pain motivates escape, while fear prevents a recurrence of pain. Fear is a response that is hard-wired into the brain, but the precise stimulus that produces the fear, like fear of heights or snakes, is not. It is something that is learned, which means it is something that can be unlearned. We know from experimental work that we readily develop a lasting fear of things like snakes, compared with, say, fear of a flower. During evolution, the regions of the brain and the body associated with fear have become appropriated by other emotions. It is because pain and fear are intimately associated with avoidance that they also produce reactions in the muscles and internal organs, and these reactions feedback into the brain. Fear can become attached to memories and psychological states, generating anxiety, and if severe, can develop into a phobia. As we have just seen, fear can also become attached to certain physical states.

There are literally hundreds of different types of fears and phobias. Some anxiety about yourself or your family or the future is perfectly normal, but nonetheless, you can reduce even these, allowing your Inner Light to shine, so that you can be happier and healthier. Ego simply means "I," but as we have seen, it has a further connotation of being the lower physical mind: The ego is designed to protect you and to enable you to function socially. Fears, like all psychological reactions, are internally generated by the ego and generate those familiar physical and emotional sensations.

But there is an important secret. Since fears, like all emotions, are being generated by the ego, a coordinated mind can control them. You can choose how you react to a fear or an emotion. What do I mean by this? When somebody says something like "I have a chronic fear of being rejected," he or she can choose whether to react or not. Learning different responses is a goal of therapy, and, unless you are in the throes of a psychiatric illness, you can learn to choose how you want to respond. It will be the key theme of the next chapter.

> "All men should strive to learn before they die, what they are running from, and to, and why."
> —James Thurber (American Writer 1894–1961)

One way of looking at fears generated by the ego is to see them as instinctual defenses. At the most basic level, there is only one type of fear, which, as we have just seen, is a hard-wired arousal response. The way in which this response is manifested is a combination of genes and experience. Fear provides the motor that becomes appropriated by the mind. We can reduce many of the fears to 12 instinctual drives that are a product of millions of years of evolution. They are present in all of us, but in most are dormant. They tend to emerge in response to life experiences, particularly in childhood. These are the 12 most common "Ego-Fears." Some overlap, but each will be modulated by your character, personality and center of gravity along the different developmental lines. Let us look at them briefly in terms of their biological and evolutionary origins, and as we do so, remember the work that you did with the Memes and see how they relate in your life.

1. **Fear of Death:** This is clearly absolutely basic, and it is genetically hard-wired. It comes out when denied food, water or relationships.

2. **Fear of Lack:** This is another basic drive, which is served by multiple neurological systems: thirst, hunger, temperature and so on.

3. **Fear of Pain:** This drive goes beyond just physical hurts, and includes fear of psychological pain, fear of aging and fear of being unable to provide value for the group or tribe.

4. **Fear of Losing Power:** This is the first of the "relationship fears." Because of the long childhood of humans, it takes most people some time to gain a measure of power in relationships and in society. If peo-

ple see themselves as "human doings" rather than as "human beings," losing power can be utterly catastrophic.

5. **Fear of Losing Control:** This is a tremendous fear that has been instilled in us from the time that the Red and Blue Memes were the dominant expressions within society.

6. **Fear of Being Abandoned or Rejected:** Being abandoned or rejected by your tribe or your mate could easily lead to your death. Because it could become a matter of life or death, this fear can easily become active.

7. **Fear of Trusting:** This is essential to protect your interests and the interests of your family and tribe. Because it is so important for survival, it can easily become activated by negative life experiences.

8. **Fear of Criticism or of Disapproval by Others:** Important for continued functioning in relationships and in society, this fear has been reinforced in most people since early childhood. It includes that most insidious drain of energy, the "disease to please." Nobody can be free so long as they are still concerned about the opinions of others.

9. **Fear of Becoming Dominant:** To become dominant in a relationship or in society does not sit well with some people. We shall see in Chapter Eleven that this has a great deal to do with a desire to reject the "dominator" model in favor of a "cooperator" model, and we see this quite commonly in people who fear success.

10. **Fear of Being Inadequate to a Task or a Role:** This can have a genetic root, but it is more often the result of negative reinforcement in childhood.

11. **Fear of the Unknown:** This fear is extremely common, and like all the others, is modulated by your personality and life experiences. Some people love playing on the edge of the unknown, but for others it can cause agony. A subtype of fear of the unknown is fear of the future.

12. **Fear of Fear Itself:** It is common to see people for whom the biggest worry is that they will become fearful. We see this most often when someone has begun to improve and is worried about sliding back down again. It can lead to a nasty vicious circle, like the person who

complains of insomnia, and in fact the insomnia is being caused by anxiety that he may not be able to sleep.

Since the ego is designed for the survival of the individual, it has no interest in your comfort, your relationships or your spirituality unless those are contributing to its primary function. It thinks that the parts of the picture that it can see are the whole picture. It is this partial view that underlies an enormous amount of needless suffering. A wise friend, competent therapist or spiritual teacher can help you put things in perspective, which means seeing the big picture. Persisting in holding onto negative thoughts, feelings and behaviors is a choice. The role of creative self-integration is not to destroy potentially useful fears or negative thoughts, but to integrate them into yourself, by transcending blind genetic programming. If turned to your advantage, each of these fears can be a powerful source of energy and motivation.

Your mind and body have a locus of control, an axis about which your life revolves. Ask yourself a question: Where do I want to have my locus of control? Do you want it to be your whole integrated being: your Overself, subtle systems, physical body and ego, or just your ego, all on its own? I am sure of your answer. So let us get to work.

Your life reflects your thoughts and feelings. Most of us take it for granted that any success, any mastery, including health mastery, has to involve struggle. The presumption has been that we cannot achieve our ideal body weight without giving something up or that we cannot stay physically healthy without sacrifice. This is an outdated notion we've held since the late Middle Ages. The truth is that life should not be a struggle. If you're struggling, it is a good indicator that something is wrong. Let's place this in an evolutionary context. It is difficult to think of any situations in nature in which animals struggle. They most certainly put effort into things like getting food, mating and migrating, but they do not struggle. Even when they fight, once it is clear who will be the victor, the battle is over. Struggle is by definition difficult, exhausting and usually prolonged. Not at all what should be happening in your life.

Your belief system is crucial to understanding why you do things, and why things happen in your life. If you were conditioned to believe that you need to struggle, then it is highly likely that this has repeated in your subconscious mind ever since. It is an important explanation for self-sabotage.

Many people enter relationships or start jobs or projects with deeply engrained notions that these are going to entail a protracted wrestling match. Thoughts and emotions like this interfere with the structure and the expression of the Information Matrix. So we need to correct the matrix. Happily there are ways of doing this.

Merely wanting to be over unhappiness or negativity is not enough. Think about it for a moment: A want is a desire, and simply replacing one desire with another is unlikely to lead to success. Happily you have yet another ally: Natural systems are designed to discard things that are no longer of value. Whether we look at dead leaves on a tree or aging skin cells, they are simply discarded. If we understand these natural principles, we can apply them to anything that is not helping us.

There are many methods for managing negative emotions and negative cognitions, but the three that we have found of greatest value have been those of liberating, affirming and Thought Field Therapy (TFT). Each works at a different level of your being, so we really turbo-charge your progress toward wellness when we combine them.

Liberating

One of the effective tools of creative self-integration is to learn to liberate yourself from the hold of negative thoughts and emotions. Negative thoughts and emotions are the source of many problems. Struggling against them can consume energy that should be going to maintain the integrity of your mind and body. Not only is it possible to let go of these negative emotions, it is essential to do so.

Liberating is exactly what it sounds like—letting go of things that are not helpful to you. Negative information and/or energy patterns in any one of the five domains that make it more and more difficult for your Inner Light to shine. I would like you to think about something. Every time you think a thought about anything, you are linked to the object of the thought. I always recommend not telling the whole world your business. Not because we want you to be secretive, but because if people know much about you, they can tie themselves to you. This is why I was initially very reluctant to write this and why many spiritual masters work in complete anonymity. If you harbor a negative emotion about anything or anyone, you are linked to that thing or person, and those negative emotions can be very harmful to you. I have seen an enormous number of people who have destroyed their minds and their bodies with constant negativity. If you liberate negativity, your Inner Light has a chance to shine, and everything in your life may come into alignment.

This is another time to use your journal. You will need to make five columns on a page. First, consider what you need to let go, and list the items one by one in a column on the left-hand side of the page. Then in the next column, write down a physical sensation associated with each item. This is because, as we saw when we discussed the somatic marker mechanism, your brain will likely have laid down a bodily marker. It is also because your subtle system contains a memory of this item. In the third column, write down why the item continues to be attached to you. In the fourth column write down why you would like to be liberated from the physical and emotional sensations. Then finally write down a precise statement of liberation: why you want to be free of this.

Let me give you an example. Imagine that you have had a relationship with someone called John, and you do not think that it is helping you to go in a direction that is helping you to grow toward expressing your Inner Light, or being able to serve. You may no longer be seeing each other, but you've still got him under your skin. You think of him and get a physical feeling, as well as some emotional attachment. You would really like to be over both. And you know that any pain or discomfort that you feel is from your *response* to the item. So you phrase your statement like this:

"John, I fully and freely liberate you. I bless you and let you go so that we can both find our Inner Light."

Having written your statements of liberation, now speak them aloud, repeating them several times.

Although we have dwelt on negative emotions, it is also a good idea to include anything or anyone about which you may feel particularly possessive. It can be very damaging for you and for another person if you make possessive statements about him or her. Besides releasing possessiveness, it is essential to liberate negative patterns in your body and needless physical items in your life. The more old and useless things you hoard, the more things there are to take up your energy and prevent the expression of new energy.

It is also important to let go of relationships that you have outgrown. I am sure that you can think of couples who have simply grown apart because the partners have grown and evolved differently. Has that happened in your life? Sometimes we get stuck in relationships as a matter of duty, even when they have become toxic for us. To stay in a dead relationship that brings nothing to either party is disrespectful to everyone involved and can be the most enormous millstone around your neck. It requires courage to liberate yourself from such a relationship, but it will often do more for your health and development than any other single thing, and it is often the catalyst to rapid internal growth. You will remain forever connected to everybody that you have ever known: That is a natural conclusion from everything that we have discovered about the interconnectedness of people and things. But that connection must not carry a powerful charge of emotional energy. That is why, when you liberate yourself from a relationship, it should be done with an attitude of gratitude that the other person was good enough to share his or her time, energy and experiences with you.

To Affirm or Not to Affirm: That Is the Question

The use of affirmations is very old but was reinvented by Emile Coue in 1924. In recent years many people have become skeptical about the use of affirmations and visualizations, either because they have tried them and found them wanting, or because they have heard of research that has shown that the mind, brain and body can distinguish between real and imagined events. One of the central concepts of some of the early writings on affirmations was that it was easy to fool the subconscious, which could not distinguish between the two. And quite obviously, your conscious mind, which is doing the affirming, can tell the difference!

The answer is that affirmations can indeed be a very helpful tool, as long as you are doing affirmations about the right thing. That may sound obvious, but I have seen countless people who have been affirming away about wanting money, when it has not actually been the main thing that they want or need. I knew somebody who was busily doing affirmations to win the affections of a famous actress, whom he had, in fact, never even met. Even if they had met, it was painfully obvious that there would not have been the slightest chance at compatibility, and on some level he knew that. So naturally his affirmations did nothing.

It is also clear that if you are harboring negative thoughts and you have negative programs running, your affirmations will likely run into the sand. Furthermore, you must take action. You have probably heard the old joke about the man who, every night for 30 years, prayed to win the lottery. Finally he heard a great voice saying, "Okay then, but just once, could you go and buy a ticket?!"

We use affirmations as tools for focusing our attention and building expectation. Why do they work? First, spoken language is very powerful because it evolved to communicate urgent and serious matters. It has been around for a long time, which is why it tends to be so much more powerful than written language. Second, words are symbols of thoughts and feelings. As you can see every day, feelings have great power. When you use the words of an affirmation, they induce thoughts, which in turn activate your feelings, which then add the power of your subtle systems to the affirmation. Together these can reshape the Informational Matrix. Third, some affirmations also have the power of having developed their own morphic fields. The only things more powerful than affirmations are the sounds of creation, some of which are captured in mantras and music.

Emotions are our subjective experience of the flow of Qi in the body. Therefore balancing these flows, or better yet the information underlying them, may provide us with a way of treating emotional disorders. And that is indeed exactly what has been shown to happen.

Thought Field Therapy (TFT)

TFT was the creation of the psychologist Roger Callahan, who discovered that stimulating a number of acupuncture points while connecting with an negative emotion, thought, impulse or memory, could initiate a cascade of healthy neurological, chemical, emotional, cognitive and even physical effects. There is an interesting side-bar here. When I first came across his work, it seemed absurd. It looked like a collection of unproven techniques cobbled together into some sort of system. I worry about sick people being treated by ineffective therapies, so I was determined to debunk TFT. I was a little taken aback when I sent for some of the Callahan materials and saw a smoker permanently cured in about five minutes. Undeterred, I flew to

California to expose what I thought might be another scam. Within two days, I discovered that it was no scam. Roger has indeed made an extraordinarily important discovery that supports the notion that the laws of healing are changing. As a simple example, I used one of Roger's simplest treatments on inveterate smokers. The first 11 whom I treated all stopped smoking and they were still not smoking almost one year later. The treatment doesn't work every time, but when it does, it can be amazing.

TFT is based on the concept that thought is a form of energy, structured by a field, and that psychological problems are manifestations of distortions within "thought fields," which Roger defines as "a complex of forces that serve as causative agents in human behavior." He conceptualizes psychological problems as the consequence of "perturbations" in the thought field. These perturbations contain the information that triggers negative emotions, and they also have relationships with specific major acupuncture points on the body. Fixing these perturbations involves tapping specific points in a specific order, while doing a series of other small tasks.

An important aspect of TFT is the concept of psychological reversal. Roger calls this the energetic blockade of natural healing, caused by reversals in the flow of Qi through the acupuncture channels. It now seems that much of what has been described as therapeutic resistance, self-sabotage or lack of willpower is a result of psychological reversal. He has devised some deceptively simple treatments that have shown us that people's difficulties were often not a matter of a lack of willpower at all, but were the result of reversed energy. Deal with that, and many problems can melt away. In Chapter Twelve I am going to show you how to use the technique yourself, and on the companion CD, I give you some further resources for exploring this intriguing form of therapy.

Earlier in this book we emphasized the importance of toxins, of extending our concept of them, so that we conceptualize them as units of rogue information. Roger Callahan has also emphasized the importance of toxins, and in recent years he has put a great deal of effort into working out how to track down and deal with them.

Not everyone will be helped with any single form of treatment, and even with the best therapists, TFT is not for everyone. However, when someone says that he or she has not been helped with TFT, it most often for one of these seven reasons:

1   The treatment has not been done quite correctly.

2   The problem has been only partially treated.

3   Psychological reversal has not been dealt with.

4   There are still some toxins lurking around.

5   There is more than one problem, and they haven't both been treated. (Somebody who said that he felt silly doing TFT needed to treat that fear of appearing foolish and then get on with the primary problem.)

6   The problem may need the help of someone trained in TFT.

7   The person may have needed a combination of therapies.

There have been a number of attempts to develop TFT in new directions, and there have been suggestions by some that the protocols can be simplified and that the order of tapping points is irrelevant. It may be so, but I am not convinced. The reason for the order of tapping, and following the prescribed patterns is that they are giving the body information, and if the tapping is done in a different order, we might expect to send a nonsense message. This is the sort of debate that will ultimately only be resolved by objective research. In Chapter Twelve I will show you how exactly to use TFT to help one common problem.

Finding and Giving Yourself Rewards

You have worked hard; you have made significant progress, so now it is time to be rewarded. As children, most of us were constantly being rewarded. For years now, there has been a lot of discussion about the motivational value of rewards. In general, they can be very useful if constructed correctly. What do I mean by "constructed correctly"? The use of rewards may sometimes come at a price. Experiments with children have shown that rewards do, for instance, encourage children to draw more. But if the rewards stop, the children completely stop drawing.

We need to learn how to reward ourselves. Simply critiquing yourself for some perceived failing is really not a good idea: You need a carrot as well as a stick. I know that you do not want to keep indulging yourself: I am sure that you have discovered that even the finest food can get boring if you have it too often, and you do not want to become a slave to an indulgence. The trick is to know a few things with which you can reward yourself. Rewards are always anchored in context: A reward for one person will not be so interesting for another. The gold stars given out in some weight management classes might seem uninteresting to some people, but for participants in the class, they can mean the world.

> "Reward sweetens labor."
> —Dutch Proverb

So your task is to identify some healthful rewards for yourself. If you insist on chocolate be one of them, then it has to be in moderation! I want you to establish your own list, because I do not want you to be like the drawing children who went on strike, and I want you to find something that is readily available and has meaning for you. It is also a good idea to establish rewards with novelty value. So something more than just going to the refrigerator and getting ice cream. And remember that I did ask that your reward be healthful!

The rewards can be solo or involve another person, if that person is agreeable. So, get to work with your Integration Journal, and start making a list. Just to get you started, I asked some folks here a few minutes ago, and the list began like this:

1 To go out for a nice meal at someplace new
2 To be recognized for something
3 To get a massage
4 To have a pedicure
5 To have my hair done
6 To buy some new shoes
7 To go to a movie
8 To play a chess game online
9 To spend an hour listening to an opera

These are simply some suggestions. I would like you to construct your own list, and to do it however you like. Keep it in a prominent place in your Journal so that you will see it often.

Naturally, we can just use our rewards for a task completed or a job well done, but I would like you to take them a step further. I would like you to identify five things that you should do but often avoid. I don't want you to focus on trivial things like emptying the dishwasher, but on things that will have a significant impact on you and your relationships. Again, list them, and consider what reward you will issue yourself for doing each task. There is one successful diet and exercise program that requires a strict regimen for six days of the week and on the seventh allows participants to indulge themselves. There are both psychological *and* physical reasons why this can work. You should also consider extending the rewards program for big projects, with commensurate big rewards.

I have been using this system for many years, ever since a friend told me that he quit smoking by each day taking all the money that he would have spent on cigarettes and putting it into a large glass jar that he kept on his desk. He saw his savings grow day by day, and in less than a year he had saved enough for his big reward: He bought a hang glider.

Chapter Eleven
Dynamic Relationships:
The Missing Key to Wellness

Of Holons and Quadrants

"Well I just called yez up
'Cause I wanted to see
A philostoper be of assistance
To me!"
—Frank Zappa (American Musician 1940–1993)

Philosophy can be the most fascinating subject, but far too many philosophy classes are dull, leaving many people wondering whether the teachings hold relevance for understanding the real, external day-to-day world. Imagine my surprise, when, a few years ago, I was participating in a project that included Oxford philosopher Rom Harre and he proceeded to tell us about a planned expedition to work with a recently discovered tribe that had no concept of a personal self. The details of the expedition are not as important as the fact that a top-notch philosopher was engaged in doing research and not just thinking about it.

Perhaps the best example of someone who started as a philosopher and is now working on practical applications of his models is Ken Wilber. His work is ambitious and is aimed toward creating an integral model containing all the key components of human existence. His work has already spawned a plethora of integrally informed fields of study in psychology, business and medicine, to name only a few. Much of his work is complex and controversial, but it provides a helpful framework with which to structure much knowledge and information that was previously scattered all over the landscape. I would like to introduce you to two of his most basic concepts, which are very relevant for us here.

First, he resurrected a 30-year-old idea, from the Hungarian/British philosopher Arthur Koestler, that reality does not consist merely of matter, energy, ideas and processes, but also incorporates *holons*. The word *holon* describes a basic unit of organization in biological and social systems, that is a whole that is at the same time a part of a larger whole. So you are a whole made of parts, like your heart, your lungs and your brain, and you are also a part of your society, and your society is part of a nation, and so on.

The second is the notion of four quadrants. Quadrants are one of the most important components of his system, together with levels, lines, waves, states and types. Each holon has an inside, or interior, perspective, and outside, or exterior, perspective. Since a holon also belongs to some larger whole, it has individual and collective perspectives. Each of these perspectives is irreducible: It cannot be broken down to something else. They each exist all the time. If you examine the figure at the end of this section, you will see that these characteristic perspectives can be mapped into four quadrants.

The reason for being interested in quadrants is this: Throughout this book we have been looking at ways of putting things together, of synthesizing and integrating models and perspectives. And this gives us another tool for doing so. Science has been trying to reduce everything to the upper right-hand quadrant: the objective "It." Yet, as we have seen, this approach leaves out a whole vast realm of human existence. This four-quadrant approach makes it clear that if we want to get a complete picture of a person, we need to adopt these four complementary perspectives. None of them contradicts the other; they each just add to the texture, the meaning and the validity of our model. All four ways of describing a person are correct, and are necessary if we want a complete account of the

Universe. So when scientists say that they have found that the temporal cortex of the brain lights up when someone is having a religious experience, that does not mean that you can reduce a person's faith and belief to a lit-up piece of brain. It is merely that the area of the brain *corresponds* to the experience. This is an incredibly important distinction: Not only are you more than your genes, you are more than your neurons, and even more than your personal experiences.

Later in this chapter, we are going to meet one of the brain's chemical messengers, dopamine. Neuroscientists have suggested that the initial excitement of an intimate relationship is caused by a surge in dopamine, while long-lasting attachment is due to the action of the hormones oxytocin and vasopressin. Although love may be associated with these chemical changes in the brain, you cannot *reduce* love to chemicals and hormones any more than you can enjoy a vacation just by looking at a map of the Caribbean. They are different but complementary ways of looking at something.

In Figure 5, I have given a brief idea of how the quadrants hang together. As a brief exercise, I would like you to think of yourself, and then place yourself in each of the four quadrants. If you look at the quadrant in the upper right-hand side, you see yourself as a person who has a body, which contains organs, tissues and cells. But you know that you are more than that. If you look at the upper left-hand side, you see yourself as someone with a self and with consciousness, who has feelings and emotions, and who, as we saw earlier, is interested in extracting meanings from the world around you. As we move to the lower right-hand side, you now see yourself as part of a social structure, a family and an ecosystem. Finally, in the lower left-hand quadrant, you can be described as someone who shares certain cultural beliefs and views of the world. The point of all this, is that we cannot reduce any one of these quadrants. We need all of them to see ourselves as we really are.

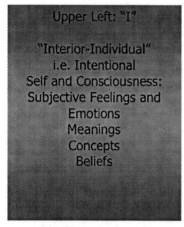 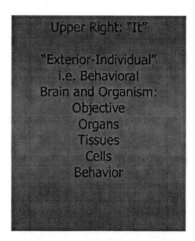

Figure 5. This diagram illustrates Ken Wilber's brilliant notion of the Four Quadrants

Relationships

When I first started looking at the hundreds of different therapeutic systems that we offer, a striking fact is that they all have at their core the development of a relationship between two or more individuals, one of whom is designated the patient or client and the other the therapist who is helping the patient cure himself or herself. Until the invention of the stethoscope, which was the first step toward separating patients from those treating them, the fundamental nature of a healing relationship was well understood, but a long time ago, orthodox medicine began to minimize the importance of relationship to cure.

Nothing in the Universe exists in isolation: We live in a Universe of relationships. It is inconceivable that anything can exist except in relationship to something else. The entire Universe is made up of integrated systems that function, develop and evolve together. A failure to construct and maintain healthy relationships can be a cause of much distress.

Several years ago I reported some interesting observations. At the time, I was doing a great deal of research on diseases of blood vessels. I had developed a laboratory method for taking some of the cells that line blood vessels from volunteers and then growing them in a cell culture dish. I discovered that if we did not have enough cells in the dish, they would all die of "loneliness." The exception is cancer cells, which in culture will grow on their own, like weeds. Next, I made an accidental and remarkable discovery. I normally cleared out our cell cultures once a week, but on this occasion I found that I had accidentally nudged one of the dishes to the back of the incubator, where it had been sitting for three weeks. Looking at the cells under the microscope, I could see that they had formed little tubes.

Now that might not sound like very much, but it was. The cells had, inside the body of the volunteer, been part of a microscopic tube called a capillary. To prepare the culture, the cells had been cleaned with all sorts of biochemical treatments to strip them away from everything else so that we would have no contaminating cells. The teaching for years has been that the development of cells and organs is a result of biochemical interactions between different cells of the body driven by the DNA inside the nucleus of the cells. But my cultured cells had no such cells to guide them. How could they "remember" that their role was to make tubes? The most likely explanation is that they are responding to morphic fields. I published the observation in a paper 14 years ago, and others have now replicated the findings.

The Status Syndrome

Sir Michael Marmot is an outstanding epidemiologist working in London, who has spent three decades examining the health consequences of differences in social standing. He has discovered that there is a social gradient that predicts health outcomes: the lower a person's social rank, the higher their risk for heart disease, diabetes, mental illness, accidents and many other health problems. But it is not only about money. Once people have passed a certain threshold of physical and material well-being, something else comes into play: other kinds of well-being that have a massive impact upon life. These are autonomy, how much control you have over your life, and opportunities for social engagement and participation. The psychological experience of inequality has profound effects on multiple body systems.

The Chalice and the Blade

The Chalice and the Blade is the title of an extraordinarily fine book by Riane Eisler, in which she shows that beliefs about society, Nature and the world around us were very different just a few years ago, and utterly different a few thousand years ago. You will see the similarity with our discussion about Spiral Dynamics, and yet she came to her conclusions by an entirely different route. What sets her work apart, and why it fits so well with the concepts that we are developing here, is that she provides a model for a livable and sustainable future, based on going back to our roots, rather than inventing an entirely new system. This "partnership model" stresses that all relationships should be expressions of partnership, containing respect, harmony and love. Growing up in one of the most patriarchal and hierarchical societies in the world, this partnership model was something for which I had been searching, and I found that it provides practical expression to all of our work on evolution, dualities and healing.

Eisler symbolizes this dominator model by the blade, and the key to her system is to discover where in our lives it is operating, and how then to move fully into partnership, symbolized by the open cup of the chalice. Most of us were taught the history of the blade: domination, warfare, generals and empires. And it is a style of thinking that still permeates much of our society. Think of the Beige, Purple and Red Memes. As we have seen, violence and domination lead to endless conflict. But Eisler provides rock-solid evidence that very different societies, based on partnership rather than domination, flourished before these dominator cultures, some coexisted with them, and some have persisted into modern times.

It has been said many times, and it is true, that humans are one of less than 10 species that kill others of their own species, implying that this is not the natural order of things. A point that we have made, and which needs repeating, is that successfully maintaining and managing our lives, and the lives of those around us, requires us to live consistently, applying natural principles to everything that we do. We need to apply the principles of partnership to every aspect of our lives and to all our relationships. This is the way of ensuring a constant dynamic interplay of our dualities. The more we live in partnership, the more we create harmony instead of conflict in our lives and in the world. The partnership model is based on respect and reverence, and on an awareness of the sanctity of all life.

Relationships are a lens through which your Overself teaches. It is exceedingly powerful to examine all your relationships and to see whether the key dynamic is partnership or domination. I would like you to take the categories described below and to make a deliberate effort to see where you are in each of these domains. If you find that some aspects of your relationships are fixed in dominator mode, always see that as an opportunity to improve something. Elite sports and business people are always on the look-out for something that isn't working as it should, for therein lies the opportunity for growth. If you find the spoor of domination, do not feel that you need to destroy it, instead plan effortlessly to integrate and evolve it. With all these relationships, I hope that you will soon see the value of keeping a watchful eye over them, exactly in the same way that you notice if your car suddenly starts to make a strange noise.

Your Relationship with Your Cells and Organs

It is good to know a little about how you body works. Where are your main organs located, and what do they do? In a normal state of healthy dynamic functioning, all your cells and organs run in homeostatic harmony, going about their business and dancing to the tune of the Informational Matrix. I believe that with proper care, your body should be able to live for at least one hundred years.

Are you living in partnership with your cells and the organs of your body, or is something dominating you?

Your Relationship with Yourself

Do you have a partnership with yourself? Are you nurturing and supporting yourself? Are you living a life of joy and creativity? Or is some inner critic running your life? What is the nature and content of your inner conversation? Is it positive and kind, or is it scattered with self-deprecating comments? If you have followed everything we have covered in our time together, you will see that you need to forge balanced and integrated relationships.

Your Relationship with Subtle Energy Systems

Do you feel the presence of your subtle systems? Are your subtle systems working with you or against you? Can you sense the subtle systems in other people? Would you like to learn to do so? Sometimes people with very negative subtle systems can be utterly draining. I have met a lot of people whom we might describe as "psychic vampires." It was very helpful to learn how to deal with them. Is that a skill that you should learn?

Your Intimate Relationships

When you think about your relationships with your family, close friends and lovers, is there domination, or do you have genuine partnerships with them? Are the relationships respectful and does everyone have a voice? Whatever the nature of your intimate relationships, do you feel the continuous dance of male and female essences, or are you stuck in one dominant pole or the other? As with all the pathologies of dichotomy, an enormous amount of distress in relationships is the consequence of becoming stuck in roles that no longer suit the people in the relationship. On the other hand, a healthy partnership in your intimate relationships forms the essence of sexual healing that can serve to repair and rebalance many aspects of your life.

It is sometimes extraordinary to realize that in the midst of an avalanche of information about sex, many people have still not equipped themselves with basic knowledge that could help develop their relationships. A young man working in the medical field once consulted me. An international rugby player, he came complaining of anxiety and impotence. He was totally locked into the dominator mindset, and it had come back to bite him. He had recently become romantically involved with a woman who was herself successful, self-confidant and centered, and she was expecting a balanced partnership. When she communicated her wants and needs, he found it very difficult to cope. Despite having had a medical training, when it came to intimate relationships, he was still relying upon advice garnered in the locker room, and it nearly destroyed the relationship. Fortunately, they were both committed to dealing with the difficulty, and it was not difficult to help them. It certainly made me wonder how many other people may be suffering in silence.

The most valuable thing to ensure the viability of intimate relationships is not so much to try to learn lots of different techniques, but instead to make the time together really count. There is nothing quite as attractive as an intimate occasion marked by complete focus on and awareness of the other person. Feeling the dance of the duality, focusing on *all* your senses, and, if you can, feeling the subtle systems of the other person.

One of the *many* unconscious reasons for why most people favor monogamy is that having multiple relationships, or even fantasies, can divert energy from the focus needed to maintain an intimate relationship. Some people advocate the use of fantasy to bolster crumbling relationships. I do not, simply because it is a poor substitute for a genuine energetic exchange between partners. If you find that your partner is unsympathetic or disinterested in you, no amount of fantasy is going to solve that. It is all about attention. If you are fantasizing about someone else, then you are not putting your energy into the relationship before you. Focus instead upon the myriad shifts and changes that both of you experience minute to minute, and it is not necessary to be thinking about someone else to get variety in your life.

Maintaining an intimate relationship really benefits from an understanding of the interplay of the dualities and subtle systems, and a sharing of life experiences. One of the most valuable predictors of long-term success of an intimate relationship is that the couple shares spiritual values.

Your Workplace and Community Relationships

How would you rate your relationships in the workplace? Are they supportive partnerships, or can you still see systems of domination? One of the revolutions of recent years has been the gradual transition of employers from being people who dominated and directed into being individuals who coach their employees and have partnerships not just with every employee, but also with every supplier and customer and with everyone with whom they interact in the community. Is there a culture of respect? Does everyone have a voice? Is everybody being heard? How do we get everyone involved in finding creative solutions to problems? How can businesses and the community partner to bring forth mutually supportive relationships?

Your Relationship with Your National Community

Do you have a sense of belonging to a nation? Are we working together? Where do you sense the dominator at work? Do we have partnerships with the organs of government? Do you feel that government is acting as a dominator or as a visionary partner? Where do you feel that partnership is operating, or is the entire system one of domination? How can we move toward a system of greater partnership? Do you feel that you personally have any ability to evolve the system? If you recall our statement that the Enlightenment was the fruit of the labors of only one thousand people, does that have any impact on your answer to the last question? How do your answers relate to the predominant Meme in your personality?

Your International and Multicultural Relationships

How would you characterize your nation's relationships with others outside your country? Where do you discern cooperation, and where domination? What can you do to bring your nation's actions closer to partnership with others? What can you do personally to live in greater partnership with people of other nationalities?

Your Relationship with Nature and the Living Environment

What do think of your relationship with the natural environment: Is it one of partnership or of domination? Are we living within the parameters of the ecosystem, or are we consuming too many resources? What can you do personally to improve your relationship with the living environment? What can you do to improve the way in which we are collectively attempting to dominate nature?

Your Relationship with Other Living Creatures

One of the most helpful and yet neglected things we can do for ourselves and for others is to explore our relationships with other living things. Do you have any relationships with animals? Are they dominator or partnership? Since our language is so important, do you talk about owning an animal or of sharing your life with one? Do you make time to be with animals? Do you notice any differences in the animals after they have spent time with you? Do you notice any difference in yourself? There has been a lot of work on using horses and dolphins in therapy, and there is good evidence that they can bring a wonderful new dimension to treatment. Some therapists have introduced visualization exercises based on horse riding to help people cope with anxiety, and have found that not only did it help with anxiety, it also deepened peoples' sense of connection with themselves and with nature. Apart from relationships with furry animals, have you explored your feelings and your relationships with insects? This is by no means a flippant question. Do you have a dominator relationship with them? I used to have an irrational dislike of spiders until Roger Callahan cured me of it using TFT. I now quite like the little creatures, keep a photo of a tarantula on my desk and would never allow anyone to squash a spider. It can be a major revelation to come to terms with your feelings about all creatures. Particularly the ones that you might not especially like.

"There's something about the outside of a horse that's good for the inside of a man."
—Winston Churchill (English Statesman, British Prime Minister, 1940–1945 and 1951–1955, and, in 1953, Winner of the Nobel Prize in Literature, 1874–1965)

Your Relationship with Spirit

Do you feel that you are in partnership with your spirit, with your Overself? Are you fully aware that you have a spiritual nature, as well as physical, psychological, subtle and social? Are you prepared to let it guide your life? How do you acknowledge, respect and revere your spiritual nature? Are you able to respect the spiritual choices made by others? The prepared mind can find spiritual truth anywhere. It need not be in a place of worship. Where, today, have you seen evidence of spirit at work in the world around you, or in yourself?

Reward, Reward Deficiency and Salience Disruption Syndrome

In the last chapter I asked you to explore the use of creating rewards for yourself. But what exactly is a reward? It is anything providing a direction to behavior. Such events include pleasurable experiences, but they can also be associated with things that remove negative stimuli. Rewards have two key functions: They energize and they reinforce behavior. If you think back to the rewards list that you created, you will have noticed that rewards are dynamic. Different things will act as rewards at different times. Your state of motivation has a lot to do with them: Food is more likely to be a reward if you are hungry. Learning is also a factor that can affect reward: When the reward systems malfunction, they can contribute to addictive behavior, and people can develop addictions to virtually anything.

Addictive habits access some of the deepest drives with us: the drive for novelty and the drive for an intense experience of the Universe.

There is a link between addictions and the chemical neurotransmitter in the brain, dopamine. No chemical works alone, but we do know dopamine to be a key player in motivation, in pleasure and in learning. For a long time, researchers thought that dopamine was simply the reward chemical in the brain, and that premise has been repeated in countless popular books and articles. But that concept cannot be correct, since dopamine rises in key regions of the brain not only in response to a pleasurable stimulus, but also in response to a threat. Not only that, but since drugs like cocaine and amphetamine increase the levels of dopamine in the brain, you would also expect that drug addicts would be in permanent bliss. Instead, most of them are thoroughly miserable, and hardly any actually want to be addicted.

We now see dopamine as a key player in salience: in deciding what is important, and what we need to pay attention to in order to survive. Whenever something novel occurs, dopamine rises in key regions of the brain: It alerts us to food and sex, as well as danger and pain. If you are hungry and you smell food, the dopamine levels in the brain instantly start to rise. They also rise if you are confronted by a threat. It may well be that addicts' brains have learned to pay attention to drugs rather than to food, sex and survival. The whole notion of dopamine and salience may provide explanations for other self-destructive behaviors, from gambling to aggression and sexual deviance. When the brain is bathed in dopamine, over time it develops tolerance, and so the now under stimulated brain needs more of the stimulus to feel anything at all, which is why the addict needs more drug to get the same effect. What is even worse is that dopamine is key to the normal functioning of parts of the frontal lobes involved in the monitoring and control of behavior, so the addict begins to show impulsivity and impaired judgment.

Some people seem to be genetically predisposed to become addicted. If they have fewer dopamine receptors, they are more likely to get a bigger effect from drugs. And it is not just drugs. We think that there is a close relationship between addictive eating and salience. Gene-Jack Wang at the Brookhaven National Laboratory has discovered that the brains of morbidly obese people seem constantly to be turned toward finding food: The regions of the brain connected to the mouth, lips and tongue are overly active, and, like the addicts who get the biggest rush from drugs, they seem to have fewer dopamine receptors in the reward systems. Perhaps like the addict, the morbidly obese eat to compensate for an under active dopamine system.

Addictions do not just occur with heroin, cigarettes and food. Many people become so wrapped up in things like watching television, surfing the Internet or reading things that will do little to feed them, that it can almost be at the level of an addiction, an addiction that can drain your energy drive and motivation. It is important to recognize if you may have some of these at play in your life. Happily, there is also good news: One of the potent ways of helping people help themselves is by using the addiction mechanisms to program positive addictive behaviors. Simple examples that we have used extensively are running, weight training, T'ai Chi Ch'uan and meditation.

You know what it feels like if you get a reward: food, warmth and a kindness. You get a sort of warm fuzzy feeling. You also know the opposite. You are cold, wet and hungry, or your significant other has departed. You will likely be feeling anxious, angry or even empty. Now imagine that the reward systems are not working properly. You may be getting all the positive reinforcers imaginable, but you still feel the anxiety. Fifteen years ago, Kenneth Blum first proposed the idea of a "Reward Deficiency Syndrome," in which there is a type of sensory deprivation involving dopamine receptors in the reward systems, and the concept allows us to link together several illnesses. If we think about it for a moment, it is extremely uncommon to find an alcoholic individual who does not smoke, and when people quit smoking, only five or six pounds of any subsequent weight gain are due to the metabolic effects of nicotine; the rest is behavioral, presumably driven by dopamine. One of the many advantages of exercise is that it is a natural way of increasing dopamine in the brain. There is actually some decent evidence to support the idea of a link, and in recent years Blum has been working on various types of supplements to combat the problem. Given the new insight about salience, it might now be more accurate to describe a "Salience Disruption Syndrome."

There is a final piece to this concept, which will lead us into the final chapter. The Salience Disruption Syndrome, substance abuse and obesity are associated with what we call the "Overload Syndromes."

The Overload Syndromes

These are a set of problems that are normally thought to be separate entities, but in each of them there is an oversensitivity to the environment. This remains a controversial topic, and the research has not been completed, but we have enough evidence to draw up this tentative list:

- Attention deficit disorder
- Migraine headaches
- Social phobia
- Anxiety
- Bipolar mood disorders
- Dislike of loud sounds or bright lights
- Overly sensitive sense of smell
- "Highly sensitive person" type
- Some types of insomnia
- Multiple environmental sensitivity
- Sensitivity to geopathic stress
- Food sensitivity

It would be a good idea to see whether any of these apply to you, for as we will see in the next chapter, we now have some new ideas for helping these problems.

Chapter Twelve
Putting the Pieces Together

The Steps of Creative Self-Integration

When all the components of your body, mind, relationships, subtle systems and spirit are operating in coordinated harmony, you can move forward by leaps and bounds. So that you can see this novel process in action, I am going to select a problem area in which I have been working for more than 25 years: obesity. Even if this is not an issue for you or for anyone in your family, this process will show you how to apply this new system. I hope that my being an endocrinologist and metabolic physician, as well as a psychiatrist and complementary therapist, can help you look at the problem with fresh eyes.

It might surprise you that in a book dedicated to the cultivation of wellness and enhancing performance, I have waited until now to discuss your physical body, particularly given that I have been working in several branches of academic medicine for 35 years. The reason is simply this: You can learn everything there is to know about diet, exercise and breathing techniques, but unless you have first prepared yourself with the background knowledge and techniques that we have been building up, your results will likely not be that good. The key to success is to combine and integrate our approaches.

Your body is a natural system following natural laws that have been evolving in recent centuries. To use an analogy, treat your body like a garden. If your personal garden is to grow, it needs a judicious mixture of the five elements of Earth, Fire, Air, Water and Spirit, Etheric or Subtle.

First, we shall see why it is inaccurate to think about obesity as having just one cause. We shall then apply the IPCRESS system, before going ahead and following the key steps:

1 Coordinate all your resources and coordinate all the holons

2 Stabilize and harmonize each level of your being: gross, subtle and causal, correct the Informational Matrix, which enables you to reorganize all the energy fields of your body.

Information: Your Resources

Following the exercises that we did in Chapter Nine, you have already assembled your tools, but you also need to know something more about weight.

The New Causes of Obesity

To the question "What causes obesity?" the conventional answer is, of course, overeating and lack of exercise. If the number of consumed calories exceeds the number expended, you will gain weight. With more than 200 recognized hormones and chemical messengers involved in controlling weight, one dietary approach or exercise plan, or dealing with one hormone or chemical won't provide "The Answer" to today's worldwide obesity epidemic. It is also important to bear in mind that your body is designed to *gain* weight.

Although I'm sure that you have heard and read a great deal about weight problems and obesity, there are four contributors to weight gain that are not usually recognized:

1 Stress

2 Salt

3 Environmental toxins

4 Viruses

Stress

For the last two decades, one of the world's foremost authorities on obesity, Professor Per Bjorntorp, of the Karolinska Institute in Stockholm, has been suggesting that chronic stress and elevations of the hormone cortisol, along with the over-consumption of high-calorie, high-fat foods, cause obesity. That is why a stress management program is an essential part of dealing with obesity. The worst type of fat lives around the organs in the abdomen. These fat cells are metabolically active and covered in cortisol receptors, which explains why cortisol causes fat deposition here.

Salt

Too much common salt in the diet can lead to an over production of the hormones aldosterone and cortisol by the adrenal glands, leading to the increase in intra-abdominal fat, as well as fluid retention. A physician named Richard Moore has produced evidence to suggest that changing the balance of potassium and sodium in the diet, together with exercise, can reduce blood pressure. So the next question is whether the same sort of approach might also help with obesity.

Environmental Toxins

It is impressive that many people lose a great deal of excess weight *after* they have completed a detoxification program, leading to the obvious question of whether detoxification rids the body of something causing weight gain.

The reason that so many prescription medicines and illicit drugs cause weight gain is partially because the same regions of the brain that modulate emotion are also involved in the control of metabolism and of many hormones, and in the control of weight. There is also a link between medicines that are fat-soluble and weight gain. Fat-soluble medicines become deposited in the body's fat stores. Since women tend to have more subcutaneous fat than men, it is also one of the many reasons the bodies of men and women handle many medicines differently.

Another line of evidence has been the worrying data of the effects of environmental toxins on the endocrine system. Some of the most common toxins, which are found in food, water and the air we breathe, are:

1   Estrogens and estrogen-like compounds

2   Organochlorines

3   Organophosphates

4   Carbamates

5   Heavy metals

In addition, in many parts of the world, animals are also fed corticosteroids, antibiotics and even antithyroid drugs. This is far from being the complete list, but the key point here is that all of these are fat soluble, and they can all disrupt different parts of the endocrine system, including some of the mechanisms involved in the control of appetite and metabolism. And some have indeed been detected in the fat of healthy volunteers. Apart from being a possible cause of metabolic disruption, there is something else: If you lose a lot of fat very quickly, these toxins are going to be released into the circulation. A doctor in Scotland, Paula Baillie-Hamilton, has made the very interesting suggestion that small amounts of toxic chemicals are a central cause of the global pandemic of obesity. Though the hypothesis is not proven, what is clear is that cleaning out the system by some sensible detoxification can be very helpful indeed. Not for everyone, detoxification requires the sanction and supervision of a healthcare professional. I will be showing you our own method in a moment.

Viruses

The idea that obesity might be caused by viruses may sound absurd, but in fact it is a very hot area of research. There are now seven viruses that have been shown to cause obesity in animals, two of which may produce obesity in humans. Recall that viruses and toxins are the vehicles of disease because they carry information that distorts the Informational Matrix of one or more of the bodies.

Armed with this information, we've taken the first step, and now let's continue with the rest of the IPCRESS System:

Planning

In earlier chapters we helped you find your Purpose. Now we manifest your Purpose by setting clear, realistic and doable goals. What single action can you take every day to help yourself deal with your weight? How much healthier will you be each week? (Notice how we are not using words like "loss" of weight!) Your goal should be to become more toned and one pound per week healthier, which translates to exercising or saving 500 calories per day.

Coordination

Many weight-management attempts founder because they work with only one side of the problem. By coordinating systems that tackle the physical, psychological, social, subtle and spiritual, the whole process becomes much easier.

Relevance to Your Outcome

Which of the approaches that we are considering feel best to you? Does it feel comfortable to use this integrated approach? Apply your burgeoning intuitive skills to answering the question.

Effectiveness

Ask yourself, Am I sure that the techniques are going to be worth my time, and will help me?

Setting End Points

What are you aiming to achieve? Remember how we discussed the importance of Higher Purpose? Your chance of success is greatly improved if you
are doing something not just for yourself, but for someone or something
else as well.

Strategy

Ask, What exactly am I going to be doing on a day-to-day basis to move
myself toward a goal of greater health and effectiveness?

Getting Started

In order to start this process, we need to activate several key resources
available to you now. They came as part of the extraordinary package that
we call your body, mind, subtle systems and soul. It is simply that in most
people these attributes are atrophied. But the real trick is to use these in
the right combination.

The geniuses before us left their mark in the morphic fields, and you
can access them.

"Do, or do not. There is no try"
—Yoda (The Sage of *Star Wars*)

Napoleon Hill popularized the idea of a Mastermind group: a group of
like-minded people who could help and support each other and brainstorm
together. Neurolinguistic programming taught the idea of "modeling." I
suggest using the two together. I have an internal Mastermind group, all of
whom I know well and whose skills I can recruit when I need them.

Let me give you an example that you can adapt for your own use. I was
once playing in a chess tournament in Las Vegas. My opponent was

extremely strong, and he was gradually getting the upper hand. So, while sitting at the chessboard, I sank into a deep meditative state, and I asked the question, "Gary Kasparov, what would you do now?" Kasparov is probably the strongest chess player in history, and I have spent a great deal of time reading his books and watching him play in person, as well as on television and in videos. My trainer was watching, and he said that he saw me gradually change the way that I was sitting, and then my entire body language changed. All I knew was that the question prompted a cascade of new thoughts and insights. I came up with a plan that I hadn't even considered before, and an hour later my opponent resigned.

> "That is why you fail" Yoda to Luke Skywalker, after Luke had said, "I don't believe it"

Programming Your Mind

I have had a lot of success using self-hypnosis, subliminal tapes and CDs to assist the subconscious mind with mental blocks that may hinder our efforts to help ourselves. Earlier we looked at some of the ego-fears, and when we are working on weight management, there are some specific fears and other emotional reactions that can sabotage all your efforts. Sometimes they appear in a sequence, but often they do not. They sometimes appear as toxins are leaving your system, or in response to low blood sugar.

What are some of the psychological barriers to weight loss?

1 **Fear:** Although fear is often the motivation to start doing something serious to help yourself, several of the ego-fears can sabotage any attempts that you might make. Take the fear of death. It is important that your body and mind don't think that they might die, or your diet will not work. Think of the next largest fear: Fear of lack. That one developed during evolution with the precise objective of making you do something if you face a shortage or a deficiency. Which of the other ego-fears might be holding you back?

2   **Anxiety:** Ask yourself: What is happening to me? Do I really want to look and feel different? Perhaps the way that I was really was okay? Roger Callahan has for years now championed the notion that many addictions are a pathological response to anxiety.

3   **Anger:** Ask yourself this: Am I angry about the way I look or feel? Angry at society's preoccupations with weight? Angry that I am doing this for someone else? Angry at my genes? Angry with my parents for not having taught me proper eating habits when I was a kid?

4   **Frustration:** Am I frustrated with myself; why can some people eat with abandon and I can't? Why am I not losing as much or as fast as I want?

5   **Sadness:** This can be a physical consequence of being overweight. Forget the myth about heavy people being jolly, developed from flawed research nearly one hundred years ago. People with chronic illnesses often go through the classic stages of mourning. As they recover, they often have to learn a whole new set of coping skills. People who have struggled with weight often go through the same thing as they progress.

6   **Envy:** Ask yourself: Why has someone else been able to lose more than me? Why is it a struggle for me?

7   **Boredom:** Have you felt as if: This whole thing is boring! I want to go out and eat everything in sight!

8   **Oral Fixation:** Some people really do enjoy the experience of having something in their mouths. This observation spawned innumerable strange theories in the early days of psychoanalysis. It is good to know if you have this problem, because you can then direct our efforts toward dealing with it.

9   **Salience Disruption Syndrome:** We introduced this novel concept at the end of the last chapter. Do not even consider that you have to conquer this problem, because it has a powerful "up" side. You are going to integrate this into your being, by grasping and engaging with it. If this

is the key issue for you, then the TFT strategy that we are going to adopt is focused upon this.

10 **Sublimation:** Do any of these statements resonate with you? I overeat because it is better than smoking; I overeat because it makes me feel comfortable; I overeat because I am missing a relationship; I overeat because of the dominance of my female essence.

11 **Rationalization:** Have you ever said to yourself: Being heavy isn't so bad; what if my clothes don't fit any more? I've heard of people getting irritable and forgetful on diets; will I still be able to think straight?

12 **Comfort:** I am sure that you have known people who eat comfort foods. In many cases they actually produce a chemical effect in the brain: Apart from the evidence of our senses, there is a substantial body of research showing the specific effects of certain foods on mood. Not surprisingly, the possible loss of comfort foods could present a major barrier to sensible eating. If you find that any of these are predominating in your mind, then just identifying them will help. You can also use TFT and flower essences to defuse the impact that they are having upon you.

Detoxification

The body has seven interlinked physical systems for ridding itself of harmful substances:

1 Liver
2 Gallbladder
3 Intestines
4 Lungs
5 Urinary system
6 Skin
7 Lymphatic system

That does not count systems that are able to rapidly expel toxins, like the stomach and the nose.

There are many methods of detoxifying your body, from the mild daily cooked brown rice regimen, to stringent types of fasting. Usually we see detoxification recommended as a single practice. However, remember what we have said about combinations being key. What we are doing here is using the detoxification as a base from which to move forward. The best approach that we have found is to use a combination of herbal supplements, together with pure organically grown vegetables, and plenty of pure spring, or better yet, distilled water: 120 to 140 fluid ounces per day during the detoxification. The biggest problem with herbal supplements is that not all manufacturers guarantee their purity or contents, and some herbs are not at all pure. There are some good sources of herbs, and I have listed some of the best sources in the appendix.

These are the most useful herbs for cleansing:

1   **Milk thistle.** This has been used for centuries as a liver cleanser, and there is some decent research on it. In tablet form, use 300mg/day for one week, or alternatively take two teaspoons of the ground seeds twice a day.

2   **Dandelion.** This is one of the oldest diuretics known, and it stimulates the liver and the gallbladder. Experts like to harvest the leaves themselves, but I would not do that unless you are 100 percent sure that you can identify the leaves. You can easily purchase some and take them as a tea, for five days. You can keep taking dandelion long term: Dandelion leaves are good in salads.

3   **Licorice.** This also is described a liver support, and it is thought to have a lot of actions on the immune system. It is of value to us here because of its mild laxative properties. It can make some people's blood pressure go up, so care is needed.

4   **Burdock root.** This is also regarded as an herb for detoxifying the liver. After centuries of people using this herb, research has now found that it does indeed have some potent effects. It is sold in Oriental markets,

and if you live somewhere that it's available, you can cook it as a vegetable. Alternatively you can buy a tincture of it, and take 20 to 30 drops each day for five days.

5   **Chickweed.** This has been used as a detoxifier and diuretic for centuries. It is readily available and has an added benefit of gently reducing the appetite and having anti-inflammatory properties.

6   **Aloe vera.** Best known for its soothing properties on the skin, aloe vera extract is widely available in health food stores, and it can be excellent to help cleanse the intestines. It is so effective that it can prevent the absorption of medicines, which is another reason for seeking expert help. It is best used for five to seven days at a time, since some people with "lazy intestines" can find themselves becoming dependent on it for a normal bowel action.

7   **Ginger root.** This helps to cleanse the intestines, bladder and skin. It also accelerates the action of some other herbs. In the Chinese system, it is used to restore depleted spleen qi and expel excess phlegm. It is also of value in motion sickness. You can either buy capsules, or better yet, buy some fresh organic ginger root and cut and peel one-inch lengths, which you infuse in hot water for five minutes. Take that three times and day, and feel the effect!

There are many other useful herbs, but these are the central seven. During the five to seven days of your detoxification program, you will only be eating only high-fiber organic fruits and vegetables because they are less likely to be covered in pesticides. When it comes to food, everybody has his or her own likes and dislikes. If there is something here that you do not like or that causes you problems, do not worry: You have plenty of options. We particularly recommend these:

1   Apples and grapes: as many as you would like

2   Leafy greens like chard, spinach, kale: as much as you'd like

3   Artichokes: as many as you would like, prepared however you would like

4   Blueberries and/or cranberries: one carton a day for five days

5   Citrus fruit: So long as you are not sensitive to citrus, you should aim
     to eat two to three lemons a day; a grapefruit and four to six oranges a
     day.

6   Celery: as much as you would like

7   Asparagus: as much as you would like

I am enthusiastic about using juices of all of these, but it is important to
maintain a high fiber content in your diet.

If you recall the other routes of elimination of toxins, during the detoxification, if you possibly can, it is extremely useful to take a sauna, have
several massages and do aerobic exercise to get the lymphatic system moving more vigorously.

The Composition of Your Diet: The Fad-Free Diet

There has been so much discussion about what sort of diet is best, and
people have become confused by the constant arguments. Any diet will
work for some people. The question is what makes the most sense, and is
there some way to reach a consensus? Always remembering that our bodies
are designed to be fat-storage machines. I suggest the following:

1   Energy balance is important: You lose weight when you burn more
     calories than you consume.

2   Calories do count: It is not simply a matter of deciding whether to go
     low fat or low carbohydrate. You can lose weight on any diet that
     restricts entire categories of foods or limits portion sizes. But you may
     get hungry and gain it back. Fat has nine calories per gram, but protein
     and carbohydrates have only four calories per gram, so eating less fat
     means consuming fewer calories without having to eat less food. So it
     is best to eat less fat and fewer simple carbohydrates.

3   What you include in your diet is as important as what you exclude.
     There are hundreds of natural substances that help protect against

chronic diseases like heart disease and cancer, and these substances are found primarily in fruits, vegetables, whole grains and legumes. These foods are also rich in fiber, which is exceedingly important for healthy digestion and to help remove unnecessary fats. The volume of what is in the stomach is also a key satiety stimulus, which is why increasing the bulk of what you eat is so helpful. There is solid evidence that the protective effects of many foods only become evident when they are consumed in combination. (Combinations are key!)

4   Always begin by making moderate changes in your diet. If you want to lower your cholesterol level or weight even more, or if you have heart disease and want to reverse it, you may need to make bigger changes. But remember that reducing your intake by only 100 calories a day could theoretically translate into a weight loss of 10 pounds in one year.

5   Avoid "trans-fatty acids" and partly hydrogenated fats. They are used to increase the shelf life of food products. But as Dean Ornish once quipped, they may decrease the shelf life of people who eat them!

6   Try to consume some omega-3 fatty acids every day. As little as three grams a day may halve your risk of sudden cardiac death, as well as lowering triglycerides, reducing inflammation, reducing the risk of depression and perhaps helping prevent some forms of cancer. You can eat fish, including salmon, mackerel and halibut, or take contaminant-free fish or flaxseed-oil capsules.

7   Eat fewer simple carbohydrates. I always tell people that they should eat nothing white unless it's a prescription medication!

8   Whatever weight loss strategy you favor, do it in a way that enhances health rather than harms it. You can lose weight by smoking cigarettes or taking such stimulants as amphetamines, but that hardly makes sense.

9   Exercise more. Simple changes like taking the stairs, parking a little farther away and walking 30 minutes a day can make a difference. Small increases can lead to big improvements over time.

Don't Eat. Dine.

Taking a little longer to eat allows you to show gratitude, appreciation and reverence for the food and is good for your digestion. Eating in an esthetically pleasing environment is a tremendous aid to digestion, assimilation of not just the nutrients, but the subtle energies of food. Before you eat anything, listen to your body to find out what you actually want to eat.

The Power of Light

In Chapter Four we discovered that there is increasing evidence that overexposure to light can be associated with a number of illnesses. Excess light has been implicated in the development of insulin resistance that can lead to type 2 diabetes and coronary artery disease. There is also evidence that insomnia can be associated with obesity. Light controls many rhythms of our bodies and is involved in the formation of vitamin D, which is key in calcium metabolism and the functions of cell membranes. It may be that part of the reason for higher rates of diabetes and of schizophrenia in recent dark-skinned migrants to temperate regions may be a consequence of vitamin D deficiency. So we need light. You have probably also heard of seasonal affective disorder (SAD). This can be a nasty illness: depression, often associated with carbohydrate craving, that is thought to be a kind of abnormal hibernation response. Fortunately it often responds to light therapy. Both too much and too little light can lead to problems. It is important not to spend any longer than you have to in high-illumination environments.

Exercise

There has probably been more written about the merits of exercise than almost any other subject. Aerobic exercise and weight training are essential parts of successful body management, and so is stretching, which, on its own, has enormous health benefits. Simply walking can be very valuable indeed. Good T'ai Chi Ch'uan instructors will often teach you to do a walking meditation, which enables you to get the benefits of both. I have also been particularly impressed by the health benefits of Pilates.

Something that I have found extremely helpful is a simple Qigong practice that seems to help gently stimulate the metabolism. I have recorded the practice as a podcast, and you can download it for free from my website, RichardGPettyMD.com

Using Thought Field Therapy

I want first to show you the precise stages that we go through.

1 Tuning: This involves intentionally concentrating upon your problem. People often don't want to do this: "Why would I want to think about something unpleasant?" Yet it is an essential step, because it brings up the specific perturbations and doesn't allow them to hide out of sight.

2 Rate your level of distress on a scale of 1-10, 10 being the most stressed. (This can be another valuable use of your Integration Journal.)

3 Tapping: Roger Callahan and his collaborators have devised and published a large number of treatment algorithms that correspond to different types of psychological disturbance. You gently, but firmly, tap away at the indicated points.

4. Perform the "Gamut series" of nine rapid treatments. This means tapping the "Gamut point" on the back of the hand while doing the eye movements, humming and counting which we are going to describe in a moment. The Gamut point is there on the diagram of the hand (Figure 7). To locate it, make a fist with your non-dominant hand (the left hand if you are right-handed). Put the index finger of your dominant hand between the knuckles of the ring and little fingers. Then open out the hand and run your finger about an inch in the direction of the wrist. Notice how more than once I have said "about." Few acupuncture points and few TFT points are very precisely located. Tap this point continuously with two fingers of your dominant hand while performing the following nine steps. The first time that you do them, you may feel a little silly: I know that I did! Persist, and you will likely find rapid benefits.

1. Open your eyes.
2. Close your eyes.
3. Open your eyes and point them down and to the left side.
4. Point your eyes down and to the right side.
5. Roll your eyes around in a circle in one direction.
6. Roll your eyes around in a circle in the opposite direction, and then look straight forward.
7. Hum a few bars of a tune.
8. Count aloud from one to five.
9. Hum the tune again.

And that's it! Interestingly Roger has discovered that if someone has a disability that prevents him or her from moving the eyes, even imagining the eyes moving seems to help, and imagining humming and counting also seems to do the trick.

Now let's look at exactly how we use TFT to deal with the urge to overeat.

1　Tune the Thought Field: Think as hard as you can about eating something you should not.
2　Rate the level of your distress about eating when you should not, on the 1-10 scale, and write it down.
3　Using two fingers of your dominant hand, tap five times under the eye, at the point shown in Figure 6. Just a firm tap: I do not want you to feel any discomfort.
4　Now tap five times under the armpit at the point shown in Figure 8.
5　Now tap one of the "collarbone points" five times.
6　Again evaluate your level of distress from 1-10. If it is unchanged, then you will need to do the tapping procedure for psychological reversal on the edge of your hand, as shown in Figure 7, and then repeat the first

five steps. If you are feeling any improvement, than proceed to the next steps.

7 Perform the nine Gamut treatments: Keep tapping the gamut point on the back of the hand, while doing that odd-looking series of routines:

Open your eyes.
Close your eyes.
Open your eyes and point them down
and to the left side.
Point your eyes down and to the right side.
Roll your eyes around in a circle in one direction.
Roll your eyes around in a circle in the opposite direction. Then look straight forward.
Hum a few bars of a tune.
Count aloud from one to five.
Hum the tune again.

8 Tap under the eye five times.
9 Tap under the arm five times.
10 Tap the collarbone point five times.
11 Now see how you feel. If there is still a problem, try tapping the psychological reversal point again.
12 Finally, holding your head steady, look down, and gradually roll your eyes toward the ceiling while tapping the Gamut point.

This technique, together with the others that we have looked at in this book, can and will help many, many people.

Flower Essences

The original flower essences were 38 remedies developed over 70 years ago by a Welsh physician named Edward Bach. Since his time, many new and powerful remedies have been discovered. The Bach Flower Essences are easy to obtain, surprisingly powerful, and are a useful addition to your household.

The Bach Remedies can be divided into seven primary groups, based on the emotions they most help. If you find that any of these emotions is involved in sabotaging you, the remedies could be most helpful for you.

1   Fear: Rock Rose, Mimulus, Cherry Plum, Aspen, Red Chestnut

2   Uncertainty: Cerato, Scleranthus, Hornbeam, Gentian, Gorse, Wild Oat

3   Disinterest: Clematis, Olive, Honeysuckle, Mustard, Chestnut Bud, White Chestnut, Wild Rose

4   Loneliness: Water Violet, Impatiens, Heather

5   Oversensitivity: Agrimony, Centaury, Walnut, Holly

6   Despondency: Larch, Pine, Elm, Star of Bethlehem, Sweet Chestnut, Willow, Oak, Crab Apple

7   Over-concern: Chicory, Vervain, Vine, Beech, Rock Water

So there you have it: a combination of approaches that have already helped huge numbers of people around the world. By following me this far, you are already participating in a revolutionary approach to health care.

I hope that you have found this worthwhile, and it only remains for me to wish you the very best of good health, peace and happiness.

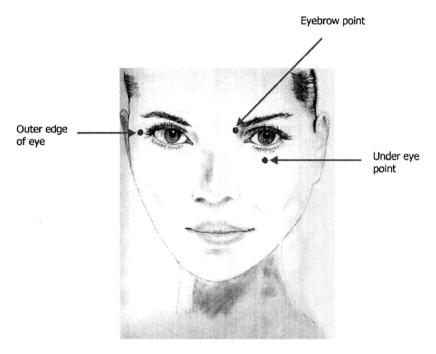

Figure 6. Some of the key points on the face that we use in Thought Field Therapy (TFT). Each is also an important acupuncture point

The "Gamut" point

The Psychological reversal point

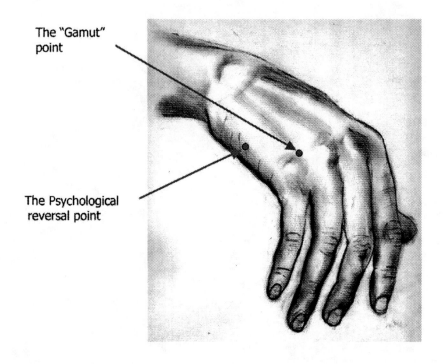

Figure 7. Key TFT points on the hand that also correspond to major acupuncture points

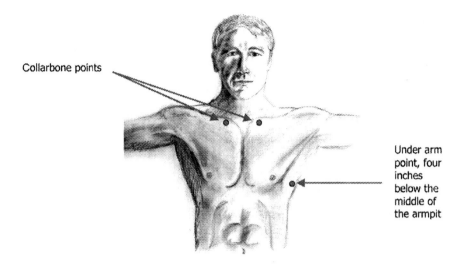

Collarbone points

Under arm point, four inches below the middle of the armpit

Figure 8. This diagram shows some of the key points on the torso that we use in Thought Field Therapy. Use this diagram when you are following the exercises in the text

Figure 9: These are the eye positions that we use when using Thought Field Therapy. Use these pictures as a guide when following the instructions in the text.

Acknowledgments

As the time comes to express my indebtedness to many people, I am reminded of something that Winston Churchill once said: "*I have never accepted what many people have kindly said namely, that I inspired the nation. It was the nation and the race dwelling all round the globe that had the lion's heart. I had the luck to be called upon to give the roar.*"

Although it is my name on the cover of this book, I am only giving voice to a massive global effort by a great many people over the last three decades, some working alone, and generously sharing their insights, others working cooperatively in University departments, in industry, in government and in many different healing professions. It has been a privilege knowing and learning from them all. My major contribution has been to put a large number of pieces together and to come up with some rather astonishing conclusions that we have been able to test and confirm with thousands of people around the globe.

If I named everyone who has helped with ideas, concepts and conversations, these acknowledgments would be inordinately long. But I must thank the librarians at the Royal Society of Medicine, the University of London, the Clinical Research Centre at Northwick Park, the Institute of Psychiatry in London, Johns Hopkins University, the University of Pennsylvania and Georgia State University. They have all been immensely helpful in tracking down the literally thousands of books and research papers that underlie everything in this book.

I would also like to thank the many people who trained me in biochemistry, in molecular and cellular biology, in clinical medicine and in an array of unorthodox healing modalities. I have also had the privilege to study with many spiritual teachers, some of whom wish to remain anonymous, not because of some desire to be coy or mysterious, but instead so that they can continue their work.

His Royal Highness, Prince Charles, the Prince of Wales, has, over the last two decades, been extraordinarily supportive of all our attempts to create a new vision of integrated healthcare. Without his help we would never have got as far as we have. Thank you, Sir.

Cheryl Sweet has been a terrific editor, Cali Lubrant produced the lovely drawings of the human form, and Joann Rompella did a fantastic job of proof-reading the entire manuscript.

Without the skill and gentle prodding of Robert Stuberg, this book, and those that will follow over the next three years, would still be sitting on the hard drive of my computer!

I am indebted to Inner Traditions of Rochester, Vermont, for their generosity in permitting me to quote from *Science and the Akashic Field*, by Ervin Laszlo.

And finally, my heartfelt thanks to Kim and Callan, who have been incredibly supportive and given me the time necessary to complete this project.

RP
Atlanta, June 2007

Further Reading

For more than three decades I have had access to resources that most people have not: books in many languages, research papers and field reports. I would like you to have the fruits of my labors. In this program we are sharing many new concepts, ideas and methods, as well as putting a different spin on some more familiar concepts. However, everything is rooted in material already available and most of it is in the public domain. This is important, first because when you are starting out on a new course in life, it is vital for you to know that you are going in the right direction, and second, it is inevitable that people will sometimes try to deflect you with well-meaning criticism. It is good for you to be able to point at a reference list like this to show others that what you are doing is not something "far out", but rooted in the highest-quality scientific and spiritual traditions. I could easily have put in hundreds of scientific papers as well, but that would take us too far beyond my intention, which is to provide you, dear reader, and a new way of looking at your life, and a set of tools to help you live it to the full.

I have also included some websites. Anyone who has tried to do research using the Internet knows that there is a great deal of variation in the quality of websites and the information in some is more reliable than others. For several years now, I have been collecting useful websites, those for which I have been able to check the information. At the end of some of the Chapters' bibliographies are some that I have checked myself. But also bear in mind that the Internet continues to be very fluid: Websites sometimes vanish for no readily apparent reason!

I use my own website—RichardGPettyMD.com—and blog—RichardGPettyMD.blogs.com—to regularly update all the material in this book and to answer questions about topics that I have discussed.

This is a little different from a traditional bibliography. First, it is long so that it may buttress your new approach to life. From the thousands of books that I have studied and analyzed, I have highlighted some of the major ones that have provided the background material, and these can form the basis for further study and reflection. I have left out difficult, academic works that need a lot of background information.

And there is a second reason for presenting you with this list. In the body of the program, I have made some suggestions for experiments to enhance your intuitive abilities. I suggest that we have here an excellent opportunity to practice. Start to use your intuition to find which books you would most like to examine. I have my favorites, but the moment that I start saying that they are, it could interfere with your own intuition and your power to choose. And above all, I want you to find freedom from which to grow. So have a little fun finding new sources of information and inspiration.

Chapter One: Setting the Scene

Aczel, Amir D. 2001. *Entanglement: The Greatest Mystery in Physics*. New York: Four Walls Eight Windows

Aggleton, John P. (Editor). 2000. *The Amygdala: A Functional Analysis*. Oxford: Oxford University Press

Al-Khalili, Jim. 2003. *Quantum: A Guide for the Perplexed*. London: Weidenfeld & Nicolson, Limited

Albert, David Z. 1992. *Quantum Mechanics and Experience*. Cambridge, Massachusetts: Harvard University Press

Amen, Daniel G. 1998. *Change Your Brain, Change Your Life: The Breakthrough Program for Conquering Anxiety, Depression, Obsessiveness, Anger, and Impulsiveness*. New York: Three Rivers Press

Anderson, Walter Truett. 2001. *All Connected Now: Life in the First Global Civilization*. Cambridge, Massachusetts: Westview Press

Anderson, Walter Truett. 2003. *The Next Enlightenment: Integrating East and West in a New Vision of Human Evolution*. New York: St. Martin's Press

Appleyard, Bryan. 1993. *Understanding the Present: Science and the Soul of Modern Man.* New York: Anchor Books

Arntz, William (Editor), Chasse, Betsy (Editor). 2004. *The Little Book of Bleeps: "Ponder these for a While!" Quotations from the Movie. What the Bleep do we Know!* Captured Light Distribution

Baeyer, Hans Christian von. 2004. *Information: The New Language of Science.* Cambridge, Massachusetts: Harvard University Press

Bailey, Alice A. 1922. *Initiation, Human and Solar.* London: Lucis Press

Bailey, Alice A. 1936. *A Treatise on the Seven Rays, Volume 1: Esoteric Psychology Part 1.* London: Lucis Press

Bailey, Alice A. 1942. *A Treatise on the Seven Rays, Volume 2 Esoteric Psychology Part 2.* London: Lucis Press

Bailey, Alice A. 1947. *The Reappearance of the Christ.* London: Lucis Press

Bailey, Alice A. 1953. *A Treatise on the Seven Rays. Volume 4: Esoteric Healing.* London: Lucis Press

Bak, Per. 1996. *How Nature Works: The Science of Self-Organized Criticality.* New York: Copernicus Springer-Verlag New York Inc.

Baker, Douglas M. 1976a. *Esoteric Anatomy, Part One.* Essendon, Hertfordshire: Baker Publications

Baker, Douglas M. 1976b. *Esoteric Healing, Part One.* Essendon, Hertfordshire: Baker Publications

Baker, Douglas M. 1976. *Esoteric Healing, Part Two.* Essendon, Hertfordshire: Baker Publications

Baker, Douglas M. 1978. *Esoteric Healing, Part Three.* Essendon, Hertfordshire: Baker Publications

Baker, Robin. 2001. *Fragile Science: The Reality Behind the Headlines.* London: Macmillan

Baldi, Pierre. 2001. *The Shattered Self: The End of Natural Evolution.* Cambridge, Massachusetts: Bradford Books/The MIT Press

Ball, Philip. 2004. *Critical Mass: How One Thing Leads to Another.* New York: Farrar, Straus and Giroux

Barabási, Albert-László. 2002. *Linked: How Everything Is Connected to Everything Else and What It Means.* Cambridge, Massachusetts: Perseus Publishing

Barrow, John D. (Editor), Davies, Paul C.W. (Editor), Harper, Charles L. 2004. *Science and Ultimate Reality: Quantum Theory, Cosmology and Complexity.* New York: Cambridge University Press

Bateson, Patrick, Martin, Paul. 2000. *Design for a Life: How Biology and Psychology Shape Human Behavior.* New York: Touchstone Books/Simon and Schuster

Baudry, Michael (Editor), Davis, Joel L. (Editor), Thompson, Richard F. (Editor). 2000. *Advances in Synaptic Plasticity.* Cambridge, Massachusetts: Bradford Book/The MIT Press

Baumann, Lee, T. 2001. *God at the Speed of Light: The Melding of Science and Spirituality.* Virginia Beach, Virginia: A.R.E. Press

Becker, Robert O., Selden, Gary. 1985. *The Body Electric: Electromagnetism and the Foundation of Life.* New York: Quill

Behe, Michael. 1996. *Darwin's Black Box: The Biochemical Challenge to Evolution.* New York: The Free Press

Bell, John. 1987. *Speakable and Unspeakable in Quantum Mechanics.* Cambridge: Cambridge University Press

Bernal, J.D. 1973. *The Extension of Man: A History of Physics Before the Quantum.* Cambridge, Massachusetts: The MIT Press

Blaha, Stephen. 2002. *Cosmos and Consciousness: Quantum Computers, Superstrings, Programming, Egypt, Quarks, Mind Body Problem, and Turing Machines.* Bloomington, Indiana: 1st Books Library

Bohm, David. 1967. *Causality and Chance in Modern Physics.* London: Routledge & Kegan Paul

Bohm, David. 1980. *Wholeness and the Implicate Order.* London: Routledge & Kegan Paul Ltd.

Bohm, David. 1987. *Unfolding Meaning: A Weekend of Dialogue With David Bohm.* London and New York: Routledge

Bohm, David, Hiley, B.J. 1993. *The Undivided Universe.* London: Routledge

Bohm, David. 1996. *The Special Theory of Relativity.* London: Routledge

Braden, Gregg. 2004. *The God Code.* Carlsbad, California: Hay House Inc.

Briggs, John, Peat, F. David. 1999. *Seven Life Lessons of Chaos: Spiritual Wisdom from the Science of Change.* New York: HarperPerennial

Bruce, Colin. 2004. *Schrödinger's Rabbits: The Many Worlds of Quantum.* Washington, D.C.: Joseph Henry Press

Brune, Martin (Editor), Ribbert, Hedda (Editor), Schiefenhovel, Wulf (Editor). 2003. *The Social Brain: Evolution and Pathology.* Chichester, West Sussex: John Wiley and Sons Ltd.

Brunton, Paul. 1936. *A Message from Arunachala.* London: Rider

Brunton, Paul. 1937. *The Quest of the Overself.* London: Rider

Brunton, Paul. 1939. *The Inner Reality.* London: Rider

Brunton, Paul. 1943. *The Wisdom of the Overself.* London: Rider

Brunton, Paul. 1969. *The Secret Path.* London: Rider

Brunton, Paul. 1988. *The Notebooks of Paul Brunton. Volume 14. Inspiration and the Overself.* Burdett, New York: Larson Publications

Buchanan, Mark. 2001. *Ubiquity: The Science of History or Why the World Is Simpler Than We Think.* New York: Crown Publishers

Campbell, Jeremy. 1982. *Grammatical Man: Information, Entropy, Language and Life.* Harmondsworth, Middlesex, England: Penguin Books, Ltd.

Capra, Fritjof. 1975. *The Tao of Physics.* New York: Bantam Books

Capra, Fritjof. 1983. *The Turning Point: Science, Society and the Rising Culture.* London: Flamingo/Fontana Paperbacks

Capra, Fritjof. 1996. *The Web of Life: A New Understanding of Living Systems*. New York: Anchor Books

Capra, Fritjof. 2002. *The Hidden Connections: Integrating the Biological, Cognitive, and Social Dimensions of Life into a Science of Sustainability*. New York: Doubleday

Casti, John L. 2003. *One, True Platonic Heaven: A Scientific Fiction of the Limits of Knowledge*. Washington, D.C.: Joseph Henry Press

Chance, MRA (Editor). 1988. *Social Fabrics of the Mind*. Hillsdale, New Jersey: Lawrence Erlbaum Associates, Publishers

Chopra, Deepak. 1990. *Quantum Healing*. New York: Harmony Books

Chopra, Deepak. 1993. *Ageless Body, Timeless Mind: The Quantum Alternative to Growing Old*. New York: Harmony Books

Close, Edward R. 2000. *Transcendental Physics: Integrating the Search for Truth*. Lincoln, Nebraska: iUniverse

Cole, K.C. 2001. *The Hole in the Universe: How Scientists Peered Over the Edge of Emptiness and Found Everything*. San Diego: Harvest Books/Harcourt Inc.

Collinge, William. 1998. *Subtle Energy: Awakening to the Unseen Forces in Our Lives,* New York: Warner Books

Cranston, Sylvia. 1993. *HPB. The Extraordinary Life & Influence of Helena Blavatsky*. New York: Tarcher/Putnam

Crook, John. 1980. *The Evolution of Human Consciousness*. Oxford: Clarendon Press

Crow, T.J. (Editor). 2002. *The Speciation of Modern Homo Sapiens*. Oxford: Oxford University Press

Cummings, Jeffrey L., Mega, Michael S. 2003. *Neuropsychiatry and Behavioral Neuroscience*. New York: Oxford University Press

Davies, Paul. 1983. *God and the New Physics*. London: J.M. Dent and Sons Ltd.

Davies, P.C.W. 1987. *The New Physics*. London: Unwin Hyman

Dossey, Larry. 1982. *Space, Time and Medicine.* Boulder, Colorado: Shambhala Publications Inc.

Dossey, Larry. 1989. *Recovering the Soul: A Scientific and Spiritual Approach.* New York: Bantam Books

Earman, John. 1995. *Bangs, Crunches, Whimpers and Shrieks.* New York: Oxford University Press

Eastaway, Rob, Wyndham, Jeremy. 1999. *Why Do Buses Come in Threes? The Hidden Mathematics of Everyday Life.* New York: John Wiley & Sons

Endler, P.C. (Editor), Schulte, J. (Editor). 1994. *Ultra High Dilution: Physiology and Physics.* Dordrecht: Kluwer Academic Publishers

Ernst, Edzard (Editor), Hahn, Eckhart G. (Editor). 1998. *Homoeopathy: A Critical Appraisal.* Oxford: Butterworth Heinemann

Factor, Donald. 1985. *Unfolding Meaning: A Weekend of Dialogue with David Bohm.* Mickleton, Gloucestershire, England: Foundation House Publications

Farwell, Larry. 1999. *How Consciousness Commands Matter: The New Scientific Revolution And the Evidence That Anything Is Possible,* Fairfield, Iowa: Sunstar Publishing Ltd.

Feinberg, Todd E. 2001. *Altered Egos: How the Brain Creates the Self.* New York: Oxford University Press

Flandern, Tom Van. 1993. *Dark Matter, Missing Planets and New Comets.* Berkeley, California: North Atlantic Books

Ford, Kenneth W. 2004. *The Quantum World: Quantum Physics for Everyone.* Cambridge, Massachusetts: Harvard University Press

Forrest, Peter. 1988. *Quantum Metaphysics.* Oxford: Basil Blackwell

Foster, David. 1985. *The Philosophical Scientists.* New York: Dorset Press

Fraser, Gordon. 2000. *Antimatter: The Ultimate Mirror.* Cambridge: Cambridge University Press

Fraser, Gordon, Lillestol, Egil, Sellevag, Inge. 1995. *The Search for Infinity: Solving the Mysteries of the Universe.* New York: Facts On File Inc.

Friedman, Norman. 1990. *Bridging Science and Spirit: Common Elements in David Bohm's Physics, The Perennial Philosophy and Seth.* St. Louis, Missouri: Living Lake Books

Fuller, Jean Overton. 1988. *Blavatsky and her Teachers.* London: East-West Publications

Furman, Mark Evan, Gallo, Fred P. 2000. *The Neurophysics of Human Behavior: Explorations at the Interface of the Brain, Mind, Behavior, and Information.* Boca Raton, Florida: CRC Press

Galanter, Marc. 2005. *Spirituality and the Healthy Mind: Science, Therapy, and the Need for Personal Meaning,* New York: Oxford University Press Inc.

Gazzaniga, Michael S. 2005. *The Ethical Brain,* New York: Dana Press

Gilmour, Robert. 1995. *Alice in Quantumland: An Allegory of Quantum Physics.* New York: Copernicus Book/Springer-Verlag

Giovannoli, Joseph. 2001. *The Biology of Belief: How Our Biology Biases Our Beliefs and Perceptions.* Rosetta Press Inc.

Glaskin, G.M. 1974. *Windows of the Mind: Consciousness Beyond the Body.* London: Arrow Books

Godfrey-Smith, Peter. 1998. *Complexity and the Function of the Mind in Nature.* Cambridge: Cambridge University Press

Goerner, S.J. 1999. *After the Clockwork Universe: The Emerging Science and Culture of Integral Society.* Edinburgh: Floris Books

Goldner, Diane. 1999. *Infinite Grace: Where the Worlds of Science and Spiritual Healing Meet.* Charlottesville, Virginia: Hampton Roads Publishing Company Inc.

Goldstein, Rebecca. 2005. *Incompleteness: The Proof and Paradox of Kurt Godel.* New York: W.W. Norton & Company

Goodwin, Brian. 1994. *How the Leopard Changed Its Spots: The Evolution of Complexity.* New York: Charles Scribner's Sons

Gordon, Richard. 2002. *Quantum-Touch.* Berkeley, California: North Atlantic Books

Goswami, Amit. 2000. *The Visionary Window: A Quantum Physicist's Guide to Enlightenment.* Wheaton, Illinois: Quest Books/Theosophical Publishing House

Goswami, Amit. 2001. *Physics of the Soul: The Quantum Book of Living, Dying, Reincarnation and Immortality.* Charlottesville, Virginia: Hampton Roads Publishing Company Inc.

Goswami, Amit. 2004. *The Quantum Doctor: A Physicist's Guide to Health and Healing.* Charlottesville, Virginia: Hampton Roads Publishing Company

Gray, Bill. 2000. *Homeopathy: Science or Myth?* Berkeley, California: North Atlantic Books

Greenia, Mark. 2002. *Living from the Heart: Exploring Subtle Energy in the New Millennium: Blending Quantum Physics and the Energy of Compassion.* Bloomington, Indiana: Unlimited Publishing

Gribbin, John R. 1998a. *Q is for Quantum. An Encyclopedia of Particle Physics.* New York: The Free Press

Gribbin, John R. 1998b. *The Search for Superstrings, Symmetry, and the Theory of Everything.* Boston: Little, Brown and Company

Griffin, David Ray. 1986. *Physics and the Ultimate Significance of Time: Bohm, Prigogine, and Process Philosophy.* Albany, New York: State University of New York Press

Guth, Alan H., Lightman, Alan P. 1997. *The Inflationary Universe.* Cambridge, Massachusetts: Perseus Books Group

Halpern, Paul. 2004. *The Great Beyond: Higher Dimensions, Parallel Universes and the Extraordinary Search for a Theory of Everything.* Hoboken, New Jersey: John Wiley & Sons Inc.

Harman, Willis, Clark, Jane (Editors). 1994. *New Metaphysical Foundations of Modern Science.* Sausalito, California: Institute of Noetic Sciences

Harman, Willis W., Sahtouris, Elisabet. 1998. *Biology Revisioned.* Berkeley, California: North Atlantic Books

Hassin, Ran R., Uleman, James S. and Bargh, John A. (Editors). 2005. *The New Unconscious,* New York: Oxford University Press Inc.

Haught, John F. 2001. *God After Darwin: A Theology of Evolution.* Boulder, Colorado: Westview Press

Hawking, Stephen W. 2002. *The Theory of Everything: The Origin and Fate of the Universe.* Beverley Hills, California: New Millennium Press

Hayes, Michael. 2004. *High Priests, Quantum Genes: Religion, Science and the Theory of Everything.* London: Black Springs Press

Healey, Richard. 1989. *The Philosophy of Quantum Mechanics: An Interactive Interpretation.* New York: Cambridge University Press

Herbert, Nick. 1987. *Quantum Reality: Beyond the New Physics.* New York: Anchor

Herbert, Nick. 1993. *Elemental Mind: Human Consciousness and the New Physics.* New York: Plume Books

Hey, Tony, Walters, Patrick. 2003. *The New Quantum Universe.* Cambridge: Cambridge University Press

Ho, Mae-Wan. 1998. *Genetic Engineering: Dream or Nightmare? The Brave New World of Science and Business.* Bath, UK: Gateway Books

Ho, Mae-Wan. 1999. *The Rainbow and the Worm: The Physics of Organisms.* River Edge, New Jersey: World Scientific Publishing Company

Hobson, J. Allan. 2005. *13 Dreams Freud Never Had: The New Mind Science.* New York: Pi Press

Hodson, Geoffrey. 1977. *Seven Human Temperaments.* Adyar, Madras, India: The Theosophical Publishing House

Horgan, John. 2000. *The Undiscovered Mind: How the Human Brain Defies Replication, Medication, and Explanation.* New York: The Free Press

Horgan, John. 2003. *Rational Mysticism: Dispatches from the Border Between Science and Spirituality.* Boston: Houghton Mifflin Company

Hull, D.L. 1988. *Science as a Process—An Evolutionary Account of the Social and Conceptual Development Of Science.* Chicago: Chicago University Press

Humphrey, Nicholas. 1992. *A History of the Mind: Evolution and the Birth of the Consciousness.* New York: Simon & Schuster Inc.

Jahn, Robert G., Dunne, Brenda J. 1987. *Margins of Reality: The Role of Consciousness in the Physical World.* San Diego, California: Harvest Books

Joos, E., Zeh, H.D., Kiefer, C., Giulini, D., Kupsch, J., Stamatescu, I.-O. 2003. *Decoherence and the Appearance of a Classical World in Quantum Theory.* Berlin: Springer-Verlag

Joseph, Rhawn. 1996. *Neuropsychiatry, Neuropsychology, and Clinical Neuroscience: Emotion, Evolution, Cognition, Language, Memory, Brain Damage, and Abnormal Behavior.* Baltimore, Maryland: Williams & Wilkins Company

Joseph, Rhawn (Editor). 2002. *NeuroTheology. Brain, Science, Spirituality, Religious Experience.* San Jose, California: University Press, California

Kaku, Michio. 1998. *Visions: How Science Will Revolutionize the 21st Century.* New York: Anchor Books

Kaku, Michio. 2005. *Parallel Worlds: A Journey Through Creation, Higher Dimensions, and the Future of the Cosmos,* New York: Doubleday

Kaku, Michio, Thompson, Jennifer. 1995. *Beyond Einstein: The Cosmic Quest for the Theory of the Universe.* New York: Anchor Books

Kauffman, Stuart. 1993. *The Origins of Order: Self-Organization and Selection in Evolution.* Oxford: Oxford University Press

Koestler, Arthur. 1972. *The Roots of Coincidence.* London: Hutchinson and Co. (Publishers) Ltd.

Koestler, Arthur. 1974. *The Challenge of Chance.* London: Hutchinson

Koestler, Arthur. 1979. *Janus: A Summing Up.* London: Picador

Koestler, Arthur (Editor), Smythies, J.R. (Editor). 1969. *Beyond Reductionism: The Alpbach Symposium.* London: Hutchinson & Co (Publishers) Ltd.

Konner, Melvin J. 1990. *The Tangled Wing: Biological Constraints on the Human Spirit.* New York: Henry Holt & Company Inc.

Krauss, Lawrence. 1991. *The Fifth Essence: The Search for Dark Matter in the Universe.* New York: Basic Books

Laszlo, Ervin. 1987. *Evolution, the Grand Synthesis.* Boston, Massachusetts: New Science Library

Laszlo, Ervin (Editor). 1993. *The Evolution of Cognitive Maps.* Amsterdam: Gordon and Breach Publishers

Laszlo, Ervin, Abraham, Ralph H. 2003. *The Connectivity Hypothesis: Foundations of an Integral Science of Quantum, Cosmos, Life and Consciousness.* Albany, New York: State University of New York Press

Laszlo, Ervin. 2004. *Science and the Akashic Field: An Integral Theory of Everything.* Rochester, Vermont: Inner Traditions

Laughlin, Robert B. 2005. *A Different Universe: Reinventing Physics from the Bottom Down,* New York: Basic Books

Leary, David E. (Editor). 1990. *Metaphors in the History of Psychology.* Cambridge: Cambridge University Press

Lederman, Leon M., Hill, Christopher T. 2004. *Symmetry and the Beautiful Universe.* Amherst, New York: Prometheus Books

Lewin, Roger. 1993. *Complexity: Life at the Edge of Chaos.* Chicago: University of Chicago Press

Lipton, Bruce. 2005. *The Biology of Belief: Unleashing the Power of Consciousness, Matter, and Miracles,* Santa Rosa, California: Mountain of Love/Elite Books

Lockwood, Michael. 1989. *Mind, Brain and the Quantum: The Compound "I".* Oxford: Basil Blackwell Ltd.

Loewenstein, Werner R. 1999. *The Touchstone of Life.* New York: Oxford University Press

Lorimer, David (Editor). 1998. *The Spirit of Science. From Experiment to Experience.* Edinburgh: Floris Books

Lorimer, David (Editor). 2001. *Thinking Beyond the Brain: A Wider Science of Consciousness.* Edinburgh: Floris Books

Lorimer, David (Editor). 2004. *Science, Consciousness and Ultimate Reality,* Charlottesville, Virginia: Imprint Academic

Macdonald, Copthorne. 2004. *Matters of Consequence: Creating a Meaningful Life and a World That Works.* Charlottetown, Prince Edward Island, Canada: Big Ideas Press

McFadden, Johnjoe. 2002. *Quantum Evolution: How Physics' Weirdest Theory Explains Life's Biggest Mystery.* New York: W. W. Norton & Company

McTaggart, Lynne. 2001. *The Field: The Quest for the Secret Force of the Universe.* London: HarperCollins

Mallove, Eugene J. 1991. *Fire from Ice: Searching for the Truth Behind the Cold Fusion Furor.* Concord, New Hampshire: Infinite Energy Press

Mandler, Jean Matter. 2004. *The Foundations of Mind: Origins of Conceptual Thought.* Oxford: Oxford University Press

Manning, Jeane. 1996. *The Coming Energy Revolution: The Search for Free Energy.* Garden City Park, New York: Avery Publishing Group

Marcus, Gary F. 2001. *The Algebraic Mind: Integrating Connectionism and Cognitive Science.* Cambridge, Massachusetts: Bradford Books/The MIT Press

Marcus, Gary F. 2004. *The Birth of the Mind: How a Tiny Number of Genes Creates the Complexity of Human Thought.* New York: Basic Books

Marshall, Louise H. (Editor), Magoun, Horace W. (Editor). 1998. *Discoveries in the Human Brain: Neuroscience Prehistory, Brain Structure, and Function.* Totawa, New Jersey: Humana Press

Martensen, Robert L. 2004. *The Brain Takes Shape: An Early History.* New York: Oxford University Press

Martinez, Ignacio, Arsuaga, Juan Luis. 2004. *Green Fire: The Life Force, from the Atom to the Mind.* New York: Thunder's Mouth Press

Maturana, Humberto R., Varela, Francisco J. 1980. *Autopoiesis and Cognition: The Realization of the Living.* Dordrecht, Holland: D. Reidel Publishing Company

Maturana, Humberto R., Varela, Francisco J. 1988. *The Tree of Knowledge*. Boston, Massachusetts: New Science Library/Shambhala

Miller, William R, C'de Baca, Janet. 2001. *Quantum Change*. New York: Guilford Press

Mindell, Arnold. 2000. *Quantum Mind: The Edge Between Physics and Psychology*. Portland, Oregon: Lao Tse Press

Mindell, Arnold. 2004. *The Quantum Mind and Healing*. Charlottesville, Virginia: Hampton Roads Publishing Company Inc.

Mitchell, Edgar D., White, John (Editor). 1976. *Psychic Exploration: A Challenge for Science*. New York: Capricorn Books/G.P. Putnam's Sons

Moore, David S. 2001. *The Dependent Gene: The Fallacy of "Nature vs. Nurture"*. New York: A.W.H. Freeman Books/Henry Holt and Company

Morowitz, Harold J. 2002. *The Emergence of Everything: How the World Became Complex*. Oxford: Oxford University Press

Morse, Melvin, Perry, Paul. 2000. *Where God Lives: The Science of the Paranormal and How Our Brains are Linked to the Universe*. New York: Cliff Street Books

Moskowitz, Gordon B. 2005. *Social Cognition: Understanding Self and Others,* New York: The Guilford Press

Murphy, Michael. 1992. *The Future of the Body: Explorations into the Further Evolution of Human Nature,* Los Angeles: Jeremy P. Tarcher Inc.

Nadeau, Robert, Kafatos, Menas. 1999. *The Non-Local Universe: The New Physics and Matters of the Mind*. Oxford: Oxford University Press

Newhouse, Flower A., Isaac, Stephen. 2001. *The 7 Bodies Unveiled*. Woodside, California: Bluestar Communications

Nichol, Lee (Editor). 2003. *The Essential David Bohm*. London: Routledge

Nicolis, Gregoire, Prigogine, Ilya, Nicolis, G. 1989. *Exploring Complexity: An Introduction*. New York: W. H. Freeman & Co.

O'Murchu, Dairmuid. 2004. *Quantum Theology: Spiritual Implications of the New Physics*. New York: The Crossroad Publishing Company

Oschman, James L. 2000. *Energy Medicine: The Scientific Basis of Bioenergy Therapies.* New York: Churchill Livingstone

Oschman, James L. 2003. *Energy Medicine in Therapeutics and Human Performance.* New York: Butterworth-Heinemann

Pearl, Eric. 2001. *The Reconnection.* Carlsbad, California: Hay House

Peat, F. David. 1997. *Infinite Potential: The Life and Times of David Bohm.* Reading, Massachusetts: Addison Wesley Publishing Company Inc.

Peat, F. David. 2002. *From Certainty to Uncertainty: The Story of Science and Ideas in the Twentieth Century.* Washington, D.C.: Joseph Henry Press

Penrose, Roger. 1997. *The Large, the Small and the Human Mind.* Cambridge: Cambridge University Press

Penrose, Roger. 2004. *The Road to Reality: A Complete Guide to the Laws of the Universe.* New York: Alfred A. Knopf

Petersen, P. Stephen. 1996. *The Quantum Tai Chi: Gauge Theory: The Dance of Mind Over Matter.* Concord, California: Empyrean Quest Publishers

Playfair, Guy Lyon. 2002. *Twin Telepathy: The Psychic Connection.* London: Vega

Popper, Karl R. 1982. *Quantum Mechanics and the Schism in Physics.* London: Routledge

Pribram, Karl. 1993. *Rethinking Neural Networks: Quantum Fields and Biological Data: Proceedings of the Second Appalachian Conference on Behavioral Neurodynamics.* Hillsdale, New Jersey: Lawrence Erlbaum Associates, Publishers

Prigogine, Ilya. 1980. *From Being To Becoming.* New York: W. H. Freeman & Co.

Prigogine, Ilya, Stengers, Isabelle. 1984. *Order Out of Chaos: Man's New Dialogue with Nature.* London: Heinemann

Quincey, Christian De. 2002. *Radical Nature: Rediscovering the Soul of Matter.* Montpelier, Vermont: Invisible Cities Press

Radin, Dean. 1997. *The Conscious Universe: The Scientific Truth of Psychic Phenomena.* San Francisco: Harper Collins

Ricard, Matthieu, Thuan, Trinh Xuan. 2001. *The Quantum and the Lotus.* New York: Crown Publishers

Ridley, B.K. 2001. *On Science (Thinking in Action).* London: Routledge

Ridley, Matt. 2003. *Nature via Nurture: Genes, Experience, and What Makes Us Human.* New York: HarperCollins

Rigden, John S. 2002. *Hydrogen: The Essential Element.* Cambridge, Massachusetts: Harvard University Press

Roney-Dougal, Serena. 1993. *Where Science and Magic Meet: Techniques for Altering States of Consciousness.* Longmead, Shaftesbury, Dorset: Element Books

Rose, Steven. 2005. *The Future of the Brain: The Promise and Perils of Tomorrow's Neuroscience.* New York: Oxford University Press Inc.

Rossi, Ernest Lawrence. 2002. *The Psychobiology of Gene Expression.* New York: W.W. Norton & Company

Saraydarian, Torkom. 1992. *New Dimensions in Healing.* Cave Creek, Arizona: T.S.G. Publishing Foundation Inc.

Satinover, Jeffrey. 2001. *The Quantum Brain.* New York: John Wiley & Sons Inc.

Schumm, Bruce A. 2004. *Deep Down Things: The Breathtaking Beauty of Particle Physics.* Baltimore, Maryland: The Johns Hopkins University Press

Schwartz, Gary E. R., Russek, Linda G.S. 1999. *The Living Energy Universe.* Charlottesville, Virginia: Hampton Roads Publishing Company Inc.

Schwartz, Jeffrey M., Begley, Sharon. 2002. *The Mind and the Brain: Neuroplasticity and the Power of Mental Force.* New York: Regan Books

Shanor, Karen Nesbit (Editor). 1999. *The Emerging Mind: New Discoveries in Consciousness.* Los Angeles: Renaissance Books

Sheldrake, Rupert. 1999. *Dogs That Know When Their Owners Are Coming Home.* New York: Crown Publishers

Sheldrake, Rupert. 2003. *The Sense of Being Stared At.* London: Hutchinson

Skolimowski, Henryk. 1994. *The Participatory Mind: A New Theory of Knowledge and the Universe.* London: Arkana

Smolin, Lee. 2001. *Three Roads to Quantum Gravity.* New York: Basic Books

Sole, Ricard, Goodwin, Brian. 2000. *Signs of Life: How Complexity Pervades Biology.* New York: Basic Books

Solms, Mark, Turnbull, Oliver. 2002. *The Brain and the Inner World: An Introduction to the Neuroscience of Subjective Experience.* New York: Other Press

Stewart, Robert A. 1989. *The Infinite Universe: God and the Quantum World of the Soul.* Tempe, Arizona: New Falcon Publications

Talbot, Michael. 1996. *The Holographic Universe.* New York: HarperCollins

Targ, Russell. 2004. *Limitless Mind: A Guide to Remote Viewing and Transformation of Consciousness.* Novato, California: New World Library

Tarnas, Richard. 1991. *The Passion of the Western Mind.* New York: Ballantine Books

Taylor, John G. 1999. *The Race for Consciousness.* Cambridge, Massachusetts: Bradford Books/The MIT Press

Taylor, Mark C. 2001. *The Moment of Complexity: Emerging Network Culture.* Chicago: University of Chicago Press

Templeton, John Marks (Editor). 1994. *Evidence of Purpose: Scientists Discover the Creator.* New York: Continuum Publishing Company

Templeton, John Marks (Editor), Hermann, Robert L. 1994. *Is God the Only Reality? Science Points to a Deeper Meaning of the Universe.* New York: Continuum Publishing Company

Thompson, Richard L. 2003. *Maya: The World as Virtual Reality.* Alachua, Florida: Govardhan Hill Publishers

Uttal, William R. 2001. *The New Phrenology: The Limits of Localizing Cognitive Processes in the Brain*. Cambridge, Massachusetts: Bradford Books/The MIT Press

Varela, Francisco J. (Editor), Shear, Jonathan (Editor). 1999. *The View from Within: First Person Approaches to the Study of Consciousness*. Thorverton, Devon: Imprint Academic

Varela, Francisco J., Thompson, Evan, Rosch, Eleanor. 1991. *The Embodied Mind: Cognitive Science and Human Experience*. Cambridge, Massachusetts: The MIT Press

Veltman, Martinus. 2003. *Facts and Mysteries in Elementary Particle Physics*. River Edge, New Jersey: World Scientific Publishing Co. Pte. Ltd.

Visser, Frank. 2003. *Ken Wilber: Thought as Passion*. Albany, New York: State University of New York Press

Walker, Evan Harris. 2000. *The Physics of Consciousness*. Cambridge, Massachusetts: Perseus Publishing

Wallenstein, Gene. 2002. *Mind, Stress, and Emotions: The New Science of Mood*. Boston: Commonwealth Press

Ward, Keith. 1996. *God, Chance and Necessity*. Oxford: Oneworld Publications Ltd.

Wassermann, Gerhard D. 1993. *Shadow Matter and Psychic Phenomena*. Oxford: Mandrake of Oxford

Webb, Stephen. 2004. *Out of This World: Colliding Universes, Branes, Strings, and Other Wild Ideas of Modern Physics*. New York: Copernicus Books/Springer-Verlag

Wheatley, Jerry Davidson. 2001. *The Nature of Consciousness The Structure of Reality: Theory of Everything Equation Revealed. Scientific Verification and Proof of Logic God Is*. Phoenix, Arizona: Research Scientific Press

Wilber, Ken. 1982. *The Holographic Paradigm and Other Paradoxes*. Boulder, Colorado: Shambhala Publications Inc.

Wilber, Ken. 1995. *Sex, Ecology, Spirituality*. Boston: Shambhala Publications Inc.

Wilber, Ken. 2000. *A Theory of Everything: An Integral Vision for Business, Politics, Science and Spirituality.* Boston: Shambhala Publications Inc.

Wilber, Ken. 2001. *Quantum Questions: Mystical Writings of the World's Greatest Physicists.* Boston: Shambhala Publications Inc.

Wolf, Fred Alan. 1984. *Star Wave: Mind, Consciousness, and Quantum Physics.* New York: Macmillan Publishing Company

Wolf, Fred Alan. 1986. *The Body Quantum.* New York: Macmillan Publishing Company

Wolfram, Stephen. 2002. *A New Kind of Science.* Champaign, Illinois: Wolfram Media Inc.

Wright, Robert. 2000. *Nonzero: The Logic of Human Destiny.* New York: Vintage Books

Wyller, Arne A. 1999. *The Creating Consciousness: Science as the Language of God.* Denver, Colorado: Divina

Zajonc, Arthur (Editor). 2004. *The New Physics and Cosmology: Dialogues with the Dalai Lama.* New York: Oxford University Press

Zee, A. 2003. *Quantum Field Theory in a Nutshell.* Princeton, New Jersey: Princeton University Press

Zeman, Adam. 2002. *Consciousness: A User's Guide.* New Haven: Yale University Press

Zohar, Danah. 1990. *The Quantum Self: Human Nature and Consciousness Defined by the New Physics.* New York: William Morrow and Company Inc.

Zohar, Danah, Marshall, Ian. 1993. *The Quantum Society: Mind, Physics and a New Social Vision.* New York: William Morrow and Company Inc.

Zohar, Danah, Marshall, Ian. 2004. *Spiritual Capital: Wealth We Can Live By.* San Francisco: Berrett-Koehler Publishers Inc.

Zukav, Gary. 1979. *The Dancing Wu Li Masters: An Overview of the New Physics.* New York: William Morrow and Company Inc.

Zukav, Gary. 1991. *The Seat of the Soul: Inspiring Vision of Humanity's Spiritual Destiny.* London: Rider

Zwiebach, Barton. 2004. *A First Course in String Theory*, Cambridge, England: Cambridge University Press

> http://fergusmurray.members.beeb.net/Causality.html
>
> http://physicsweb.org/articles/news/7/9/2
>
> http://plato.stanford.edu/entries/qt-entangle/
>
> http://whatis.techtarget.com/definition/0,sid9_gci341428,00.html
>
> http://www.cosmopolis.com/topics/quantum-nonlocality.html
>
> http://www.integralnaked.org
>
> http://www.joot.com/dave/writings/articles/entanglement/
>
> http://www.lifescientists.de/publication/pub2003-04-1.htm
>
> http://www.newscientist.com/article.ns?id=dn2564
>
> http://www.noetic.org
>
> http://www.princeton.edu/~pear/
>
> http://www.sheldrake.org/

I also highly recommend two magazines that regularly explore many of the topics that I discuss throughout the book.

> http://www.magicalblend.com
>
> http://www.spiritualityhealth.com

Chapter Two: Straws in the Wind

Baker, Douglas M. 1975. *The Jewel in the Lotus: Volume One of The Seven Pillars of Ancient Wisdom*. Essendon, Hertfordshire: Baker Publications

Barabási, Albert-László. 2002. *Linked: How Everything Is Connected to Everything Else and What It Means*. Cambridge, Massachusetts: Perseus Publishing

Beinfield, Harriet, Korngold, Efrem. 1992. *Between Heaven and Earth: A Guide to Chinese Medicine*. New York: Ballantine Books

Chia, Mantak. 2005. *Golden Elixir Chi Kung.* Rochester, Vermont: Destiny Books

Cohen, Kenneth S. 1997. *The Way of Qigong: The Art and Science of Chinese Energy Healing.* New York: Ballantine Books

Deadman, Peter, Baker, Kevin, Al-Khafaji. 1998. *A Manual of Acupuncture.* Vista, California: Eastland Press

Flaws, Bob, Sionneau, Philippe. 2001. *The Treatment of Modern Western Medical Diseases with Chinese Medicine: A Textbook and Clinical Manual.* Boulder, Colorado: Blue Poppy Press

Foss, Laurence. 2002. *The End of Modern Medicine.* Albany, New York: State University of New York Press

Foss, Laurence, Rothenburg, Kenneth. 1987. *The Second Medical Revolution: Biomedicine to Infomedicine.* New York: Random House Inc.

Laszlo, Ervin, Abraham, Ralph H. 2003. *The Connectivity Hypothesis: Foundations of an Integral Science of Quantum, Cosmos, Life and Consciousness.* Albany, New York: State University of New York Press

Laszlo, Ervin. 2004. *Science and the Akashic Field: An Integral Theory of Everything.* Rochester, Vermont: Inner Traditions

Liang, Shou-Yu, Wu, Wen-Chiang. 1997. *Qigong Empowerment: A Guide to Medical Taoist Buddhist Wushu Energy Cultivation.* East Providence, Rhode Island: The Way of the Dragon Publishing

Lin, Zixin. 2000. *Qigong: Chinese Medicine or Pseudoscience?* Amherst, Massachusetts: Prometheus Books

Maciocia, Giovanni. 1989. *The Foundations Of Chinese Medicine: A Comprehensive Text for Acupuncturists and Herbalists.* Edinburgh: Churchill Livingstone

Maciocia, Giovanni. 2004. *Diagnosis in Chinese Medicine. A Comprehensive Guide.* Edinburgh: Churchill Livingstone

Phalen, Kathleen F. 1998. *Integrative Medicine: Achieving Wellness Through the Best of Eastern and Western Medical Practices.* Boston: Journey Editions

Weil, Andrew. 1995. *Spontaneous Healing: How to Discover and Enhance Your Body's Natural Ability to Maintain and Heal Itself.* New York: Ballantine Books

Chapter Three: Our Changing Planet, Our Evolving People

Ardrey, Robert. 1976. *The Hunting Hypothesis: A Personal Conclusion Concerning the Evolutionary Nature of Man.* London: William Collins Sons & Co. Ltd.

Arsuaga, Juan Luis. 2002. *The Neanderthal's Necklace: In Search of the First Thinkers.* New York: Four Walls Eight Windows

Badcock, Christopher. 1989. *Oedipus in Evolution: A New Theory of Sex.* Oxford: Basil Blackwell

Bateson, Gregory. 1973. *Steps to an Ecology of Mind: Collected Essays in Anthropology, Psychiatry, Evolution, and Epistemology.* Frogmore, St Albans, Hertfordshire: Paladin Books

Bateson, Gregory. 1979. *Mind and Nature: A Necessary Unity.* London: Wildwood House

Boaz, Noel. 2002. *Evolving Health: The Origins of Illness and How the Modern World is making Us Sick.* New York: John Wiley & Sons Inc.

Boyd, Graham W. 1989. *On Stress Disease and Evolution.* Hobart: University of Tasmania

Brooks, Daniel R., Wiley, Edward O. 1986. *Evolution as Entropy: Toward a Unified Theory of Biology.* Chicago: University of Chicago Press

Brune, Martin (Editor), Ribbert, Hedda (Editor), Schiefenhovel, Wulf (Editor). 2003. *The Social Brain: Evolution and Pathology.* Chichester, West Sussex: John Wiley and Sons Ltd.

Burnham, Terry, Phelan, Jay. 2000. *Mean Genes: From Sex to Money to Food. Taming Our Primal Instincts.* Cambridge, Massachusetts: Perseus Publishing

Buss, David M. 1994. *The Evolution of Desire.* New York: Basic Books

Buss, David M. 1999. *Evolutionary Psychology: The New Science of the Mind*. Needham Heights, Massachusetts: Allyn and Bacon

Calvin, William H. 1990. *The Cerebral Symphony: Seashore Reflections on the Structure of Consciousness*. New York: Bantam

Calvin, William H. 2002. *A Brain for All Seasons: Human Evolution and Abrupt Climate Change*. Chicago: University of Chicago Press

Calvin, William H. 2004. *A Brief History of the Mind: From Apes to Intellect and Beyond*. Oxford: Oxford University Press

Cavalli-Sforza, Luigi Luca, Cavalli-Sforza, Francesco. 1995. *The Great Human Diasporas*. Cambridge, Massachusetts: Perseus Books

Corballis, Michael C. 1991. *The Lopsided Ape: Evolution of the Generative Mind*. New York: Oxford University Press

Coren, Richard L. 1998. *Evolutionary Trajectory: The Growth of Information in the History and Future of the Earth*. Langhorne, Pennsylvania: Gordon and Breach

Crook, John. 1980. *The Evolution of Human Consciousness*. Oxford: Clarendon Press

Dawkins, Richard. 2004. *The Ancestor's Tale: A Pilgrimage to the Dawn of Evolution*. Boston: Houghton Mifflin Company

Deacon, Terrence W. 1997. *The Symbolic Species: The Co-Evolution of Language and the Brain*. New York: W. W. Norton & Company

Donald, Merlin. 2001. *A Mind So Rare: The Evolution of Human Consciousness*. New York: W. W. Norton & Company

Dunbar, Robin. 1996. *Grooming, Gossip, and the Evolution of Language*. Cambridge, Massachusetts: Harvard University Press

Eccles, J.C. 1989. *Evolution of the Brain: Creation of the Self*. London: Routledge

Ewald, Paul W. 2000. *Plague Time: How Stealth Infections Cause Cancer, Heart Disease, and Other Deadly Ailments*. New York: The Free Press

Forbes, Nancy. 2004. *Imitation of Life: How Biology Is Inspiring Computing*. The MIT Press: Cambridge, Massachusetts

Geary, David C. 1998. *Male, Female: The Evolution of Human Sex Differences.* Washington, D.C.: American Psychological Association

Gisolfi, Carl V., Mora, Francisco. 2000. *The Hot Brain: Survival, Temperature, and the Human Body.* Cambridge, Massachusetts: Bradford Books/The MIT Press

Goertzel, Ben. 1993. *The Evolving Mind.* Langhorne, Pennsylvania: Gordon and Breach Publishers

Gould, Stephen Jay. 2002. *The Structure of Evolutionary Theory.* Cambridge, Massachusetts: Harvard University Press

Grant, Valerie J. 1998. *Maternal Personality, Evolution and the Sex Ratio.* London: Routledge

Harper, R.M.J. 1975. *Evolutionary Origins of Disease.* Barnstable, England: G. Mosdell

Harris, Marvin (Editor), Ross, Eric B. (Editor). 1987. *Food and Evolution: Toward a Theory of Human Food Habits.* Philadelphia: Temple University Press

Harrison, G.A. (Editor), Morphy, Howard (Editor). 1998. *Human Adaptation.* Oxford: Berg

Horrobin, David. 2001. *The Madness of Adam and Eve: How Schizophrenia Shaped Humanity.* New York: Bantam Press

Humphrey, Nicholas. 1992. *A History of the Mind: Evolution and the Birth of the Consciousness.* New York: Simon & Schuster Inc.

Jaynes, Julian. 1977. *The Origins of Consciousness in the Breakdown of the Bicameral Mind.* Boston: Houghton Mifflin

Katsenelinboigen, Aron I. 1997. *Evolutionary Change.* Amsterdam: Gordon and Breach Publishers

Kegan, Robert. 1983. *The Evolving Self.* Cambridge, Massachusetts: Harvard University Press

Kingdon, Jonathan. 1996. *Self-Made Man: Human Evolution from Eden to Extinction?* New York: Wiley

Klawans, Harold L. 2000. *Defending the Cavewoman: And Other Tales of Evolutionary Neurology.* New York: W. W. Norton & Company

Klein, Richard G., Edgar, Blake. 2002. *The Dawn of Human Culture.* New York: Wiley

Konner, Melvin J. 1990. *The Tangled Wing: Biological Constraints on the Human Spirit.* New York: Henry Holt & Company Inc.

Kurten, Bjorn. 1984. *Not from the Apes: A History of Man's Origins and Evolution.* New York: Columbia University Press

Laland, Kevin N., Brown, Gillian. 2002. *Sense and Nonsense: Evolutionary Perspectives on Human Behaviour.* Oxford: Oxford University Press

Laszlo, Ervin. 1987. *Evolution, the Grand Synthesis.* Boston, Massachusetts: New Science Library

Laszlo, Ervin. 1994. *The Choice: Evolution or Extinction?* New York: Jeremy P. Tarcher/Putnam Books

Laszlo, Ervin (Editor). 1993. *The Evolution of Cognitive Maps.* Amsterdam: Gordon and Breach Publishers

Lockley, Martin. 1999. *Eternal Trail. A Tracker Looks at Evolution.* Reading Massachusetts: Perseus Books

McFadden, Johnjoe. 2002. *Quantum Evolution: How Physics' Weirdest Theory Explains Life's Biggest Mystery.* New York: W. W. Norton & Company

Maclean, Paul D. 1990. *The Triune Brain in Evolution. Role in Paleocerebral Functions.* New York: Plenum Press

Moore, David S. 2001. *The Dependent Gene: The Fallacy of "Nature vs. Nurture".* New York: A.W.H. Freeman Books/Henry Holt and Company

Moore, Janice. 2002. *Parasites and the Behavior of Animals.* Oxford: Oxford University Press

Narby, Jeremy. 1998. *The Cosmic Serpent: DNA and the Origins of Knowledge.* New York: Jeremy P. Tarcher/Putnam

Nesse, Randolph M., Williams, George C. 1996. *Why We Get Sick: The New Science of Darwinian Medicine.* New York: Vintage Books

Palumbi, Stephen R. 2001. *The Evolution Explosion: How Humans Cause Rapid Evolutionary Change.* New York: W. W. Norton & Company Inc.

Pink, Daniel H. 2005. *A Whole New Mind: Moving from the Information Age to the Conceptual Age,* New York: Riverhead Books

Plotkin, Henry. 2004. *Evolutionary Thought in Psychology: A Brief History.* Oxford: Blackwell Publishing

Ratey, John J., Johnson, Catherine. 1997. *Shadow Syndromes: The Mild Forms of Major Mental Disorders That Sabotage Us.* New York: Pantheon Books

Richerson, Peter J., Boyd, Robert. 2005. *Not by Genes Alone: How Culture Transformed Human Evolution.* Chicago: The University of Chicago Press

Rose, Hilary (Editor), Rose, Steven (Editor). 2000. *Alas, Poor Darwin: Arguments Against Evolutionary Psychology.* New York: Harmony Books

Rose, Steven. 2005. *The Future of the Brain: The Promise and Perils of Tomorrow's Neuroscience,* New York: Oxford University Press Inc.

Stearns, Stephen (Editor). 1999. *Evolution in Health and Disease.* Oxford: Oxford University Press

Steiner, Rudolf. 1989. *The Evolution of the World & of Humanity.* Blauvelt, New York: Spiritual Science Library

Stevens, Anthony, Price, John. 1996. *Evolutionary Psychiatry.* London: Routledge

Stinson, Sara (Editor), Bogin, Barry (Editor), Huss-Ashmore, Rebecca (Editor), O'Rourke, Dennis (Editor). 2000. *Human Biology: An Evolutionary and Biocultural Perspective.* New York: Wiley-Liss Inc.

Trevathan, Wenda R. (Editor), Smith, E. O. (Editor), McKenna, James J. (Editor). 1999. *Evolutionary Medicine.* New York: Oxford University Press

Wilson, Edward Osborne. 2002. *The Future of Life.* New York: Knopf

Chapter Four: The Evolving Laws of Health and Healing

Aunger, Robert. 2002. *The Electric Meme: A New Theory of How We Think and Communicate.* New York: The Free Press

Beck, Don Edward, Cowan, Christopher C. 1996. *Spiral Dynamics.* Malden, Massachusetts: Blackwell Publishers Inc.

Blackmore, Susan. 1999. *The Meme Machine.* Oxford: Oxford University Press

Whiting, Lloyd Harrison. 2002. *The Complete Universe of Memes.* San Jose, California: Writers Club Press

Wilber, Ken. 2000a. *Integral Psychology.* Boston: Shambhala Publications Inc.

Wilber, Ken. 2000b. *A Theory of Everything: An Integral Vision for Business, Politics, Science and Spirituality.* Boston: Shambhala Publications Inc.

Wright, Robert. 2000. *Nonzero: The Logic of Human Destiny.* New York: Vintage Books

http://www.spiraldynamics.org/
www.spiraldynamics.net
www.spiraldynamicsgroup.com/
www.spiraldynamics.intranets.com/

Chapter Five: Beyond the Clockwork Universe

Becker, Robert O., Selden, Gary. 1985. *The Body Electric: Electromagnetism and the Foundation of Life.* New York: Quill

Dziemidko, Helen E. 1999. *The Complete Book of Energy Medicines: Choosing Your Path to Health.* Rochester, Vermont: Healing Arts Press

Eden, Donna. 1999. *Energy Medicine.* Los Angeles: J. P. Tarcher

Emoto, Masuru. 1999. *The Message from Water I.* Tokyo, Japan: HADO Kyoikusha

Emoto, Masuru. 2003. *The Message from Water II.* Tokyo, Japan: HADO Kyoikusha

Emoto, Masuru. 2004a. *The Message from Water III*. Tokyo, Japan: HADO Kyoikusha

Emoto, Masuru. 2004b. *The Hidden Messages in Water*. Hillsboro, Oregon: Beyond Words Publishing

Goerner, S.J. 1999. *After the Clockwork Universe: The Emerging Science and Culture of Integral Society*. Edinburgh: Floris Books

Jacka, Judy. 2003. *Synthesis in Healing*. Charlottesville, Virginia: Hampton Roads Publishing Company Inc.

Jonas, Wayne B., Jacobs, Jennifer. 1996. *Healing with Homeopathy: The Complete Guide*. New York: Warner Books Inc.

Lee, Richard H. 1997. *Bioelectric Vitality: Exploring the Science of Human Energy*. San Clemente, California: Chine Healthways Institute

McTaggart, Lynne. 2001. *The Field: The Quest for the Secret Force of the Universe*. London: HarperCollins

Maturana, Humberto R., Varela, Francisco J. 1988. *The Tree of Knowledge*. Boston, Massachusetts: New Science Library/Shambhala

Rubik, Beverly. 1989. *The Interrelationship Between Mind and Matter*. Philadelphia: The Center for Frontier Studies

Schlitz, Marilyn (Editor), Amorok, Tina (Editor), Micozzi, Marc S. (Editor). 2005. *Consciousness and Healing: Integral Approaches to Mind-Body Medicine*. St. Louis, Missouri: Elsevier Churchill Livingstone

Sheldrake, Rupert. 1981. *A New Science of Life*. London: Blond and Briggs

Sheldrake, Rupert. 1988. *The Presence of the Past*. London: Collins

Sheldrake, Rupert. 1994. *Seven Experiments That Could Change the World*. London: Fourth Estate Limited

Sheldrake, Rupert. 1999. *Dogs That Know When Their Owners Are Coming Home*. New York: Crown Publishers

Sheldrake, Rupert. 2003. *The Sense of Being Stared At*. London: Hutchinson

Sheldrake, Rupert, McKenna, Terence, Abraham, Ralph. 1998. *The Evolutionary Mind: Trialogues at the Edge of the Unthinkable.* Santa Cruz, California: Trialogue Press

Sperber, Dan. 1996. *Explaining Culture: A Naturalistic Approach.* Malden, Massachusetts: Blackwell Publishers Ltd.

Tiller, William A., Holland, Jack. 1997. *Science and Human Transformation: Subtle Energies, Intentionality and Consciousness.* Walnut Creek, California: Pavior Publishing

Tiller, William A., Dibble, Walter, Kohane, Michael. 2001. *Conscious Acts of Creation.* Walnut Creek, California: Pavior Publishing

> http://heartmath.org/
> http://science-spirit.org/
> http://wilber.shambhala.com/html/books/kosmos/excerptG/part1.cfm/
> http://www.bion.si/DVB03/detection_biofield_ambient_light_ijs03.htm
> http://www.datadiwan.de/SciMedNet/home.htm
> http://www.energytoolsint.com/lecture/chi_missing_link.htm
> http://www.issseem.org/
> http://www.noetic.org/publications/research/main.cfm?page=frontiers_59.htm
> http://www.sheldrake.org/
> http://www.whalemedical.com/ap1.html
> http://www.whps.com/misaha/hypot.htm

Chapter Six: Hidden Harbingers of Health

Baker, Douglas. 1976. *Esoteric Anatomy, Part One.* Essendon, Hertfordshire: Baker Publications

Baker, Douglas. 1979. *Esoteric Anatomy, Part Two.* Essendon, Hertfordshire: Baker Publications

Bek, Lilla, Pullar, Phillipa. 1995. *Healing with Chakra Energy: Restoring the Natural Harmony of the Body.* Rochester, Vermont: Inner Traditions International Ltd.

Brennan, Barbara Ann. 1988. *Hands of Light: A Guide to Healing Through the Human Energy Field.* New York: Bantam

Bruyere, Rosalyn L, Farrens, Jeanne. 1994. *Wheels of Light: Chakras, Auras and the Healing Energy of the Body.* New York: Fireside

Burger, Bruce. 1997. *Esoteric Anatomy: The Body as Consciousness.* Berkeley, California: North Atlantic Books

Carnie, L.V. 1997. *Chi Gung: Chinese Healing, Energy, and Natural Magick.* St. Paul, Minnesota: Llewellyn Publications

Eberle, Gary. 2003. *Sacred Time and the Search for Meaning.* Boston: Shambhala Publications Inc.

Frankl, Viktor E. 1952. *The Doctor and the Soul.* Harmondsworth, Middlesex, England: Penguin Books Ltd.

Frankl, Viktor E. 1992. *Man's Search for Meaning: An Introduction to Logotherapy.* Boston: Beacon Press

Galian, Laurence. 1995. *Beyond Duality: The Art of Transcendence.* Tempe, Arizona: New Falcon Publications

Gerber, Richard. 2000. *Vibrational Medicine for the 21st Century: The Complete Guide to Energy Healing and Spiritual Transformation.* New York: Eagle Brook

Groddeck, G. 1977. *The Meaning of Illness.* London: Hogarth Press

Judith, Anodea. 1987. *Wheels of Life: A User's Guide to the Chakra System.* St. Paul, Minnesota: Llewellyn Publications

Judith, Anodea. 1990. *The Truth About Chakras.* St. Paul, Minnesota: Llewellyn Publications

Judith, Anodea. 1996. *Eastern Body, Western Mind: Psychology and the Chakra System as a Path to the Self.* Berkeley, California: Celestial Arts

Kidel, Mark (Editor), Rowe-Leete, Susan (Editor). 1988. *The Meaning of Illness.* London: Routledge & Kegan Paul Ltd.

Kit, Wong Kiew. 1993. *The Art of Chi Kung: Making the Most of Your Vital Energy.* Longmead, Shaftesbury, Dorset: Element Books Ltd.

Loewer, Barry (Editor), Rey, George (Editor). 1991. *Meaning in Mind: Fodor and his Critics.* Oxford: Blackwell Publishing

MacFlouer, Niles. 1999. *Life's Meaning.* Tempe, Arizona: Ageless Wisdom Publishers

Modell, Arnold H. 2003. *Imagination and the Meaningful Brain.* Cambridge, Massachusetts: The MIT Press

Motoyama, Hiroshi. 1981. *Theories of the Chakras: Bridge to Higher Consciousness.* New Delhi, India: New Age Books

Naylor, Thomas H., Willimon, William H., Naylor, Magdalena R. 1994. *The Search for Meaning.* Nashville, Tennessee: Abingdon Press

Ottoson, David (Editor). 1987. *Duality and Unity of the Brain.* New York: Macmillan

Pattakos, Alex. 2004. *Prisoners of Our Thoughts: Viktor Frankl's Principles at Work.* San Francisco: Berrett-Koehler Publishers Inc.

Pert, Candace. 1999. *The Molecules of Emotion: The Science Behind Mind-Body Medicine.* New York: Simon & Schuster Inc.

Rosemergy, Jim. 1999. *The Quest for Meaning: Living a Life of Purpose.* Unity Village, Missouri: Unity Books

Shumsky, Susan G., Charak, K.S. 2003. *Exploring Chakras: Awaken Your Untapped Energy.* Franklin Lakes, New Jersey: New Page Books

Snow, Tiffany. 2004. *The Power of the Divine: A Healer's Guide. Tapping Into the Miracle.* San Diego, California: Spirit Journey Books

Sontag, Susan. 1989. *Illness as Metaphor, and AIDS and Its Metaphors.* New York: Anchor Books

Tansley, David. 1984. *Chakras—Rays and Radionics.* Saffron Walden, Essex, England: C. W. Daniel Company Ltd.

Taylor, Daniel. 1996. *The Healing Power of Stories: Creating Yourself Through the Stories of Your Life.* New York: Doubleday

Templeton, John Marks. 1997. *Worldwide Laws of Life: 200 Eternal Spiritual Principles.* Philadelphia: Templeton Foundation Press

Virtue, Doreen. 1998. *Chakra Clearing*. Carlsbad, California: Hay House Inc.

Whiteman, J.H.M. 1986. *Old and New Evidence on the Meaning of Life: An Introduction to Scientific Mysticism*. London: Colin Smythe Ltd

Chapter Seven: Expanding Concepts of Health and Disease

Addington, Jack Ensign. 1979. *The Secret of Healing*. Marina del Rey, California: DeVorss and Company Publishers

Assagioli, Roberto. 1965. *Psychosynthesis*. Wellingborough, Northamptonshire: Turnstone Press Ltd.

Assagioli, Roberto. 1973. *The Act of Will*. London: Wildwood House

Ballentine, Rudolph. 1999. *Radical Healing: Integrating the World's Great Therapeutic Traditions to Create a New Transforming Medicine*. New York: Harmony Books

Barasch, Marc Ian. 1993. *The Healing Path: A Soul Approach to Illness*. New York: Jeremy P. Tarcher/Putnam Books

Benor, Daniel J. 2001a. *Spiritual Healing: A Scientific Validation of a Healing Revolution*. Southfield, Michigan: Vision Publications

Benor, Daniel J. 2001b. *Spiritual Healing; Professional Edition*. Southfield, Michigan: Vision Publications

Benor, Daniel J. 2004. *Consciousness, Bioenergy and Healing. Healing Research, Volume II*. Medford, New Jersey: Wholistic Healing Publications

Caine, Kenneth Winston, Kaufman, Brian Paul. 1999. *Prayer, Faith and Healing: Cure Your Body, Heal Your Mind, and Restore Your Soul*. Emmaus, Pennsylvania: Rodale Press Inc.

Castleman, Michael. 2000. *Blended Medicine: The Best Choices in Healing. The Breakthrough System That Combines Natural, Alternative and Mainstream Medicine*. Emmaus, Pennsylvania: Rodale Press Inc.

Chia, Mantak. 1983. *Awaken Healing Energy Through the Tao*. New York: Aurora Press

Chopra, Deepak. 1990. *Quantum Healing*. New York: Harmony Books

Chopra, Deepak. 1993. *Ageless Body, Timeless Mind: The Quantum Alternative to Growing Old*. New York: Harmony Books

Deci, Edward L., Flaste, Richard. 1995. *Why We Do What We Do: Understanding Self-Motivation*. New York: Penguin Putnam Inc.

Dossey, Larry. 1993. *Healing Words*. San Francisco: Harper San Francisco

Dossey, Larry. 1999. *Reinventing Medicine*. San Francisco: Harper San Francisco

Dossey, Larry. 2001. *Healing Beyond the Body*. Boston: Shambhala Publications Inc.

Elmiger, Jean. 1998. *Rediscovering Real Medicine*. Rockport, Massachusetts: Element

Ferrucci, Piero. 2004. *What We May Be: Techniques for Psychological and Spiritual Growth Through Psychosynthesis*. New York: Jeremy P. Tarcher/Penguin

Firman, John, Gila, Ann. 2002. *Psychosynthesis: A Psychology of the Spirit*. Albany, New York: State University of New York Press

Friedman, Norman. 1990. *Bridging Science and Spirit: Common Elements in David Bohm's Physics, the Perennial Philosophy and Seth*. St. Louis, Missouri: Living Lake Books

Gerber, Richard. 2000. *Vibrational Medicine for the 21st Century: The Complete Guide to Energy Healing and Spiritual Transformation*. New York: Eagle Brook

Gerber, Richard. 2001. *Vibrational Medicine*. Santa Fe, New Mexico: Bear & Company Publishing Inc.

Gordon, Marilyn. 2000. *Extraordinary Healing: Transforming Your Consciousness, Your Energy System, and Your Life*. Oakland, California: Wiseworld Publishing

Hopking, Alan. 2005. *Esoteric Healing: A Practical Guide Based on the Teachings of the Tibetan in the Works of Alice A. Bailey*. Nevada City, California: Blue Dolphin Publishing

Koenig, Harold G. 1999. *The Healing Power of Faith: Science Explores Medicine's Last Great Frontier.* New York: Simon & Schuster

Koenig, Harold G. 2003. *Purpose and Power in Retirement: New Opportunities for Meaning and Significance.* Radnor, Pennsylvania: Templeton Foundation Press

Kohatsu, Wendy (Editor). 2002. *Complementary and Alternative Medicine Secrets.* Philadelphia, PA: Hanley & Belfus Inc.

Leider, Richard J. 1997. *The Power of Purpose: Creating Meaning in Your Life and Work.* San Francisco: Berrett-Koehler Publishers Inc.

Levesque, Lynne C. 2001. *Breakthrough Creativity: Achieving Top Performance Using the Eight Creative Talents.* Palo Alto, California: Davies-Black Publishing

Macdonald, Copthorne. 2004. *Matters of Consequence: Creating a Meaningful Life and a World That Works.* Charlottetown, Prince Edward Island, Canada: Big Ideas Press

McNamara, Rita. 1989. *Toward Balance: Psycho-Physical Integration and Vibrational Therapy.* York Beach, Maine: Red Wheel Weiser

Manning, Clark A., Vanrenen, Louis J. 1988. *Bioenergetic Medicines East and West.* Berkeley, California: North Atlantic Books

Marti, James E. 1998. *The Alternative Health and Medicine Encyclopedia.* Detroit: Visible Ink

Maslow, Abraham H. 1987. *Motivation and Personality.* New York: HarperCollins Publishers

Maslow, Abraham H., Lowry, Richard (Editor). 1968. *Toward a Psychology of Being.* New York: John Wiley & Sons Inc.

Mason, Keith. 1992. *Medicine for the Twenty-First Century: The Key to Healing with Vibrational Medicine.* Longmead, Shaftesbury, Dorset: Element Books

Matthews, Dale A., Clark, Connie. 1998. *The Faith Factor: Proof of the Healing Power of Prayer.* New York: Viking

Mellin, Laurel. 2003. *The Pathway: Follow the Road to Health and Happiness.* New York: Regan Books/HarperCollins

Micozzi, Marc S (Editor). 1996. *Fundamentals of Complementary and Alternative Medicine.* New York: Churchill Livingston

Murray, Michael, Pizzorno, Joseph. 1998. *Encyclopedia of Natural Medicine.* Roseville, California: Prima Health

Muskin, Philip R, ed. 2000. *Complementary and Alternative Medicine and Psychiatry,* Vol. 19. Washington, D.C.: American Psychiatric Association Press Inc.

Myss, Caroline. 1996. *Anatomy of the Spirit.* New York: Harmony Books

Phalen, Kathleen F. 1998. *Integrative Medicine: Achieving Wellness Through the Best of Eastern and Western Medical Practices.* Boston: Journey Editions

Pizzorno, Joseph E. (Editor), Murray, Michael T. (Editor). 1999. *Textbook of Natural Medicine.* New York: Churchill Livingstone

Rosemergy, Jim. 1999. *The Quest for Meaning: Living a Life of Purpose.* Unity Village, Missouri: Unity Books

Roth, Ron, Occhiogrosso, Peter. 1999. *Prayer and the Five Stages of Healing.* Carlsbad, California: Hay House Inc.

Samuels, Michael, Lane, Mary Rockwood. 1998. *Creative Healing: How to Heal Yourself by Tapping Your Hidden Creativity.* San Francisco: Harper

Sharma, Yubraj. 2004. *Spiritual Bioenergetics of Homoeopathic Materia Medica.* Wembley, Middlesex, England: Academy of Light Ltd.

Simon, David. 2000. *Vital Energy: The 7 Keys to Invigorate Body, Mind and Soul.* New York: John Wiley & Sons Inc.

Snow, Tiffany. 2004. *The Power of the Divine: A Healer's Guide. Tapping into the Miracle.* San Diego, California: Spirit Journey Books

Spencer, John W, Jacobs, Joseph J. 1999. *Complementary/Alternative Medicine. An Evidence-Based Approach.* St Louis: Mosby

Stanway, Andrew. 1982. *Alternative Medicine.* Harmondsworth, Middlesex, England: Penguin Books Ltd.

Sugiyama, Shojiro. 2002. *Aura, Ki, and Healing.* Chicago, Illinois: J. Toguri Mercantile Co.

Sylvest, Vernon M. 1996. *The Formula: Who Gets Sick, Who Gets Well, Who Is Happy, Who Is Unhappy, and Why.* Fairfield, Iowa: Sunstar Publishing Ltd.

Taylor, Eugene. 1997. *A Psychology of Spiritual Healing.* West Chester, Pennsylvania: Chrysalis Books

Thagard, Paul. 1999. *How Scientists Explain Disease.* Princeton, New Jersey: Princeton University Press

Vithoulkas, George. 1992. *A New Model of Health and Disease.* Berkeley, California: North Atlantic Books

Watt, James (Editor). 1988. *Talking Health: Conventional and Complementary Approaches.* London: Royal Society of Medicine Services Ltd.

Watts, Alan. 1973. *The Book on the Taboo Against Knowing Who You Are.* New York: Vintage Books

Weil, Andrew. 1983. *Health and Healing.* Boston: Houghton Mifflin

Werbach, Melvyn R. 1986. *Third Line Medicine.* London: Arkana

Wilber, Ken. 1980. *The Atman Project: A Transpersonal View of Human Development.* Wheaton, Illinois: Quest Books/Theosophical Publishing House

Wilber, Ken. 1995. *Sex, Ecology, Spirituality.* Boston: Shambhala Publications Inc.

Wilson, Colin. 1972. *New Pathways in Psychology: Maslow and the Post-Freudian Revolution.* London: Victor Gollancz

Wood, Matthew. 2000. *Vitalism: The History of Herbalism, Homeopathy, and Flower Essences.* Berkeley, California: North Atlantic Books

Wright, Machaelle Small. 1987. *Behaving as if the God in All Life Mattered.* Warrenton, Virginia: Perelandra, Limited

Young, Jacqueline. 2001. *The Healing Path: The Practical Guide to the Holistic Traditions of China, India, Tibet, and Japan.* London: Thorsons

Chapter Eight: Recruiting Your Allies

Armstrong, Thomas. 1999. *7 Kinds of Smart: Identifying and Developing Your Multiple Intelligences.* New York: Plume Books/New American Library

Baker, Douglas. 1993. *Stress Disorders.* Essendon, Hertfordshire: Baker Publications

Boyd, Graham W. 1989. *On Stress Disease and Evolution.* Hobart: University of Tasmania

Bremner, J. Douglas. 2002. *Does Stress Damage the Brain? Understanding Trauma-Related Disorders from a Neurological Perspective.* New York: W. W. Norton & Company

Brown, Jason, W. 1996. *Time, Will, and Mental Process (Cognition and Language).* New York: Plenum Press

Chia, Mantak. 1985. *Taoist Ways to Transform Stress into Vitality: The Inner Smile. Six Healing Sounds.* Huntington, New York: Healing Tao Books

Conrad, Sheree, Milburn, Michael. 2001. *Sexual Intelligence: The Groundbreaking Study That Shows You How to Boost Your "Sex IQ" and Gain Greater Sexual Satisfaction.* New York: Crown Publishers

Edwards, Paul. 1998. *The Spiritual Intelligence Handbook.* Kearney, Nebraska: Morris Publishing

Gardner, Howard. 1983. *Frames of Mind: The Theory of Multiple Intelligences.* New York: Basic Books

Gardner, Howard. 1993. *Multiple Intelligences: The Theory in Practice.* New York: Basic Books

Gardner, Howard. 1999. *Intelligence Reframed: Multiple Intelligences for the Twenty-First Century.* New York: Basic Books

Gardner, Howard. 2004. *Changing Minds: The Art and Science of Changing Our Own and Other People's Minds.* Boston, Massachusetts: Harvard Business School Press

Groves, Dawn. 2004. *Stress Reduction for Busy People*. Novato, California: New World Library

Haddock, Frank Channing. 1942. *Power of Will: A Practical Companion Book for the Unfoldment of the Powers of Mind*. Whitefish, Montana: Kessinger Publishing

Kahn, Ada P. 1998. *Stress A-Z: A Sourcebook for Facing Everyday Challenges*. New York: Facts On File Inc.

Khavari, Khalil A. 2000. *Spiritual Intelligence: A Practical Guide to Personal Happiness*. New Liskeard, Ontario: White Mountain Publications

Lenson, Barry. 2002. *Good Stress, Bad Stress: An Indispensible Guide to Identifying and Managing Your Stress*. New York: Marlowe & Company

Libet, Benjamin (Editor), Freeman, Anthony (Editor), Sutherland, Keith (Editor). 1999. *The Volitional Brain: Towards a Neuroscience of Free Will*. Thorverton, UK: Imprint Academic

Loehr, James E. 1997. *Stress for Success*. New York: Times Business

Loehr, Jim, Schwartz, Tony. 2003. *The Power of Full Engagement: Managing Energy, Not Time, Is the Key to High Performance and Personal Renewal*. New York: The Free Press

McEwen, Bruce, Lasley, Elizabeth. 2002. *The End of Stress as We Know It*. Washington, DC: National Academy Press

Mason, L. John. 1980. *Guide to Stress Reduction*. Culver City, California: Peace Press Inc.

Pelletier, Kenneth. 1977. *Mind as Healer, Mind as Slayer: A Holistic Approach to Preventing Stress Disorders*. New York: Dell Publishing Company Inc.

Sapolsky, Robert M. 1998. *Why Zebras Don't Get Ulcers: An Updated Guide to Stress, Stress-Related Diseases, and Coping*. New York: Henry Holt & Company Inc.

Saraydarian, Torkom. 1995. *The Mysteries of Willpower*. Cave Creek, Arizona: T.S.G. Publishing Foundation Inc.

Selye, Hans. 1978. *The Stress of Life*. New York: McGraw-Hill Education

Sisk, Dorothy A., Torrance, E. Paul. 2001. *Spiritual Intelligence: Developing Higher Consciousness.* Buffalo, New York: Creative Education Foundation Press

Steptoe, A, Appels, AD. 1989. *Stress, Personal Growth and Health.* Chichester: John Wiley & Sons

Wegner, Daniel M. 2002. *The Illusion of Conscious Will.* Cambridge, Massachusetts: The MIT Press

Chapter Nine: Creative Self-Integration

Adrienne, Carol. 1998. *The Purpose of Your Life: Finding Your Place in the World Using Synchronicity, Intuition and Uncommon Sense.* New York: Eagle Brook

Berger, Ruth. 1995. *Medical Intuition: How to Combine Inner Resources with Modern Medicine.* York Beach, Maine: Samuel Weiser Inc.

Capra, Fritjof. 1996. *The Web of Life: A New Understanding of Living Systems.* New York: Anchor Books

Claxton, Guy. 1999. *Wise Up: The Challenge of Lifelong Learning.* New York: Bloomsbury Publishing

Einstein, Patricia. 1997. *Intuition: The Path to Inner Wisdom. A Guide to Discovering and Using Your Greatest Natural Resource.* Rockport, Massachusetts: Element Books Inc.

Emery, Marcia. 1999. *The Intuitive Healer.* New York: St. Martin's Press

Karges, Craig. 1999. *Ignite Your Intuition.* Deerfield Beach, Florida: Health Communications Inc.

Knapp, Stephen. 2000. *How the Universe Was Created and Our Purpose in It.* Detroit, Michigan: The World Relief Network

Koenig, Harold G. 2003. *Purpose and Power in Retirement: New Opportunities for Meaning and Significance.* Radnor, Pennsylvania: Templeton Foundation Press

McCarthy, Kevin W. 1992. *The On-Purpose Person: Making Your Life Make Sense*. Colorado Springs, Colorado: Pinon Publishers

McCartney, Francesca. 2001. *Intuition Medicine: The Science of Energy*. Mill Valley, California: Academy of Intuitive Studies and Intuition Medicine

Mierswa, Ruth. 1998. *Who You Are and Why You Are Here: Find Your Life Purpose and Personality Type*. Fairport, New York: Rainbow Gateway

Millman, Dan. 1993. *The Life You Were Born to Live: A Guide to Finding Your Life Purpose*. Tiburon, California: H.J. Kramer Inc.

Roberts, Denton L., Thronson, Frances Ann. 1997. *Find Purpose, Find Power: Sing the Song in Your Heart*. Los Angeles: Human Esteem Publishing

Robinson, Lynn A. 2001. *Divine Intuition: Your Guide to Creating a Life You Love*. New York: Dorling Kindersley

Schulz, Mona Lisa. 1998. *Awakening Intuition: Using Your Mind-Body Network for Insight and Healing*. New York: Harmony Books

Sisk, Dorothy A., Torrance, E. Paul. 2001. *Spiritual Intelligence: Developing Higher Consciousness*. Buffalo, New York: Creative Education Foundation Press

Thurston, Mark. 1984. *Discovering Your Soul's Purpose*. Virginia Beach, Virginia: A.R.E. Press

Warren, Rick. 2002. *The Purpose-Driven Life: What on Earth Am I Here For?* Grand Rapids, Michigan: Zondervan Publishing House

Watts, Alan, Watts, Mark (Editor). 2003. *Become What You Are*. Boston, Massachusetts: Shambhala Publications Inc.

Wilde, Stuart. 2003. *Sixth Sense: Including the Secrets of the Etheric Subtle Body*. Carlsbad, California: Hay House Inc.

Chapter Ten: Mind Control

Arenson, Gloria. 2001. *Five Simple Steps to Emotional Healing: The Last Self-Help Book You Will Ever Need.* New York: Fireside Book/Simon & Schuster

Callahan, Roger J. 2001. *Tapping the Healer Within: Using Thought-Field Therapy to Instantly Conquer Your Fears, Anxieties and Emotional Distress.* Lincolnwood (Chicago), Illinois: Contemporary Books

Callahan, Roger J., Callahan, Joanne. 2000. *Stop the Nightmares of Trauma: Thought Field Therapy, The Power Therapy for the 21st Century.* Chapel Hill, North Carolina: Professional Press

Charlton, Bruce. 2000. *Psychiatry and the Human Condition.* Oxford: Radcliffe Medical Press

Churchland, Patricia S., Sejnowski, Terrence J. 1992. *The Computational Brain.* Cambridge, Massachusetts: Bradford Books

Damasio, Antonio R. 1994. *Descartes' Error: Emotion, Reason and the Human Brain.* New York: G. P. Putnam's and Sons

Damasio, Antonio R. 1999. *The Feeling of What Happens: Body and Emotion in the Making of Consciousness.* New York: Harcourt Brace and Company

Damasio, Antonio R. 2003. *Looking for Spinoza: Joy, Sorrow, and the Feeling Brain.* New York: Harcourt Inc.

Diepold, John H., Britt, Victoria, Bender, Sheila. 2004. *Evolving Thought Field Therapy: The Clinician's Handbook of Diagnoses, Treatment, and Theory.* New York: W. W. Norton

Durlacher, James V. 1995. *Freedom from Fear Forever: The Acu-Power Way to Overcoming Your Fears, Phobias and Inner Problems.* Tempe, Arizona: Van Ness Publishing Co.

Edelman, Gerald M., Tononi, Giulio. 2000. *A Universe of Consciousness: How Matter Becomes Imagination.* New York: Basic Books

Flint, Garry A. 1999. *Emotional Freedom.* Vernon, British Columbia: NeoSolTerric Enterprises

Friedberg, Fred. 2001. *Do-It-Yourself Eye Movement Technique for Emotional Healing.* Oakland, California: New Harbinger Publications Inc.

Furman, Mark Evan, Gallo, Fred P. 2000. *The Neurophysics of Human Behavior: Explorations at the Interface of the Brain, Mind, Behavior, and Information.* Boca Raton, Florida: CRC Press

Gallo, Fred P. 1999. *Energy Psychology.* Boca Raton, Florida: CRC Press

Gallo, Fred P. 2000. *Energy Diagnostic and Treatment Methods.* New York: W.W. Norton and Company Inc.

Gallo, Fred P. (Editor). 2002. *Energy Psychology in Psychotherapy.* New York: W.W. Norton and Company Inc.

Gallo, Fred P., Vincenzi, Harry. 2000. *Energy Tapping.* Oakland, CA: New Harbinger Publications Inc.

Gazzaniga, Michael S. 1985. *The Social Brain: Discovering the Networks of the Mind.* New York: Basic Books Inc.

Gazzaniga, Michael S. 1998. *The Mind's Past.* Berkeley, California: University of California Press

Gazzaniga, Michael S. (Editor). 2000. *The New Cognitive Neurosciences.* Cambridge, Massachusetts: The MIT Press

Gilkeson, Jim. 2000. *Energy Healing. A Pathway to Inner Growth.* New York: Marlowe and Company

Houshmand, Zara (Editor), Livingstone, Robert B. (Editor), Wallace, B. Alan (Editor). 1999. *Consciousness at the Crossroads: Conversations with the Dalai Lama on Brain Science and Buddhism.* Ithaca, New York: Snow Lion Publications

Lambrou, Peter T., Pratt, George J. 2000. *Instant Emotional Healing.* New York: Broadway Books

Ledoux, Joseph. 1996. *The Emotional Brain: The Mysterious Underpinnings of Emotional Life.* New York: Simon & Schuster

Llinas, Rodolfo R. (Editor), Churchland, Patricia Smith (Editor). 1996. *The Mind-Brain Continuum: Sensory Processes.* Cambridge: Bradford Books/The MIT Press

Lynch, Valerie, Lynch, Paul. 2001. *Emotional Healing in Minutes.* Hammersmith, London: Thorsons

Nunez, Rafael (Editor), Freeman, Walter J. (Editor). 2000. *Reclaiming Cognition: The Primacy of Action, Intention and Emotion.* Thorverton, United Kingdom: Imprint Academic

Phillips, Maggie. 2000. *Finding the Energy to Heal.* New York: W. W. Norton & Company

Sapolsky, Robert M. 2002. *A Primate's Memoir: A Neuroscientist's Unconventional Life Among the Baboons.* New York: Scribner Book Company

Smith, David Livingstone. 2004. *Why We Lie: The Evolutionary Roots of Deception and the Unconscious Mind.* New York: St. Martin's Press

Zeman, Adam. 2002. *Consciousness: A User's Guide.* New Haven: Yale University Press

Chapter Eleven: Dynamic Relationships: The Missing Key to Wellness

Aron, Elaine N. 1997. *The Highly Sensitive Person: How to Thrive When the World Overwhelms You.* New York: Bantam Dell Publishing Group

Bellack, Leopold. 1975. *Overload: The New Human Condition.* New York: Human Sciences Press

Calhoun, Marcy. 1987. *Are You Really Too Sensitive? How to Understand and Develop Your Sensitivity as the Strength It Is.* Yuba City, CA: Intuitive Development Publishing

Charles, C. Leslie. 1999. *Why Is Everyone So Cranky? The Ten Trends That Are Making Us Angry and How We Can Find Peace of Mind Instead.* New York: Hyperion

Conley, Dalton. 2004. *The Pecking Order: Which Siblings Succeed and Why.* New York: Pantheon/Random House

Eisler, Riane. 1987. *The Chalice and the Blade.* London: Harper and Row

Eisler, Riane. 2002. *The Power of Partnership: Seven Relationships That Will Change Your Life.* Novato, California: New World Library

Eisler, Riane, Loye, David. 1998. *The Partnership Way: New Tools for Living & Learning. A Practical Companion for "the Chalice and the Blade", Healing Our Families, Our Communities.* Brandon, Vermont: Holistic Education Press

Elster, Jon. 2000. *Strong Feelings: Emotion, Addiction, and Human Behavior.* Cambridge, Massachusetts: Bradford Books/The MIT Press

Heller, Sharon. 2002. *Too Loud, Too Bright, Too Fast, Too Tight: What to Do If You Are Sensory Defensive in an Overstimulating World.* New York: HarperCollins Publishers

Marmot, Michael. 2004. *The Status Syndrome: How Social Standing Affects Our Health and Longevity.* New York: Times Books/Henry Holt and Company

May, Gerald G. 1988. *Addiction and Grace: Love and Spirituality in the Healing of Addictions.* New York: HarperSanFrancisco

Miller, David, Blum, Kenneth. 1996. *Overload: Attention Deficit Disorder and the Addictive Brain.* Kansas City, Missouri: Andrews and McMeel

Ritchey, David, Ring, Kenneth. 2003. *The H.I.S.S. of the A.S.P.: Understanding the Anomalously Sensitive Person.* Terra Alta, West Virginia: Headline Books Inc.

Simons, Ronald C. 1996. *Boo! Culture, Experience and the Startle Reflex.* New York: Oxford University Press

Visser, Frank. 2003. *Ken Wilber: Thought As Passion.* Albany, New York: State University of New York Press

Wilber, Ken. 2000a. *Integral Psychology.* Boston: Shambhala Publications Inc.

Wilber, Ken. 2000b. *A Theory of Everything: An Integral Vision for Business, Politics, Science and Spirituality.* Boston: Shambhala Publications Inc.

Zeff, Ted. 2004. *The Highly Sensitive Person's Survival Guide: Essential Skills for Living Well in an Overstimulated World.* Oakland, California: New Harbinger Publications Inc.

Chapter Twelve: Putting the Pieces Together

Alexander, Jane. 1998. *The Detox Plan for Body, Mind and Spirit.* Boston: Journey Editions

Baillie-Hamilton, Paula. 2004. *The Body Restoration Plan: Eliminate Chemical Calories and Repair Your Body's Natural Slimming System.* New York: Avery

Ball, Stefan. 1997. *Bach Flower Remedies for Men.* Saffron Walden, Essex, England: C. W. Daniel Company Ltd.

Barnard, Julian. 1979. *A Guide to the Bach Flower Remedies.* Saffron Walden, Essex, England: C. W. Daniel Company Ltd.

Bear, Jessica. 1993. *Bach Flower Herbal Emotional Formulas. Revised Printing.* Las Vegas, Nevada: Balancing Essentials Press

Bear, Jessica. 1999. *Practical Uses and Applications of the Bach Flower Emotional Remedies.* Second, Revised Las Vegas, Nevada: Balancing Essentials Press

Bray, George (Editor), Bouchard, Claude (Editor), James, W.P.T. (Editor). 1998. *Handbook of Obesity.* New York: Marcel Dekker

Chancellor, Philip M. 1971. *Handbook of the Bach Flower Remedies.* Saffron Walden, Essex, England: C. W. Daniel Company Ltd.

Chuckrow, Robert. 2002. *Tai Chi Walking.* Boston, Massachusetts: YMAA Publication Center

Crompton, Paul. 1996. *Walking Meditation: Pakua. The Martial Art of the I Ching.* Longmead, Shaftesbury, Dorset: Element Books, Ltd.

Devi, Lila. 2003. *The Essential Flower Essence Handbook: Remedies for Inner Well-Being.* Carlsbad, California: Hay House

Galland, Leo. 1997. *The Four Pillars of Healing: How the New Integrated Medicine—the Best of Conventional and Alternative Approaches—Can Cure You.* New York: Random House

Haas, Elson M. 1996. *The Detox Diet.* Berkeley, California: Celestial Arts Publishing

Howard, Judy. 1990. *The Bach Flower Remedies Step by Step: A Complete Guide to Prescribing.* Saffron Walden, Essex: C. W. Daniel Company Ltd.

Howard, Judy. 1992. *Bach Flower Remedies for Women.* Saffron Walden, Essex, England: C. W. Daniel Company, Ltd.

Jones, T.W. Hyne. 1982. *Dictionary of the Bach Flower Remedies.* Saffron Walden, Essex, England: C. W. Daniel Company Ltd.

Kaminski, Patricia, Katz, Richard. 1994. *Flower Essence Repertory.* Nevada City, California: Flower Essence Society

Kramer, Dietmar, Wild, Helmut. 1996. *New Bach Flower Body Maps: Treatment by Topical Application.* Rochester, Vermont: Inner Traditions International Ltd.

Krishnamoorty, V. 1996. *Beginner's Guide to Bach Flower Remedies.* New Delhi, India: B. Jain Publishers Pvt. Ltd.

Lipman, Frank, Gunning, Stephanie. 2003. *Total Renewal: 7 Key Steps to Resilience, Vitality and Long-Term Health.* New York: Jeremy P. Tarcher/Putnam

Pallasdowney, Rhonda M. 2002. *The Complete Book of Flower Essences.* Novato, California: New World Library

Scheffer, Mechthild. 1996. *Mastering Bach Flower Therapies: A Guide to Diagnosis & Treatment.* Rochester, Vermont: Healing Arts Press

Shazzie. 2003. *Detox Your World: Quick and Lasting Results for a Beautiful Mind, Body and Spirit.* Cambridge, England: Rawcreation Limited

Simon, David. 1997. *The Wisdom of Healing: A Natural Mind-Body Program for Optimal Wellness.* New York: Harmony Books

Vohra, D.S. 1995. *Repertory of Bach Flower Remedies: A Comprehensive Study.* Reprint New Delhi, India: B. Jain Publishers Pvt. Ltd.

Websites:

http://altmedicine.about.com/od/herbsupplementguide/
http://nccam.nih.gov/health/supplement-safety/

http://www.mayoclinic.com/invoke.cfm?id=NU00205
http://www.myvitaminguide.com
http://www.phytopharmica.com/
http://www.tftrx.com

978-0-595-45801-1
0-595-45801-7

Printed in the United States
91396LV00004B/118-300/A